Rethinking Labor History

ESSAYS ON DISCOURSE AND CLASS ANALYSIS

Rethinking Labor History

Edited by Lenard R. Berlanstein

University of Illinois Press   Urbana and Chicago

This book is printed on acid-free paper.

Library of Congress Cataloging-in-Publication Data

Rethinking labor history : essays on discourse and class analysis /
  edited by Lenard R. Berlanstein.
      p. cm.
    Includes bibliographical references and index.
    ISBN 0-252-01975-X (alk. paper). — ISBN 0-252-06279-5 (pbk. :
alk. paper)
    1. Labor movement—Historiography. 2. Social classes—
Historiography. 3. Labor movement—France—Historiography.
4. Social classes—France—Historiography. I. Berlanstein, Lenard R.
HD4904.R488 1993
305.5'62—dc20   92-24297
                                                         CIP

CONTENTS

Preface   vii

Introduction   1
    Lenard R. Berlanstein

Toward a Post-materialist Rhetoric for Labor History   15
    William H. Sewell, Jr.

Reflections on Labor History and Language   39
    Donald Reid

Lifeworld, System, and Communicative Action:
    The Habermasian Alternative in Social History   55
    Christopher H. Johnson

Class Analysis, Politics, and French Labor History   90
    Ronald Aminzade

Women's Strikes and the Politics of Popular
    Egalitarianism in France, 1916–18   114
    Laura Lee Downs

Perceptions of Beauty and the Problem of
    Consciousness: Parisian Furniture Makers   149
    Leora Auslander

Commentary: For Reconstruction in Labor History   182
    Michael Hanagan

Commentary: New Labor History from the
    Perspective of a Women's Historian   200
    Gay L. Gullickson

Selected Bibliography   215

Notes on Contributors   227

Index   229

Preface

The idea for this collection arose in 1989, but it has deeper roots in my professional experience. I had moved into labor history a decade earlier, when capitalism was still the universally recognized motor of social change, and the proletarianization model was at its height of prestige. Signs of dissent were perhaps visible even then, but they were not coherent enough to pose serious challenges to the dominant interpretations established by Charles Tilly, Christopher Johnson, or Joan Scott (in *The Glassworkers of Carmaux*). I had no real grounds for questioning class analysis or the positivism that pervaded history. By the end of the 1980s, it was clear that my intellectual position had become untenable. Either I had to treat discourse analysis seriously, or I had to have good reasons for not bothering to do so. The claims and achievements of those who took "language" as their starting point were too startling to dismiss as ephemeral. Believing that many others in labor history shared my confusion, I organized a panel on "The Future of Labor History" for the Society for French Historical Studies meeting in Columbus, Ohio. Michael Hanagan, Christopher Johnson, William Reddy, Michelle Perrot, and William Sewell accepted invitations to share their views on revisionism. The success of the panel argued for expanding the scope of the debate and putting the essays into published form.

Numerous conversations with colleagues before and since the presentation convince me that ambiguity and suspicion surround the revisionism labor history is experiencing. I am constantly surprised by how many serious scholars dismiss the "linguistic turn" as a fad that may amuse them but does not really interest them. Other colleagues claim to respect efforts to introduce theory, wish to learn more, and profess to be willing to incorporate it into their own work. Of course, there is much uncertainty about how to do so. Confronting revisionism compels us to ask how much of the familiar we must discard to accommodate the new. There has been surprisingly little systematic debate, even though the controversy is central to the future of social history. My hope is that the present volume will encourage scholars finally to come to grips with the alternatives before them. The contributors make an attractive case for synthesis. Even the defenders of class analysis argue for its refashioning. In this sense the title of the collection is fully justified.

The publication of this collection is testimony to the generosity and dedication of many colleagues. Among the friends who gave me encouragement and advice, I particularly want to cite Elinor Accampo, Linda Clark, Rachel Fuchs, Lynn Hunt, Richard Kuisel, Herman Lebovics, and Judith Stone. I thank Jack Censer, Michael Hanagan, and Timothy Meagher for serving as sounding boards for my ideas. Christopher Johnson, William Sewell, and Charles Tilly provided helpful advice on the direction the project should take. I am deeply grateful to Joan Scott, Gay Gullickson, and Donald Reid for reading drafts of my introduction and providing guidance for revising it. Finally, I want to pay tribute to the contributors as a group for their cooperation and enthusiasm. They received absolutely no compensation for their hard work—not even invitations to the pleasant conference that often launches a collection of essays. Their labors arose purely from a commitment to serve the field. The truth be told, I had frequently heard that editing was a thankless and problem-laden task. All I can say is that other editors did not work with the superb collaborators I was so fortunate to have.

LENARD R. BERLANSTEIN

Introduction

This volume addresses a series of problems in labor history that have, in recent years, upset practitioners and provoked calls for the fundamental overhaul of the field. The collection draws on the thinking and work of scholars whose achievements are largely in the specialty of French labor history, but the matters under discussion are not limited to the historiography of any one country. They are conceptual issues that once were taken for granted but now seem unsettled. The concentration on France reflects the special place of its labor history at the epicenter of the controversy and the large role of scholars in that area in shaping the debate. Those working outside of France will immediately see the relevance of the essays. Indeed, the questions in dispute are so basic that all historians should be interested in the discussion. Labor history is particularly beset with contention at the moment because the field has been so receptive to interdisciplinary and cutting-edge approaches. Similar disagreement rages in intellectual and women's history for the same reasons.[1] Other fields have much to learn from the arguments. If their conventions seem more secure, it is because the barriers to innovation are higher.

The publication of E. P. Thompson's *Making of the English Working Class* in 1963 marked the coming of age for the "new labor history." What made the approach new at the time was the effort to reinterpret formal working-class institutions (trade unions or political parties) and socialist thought in terms of the authentic voices and authentic experiences of working people. Perhaps because it mobilized the idealism and antiestablishment sentiments of a generation of historians who entered the profession during and after the Vietnam War, the new labor history displayed a remarkable vitality. The field absorbed much of the energy directed at writing history "from below."[2] The scholarship quickly yielded important revelations. Previously, the Industrial Revolution and a factory labor force had dominated thinking about the working class. New labor historians challenged the textbook view that a great caesura in human history had occurred between 1780 and 1830 because of mechanized manufacturing. They stressed, instead, the durability of pre-industrial patterns of work and leisure. The handicraft workers' confrontations with capitalistic development framed much research in the field. New labor historians thus documented the struggle between employers and wage earners for control over the production process. The theme of pre-industrial laborers' facing the economic transformations of the nineteenth century encouraged studies of family life, recreation, and off-the-job solidarities. All these questions could be asked, and finally were asked, about women workers as well.[3] The rise of a class-based society and of class conflict remained the central issue of labor history, but there was also wide-spread interest in the texture of wage earners' daily lives.

The new labor history advanced largely through case studies. Often, they centered on an incidence of intense conflict; by examining the conditions that had generated the conflict, authors endeavored to shed light on the sources of class consciousness. Building on the observation that skilled workers were everywhere the backbone of labor movements, historians developed the proletarianization model as the preeminent explanation for class conflict. It holds that struggles on the part of skilled workers for control over their work were primarily responsible for gener-ating concerted class action against employers or against the established social order. Thus, Joan Scott's 1974 study of glassworkers argued they were indifferent to socialist rhetoric and to the protests of other wage earners as long as their craft control held. Only when a reorganization of production threatened to reduce the value of their skills did the glass-workers become class conscious.[4] Such findings focused attention on the shop-floor experience as a crucial factor in shaping the wage earners' political identity.

Labor historians of the 1960s and 1970s insisted on their iconoclastic role in transforming a discipline heretofore centered on diplomatic rela-tions and high politics. Innovations in methodology and conceptualization were real but ultimately more limited. New labor historians sought to expand the sort of documents that might be consulted and enthusiasti-cally explored social science models for assistance in interpreting the lives of the laboring poor. However, they largely accepted conventional use of sources and procedures for constructing narratives, while scholars in literary criticism, anthropology, and intellectual history were rejecting "positivistic" modes of inquiry.[5] Labor historians remained comfortable with at least a vague economic determinism and with base/superstructure reasoning. Some commanding figures in the field, like E. P. Thompson and Eric Hobsbawm, were Marxists of an innovative strain and sought to free class from simple economic determinism. Yet the scholarship of labor history by and large remained wedded to a definition involving the relation to the means of production.[6]

Charles Tilly had a formative influence on labor history through his voluminous writings and through training many practitioners (including two contributors to this collection, Ronald Aminzade and Michael Hanagan). Tilly is vaguely Marxist but not fully engaged with that body of thought. His landmark studies of the ways people acted together on shared interests emphasized organizational capacity as the key to protest (or "contention," as he came to call it).[7] Tilly recognized both capitalism and the development of the state's ability to coerce as the master forces of social change. He identified the loss of ownership and control over productive property as the pivotal transformation in the West over the past several centuries.[8] His views were widely diffused in the field.

Labor history was somewhat more theoretically orientated than was the discipline as a whole, but it retained plenty of room for eclecticism. Practitioners were impressed with the way Natalie Davis used concepts from cultural anthropology, such as ritual, inversion, or rites of passage, to interpret community values.[9] The influence of the Annales school created interest in material culture, demography, and population movements. Though largely indifferent to Michel Foucault's philosophy, labor historians read his historical works and derived an interpretation of liberal institutions as instruments of normalization.[10] Scholars in the field sometimes wrote as if culture or politics were independent of an economic base, but they rarely made the claim explicit.

Only with hindsight do the early 1980s appear as the moment when the self-confidence and cohesiveness of the new labor history began to founder. Donald Reid, one of the contributors to this collection, reports that in 1981 his reading of Jacques Rancière gave him second thoughts about his own commitment to the proletarianization model. Such doubts were not yet commonplace, but unorthodox approaches to labor history were beginning to appear in print. Just a year before, William Sewell, Jr., had questioned the primacy of material causality in *Work and Revolution in France.*[11] Sewell had been struck by the continuity of corporate language in laborers' pronouncements from the Old Regime well into the nineteenth century. To interpret this, he turned to the cultural anthropology of Clifford Geertz.[12] This perspective suggested to Sewell that it was hardly sufficient to document workers' conditions to understand the development of class consciousness. Labor historians must, he argued, seek to reconstruct "the words, metaphors, and rhetorical conventions that [workers] used to think about their experiences."[13] The author did not deny that changes in the work situation played a role in the development of class consciousness, but he portrayed the sense of class principally as the result of a cultural process in which new meanings were created.

Sewell's insistence on the primacy of culture acting over and above "real" economic forces in creating class found support among a few other scholars in labor history. In 1983, the British labor historian Gareth Stedman Jones, once a more conventional Marxist, published an iconoclastic study of Chartism.[14] He no longer believed Chartism to have been a response to capitalistic change. His reading of post-structuralist theory (which we will come to in a moment) convinced him that Chartism was the product of the political discourse of Radicalism, which defined the participants and their goals. Stedman Jones reversed the conventional wisdom that economic discontents produced working-class consciousness and Chartist protest by asserting that "it was not consciousness (or ideology) that produced politics but politics that produced consciousness." Even though, as Joan Scott has shown, the author does not pursue his theoretical claims to their conclusion, he does break with an enormous amount of previous work in labor history.[15]

A year later, William Reddy published a study of French textile workers that corroborated Sewell's claims for the autonomy of culture.[16] Reddy treated the market largely as a cultural construct—a nontraditional way of thinking about work and earnings on the part of mill owners and other liberals. This thinking had to be imposed on workers, who opposed it in the name of long-standing ideals regarding family, honor, and independence. Conflict arose over these tensions, but Reddy thought of it as community strife rather than class conflict. Class consciousness was not part of his conceptual framework. Indeed, Reddy argued that all such concepts deriving from nineteenth-century socialism (including Marxism) were alien to the way workers understood their lives. French labor historians have long believed that the mill hands of northern France approximated a classic Marxian proletariat, but Reddy dismissed that view, leaving a lot of labor history behind.

Such doubts and revisions have since been proliferating. As a result, the new labor history has quickly become the "old new labor history." In face of the challenges, Marxist scholars have been—to use Tilly's terms—reactive rather than proactive. Calls for fresh starts now prevail over efforts to assimilate previous scholarship. To enter the field today would require making sharp choices about training, approaches, and guiding principles. Of course, in the long run, questioning may be the mark of a certain sort of vitality. In the short run, however, such introspection sows a lot of confusion. This collection seeks to give some order and direction to the debate about renovating labor history.

Why have the challenges to the new labor history become so potent? Its crisis coincides neatly with the worldwide crises in the left and in labor politics—and for good reason. The guiding questions of the field concern what failed to happen—the creation of a majoritarian, class-conscious, workers' movement that was able to impose a new sociopolitical order. Writing labor history is inevitably influenced by perceptions of the possibility or desirability of such an outcome. In the 1960s and 1970s, historians were inspired by the work of Thompson, George Rudé, and David Montgomery when these scholars demonstrated the power of communitarian values in popular culture.[17] Documenting the potential for self-assertion among the oppressed seemed a worthwhile enterprise at the time. Recently, the collapse of Communism, the ostensibly universal enchantment with the marketplace as liberator, and the strength of ethnic over class identities do not lend credence to the role of the working class as an agent of change. At the same time, flourishing women's movements have cast doubt on the claims of a male-dominated left to speak for the emancipation of all people. The changed political climate forces historians to wonder if they have been posing the right questions.

The conscious and unconscious encouragement to revisionism that the new political situation bred went hand in hand with some imposing intellectual challenges to the new labor history. Questioning the value of class analysis has been one of these. To be sure, history has never enjoyed a consensus on what class was or how it was formed.[18] There was, however, agreement that class was an essential tool of analysis. No longer does the agreement hold. Reflecting a growing sensitivity to the instability and unpredictability of class identity, William Reddy denies that the relation to the means of production provides a usable guide to class. He proceeds to cast doubt on class analysis by showing how difficult it is to discern a "socially distinct set of individuals, united by some identifiable trait or traits, as having shared intentions." Not that ways are lacking to rework class analysis to meet this objection. The problem, Reddy finds, is that there are all too many ways, so that class loses all rigor as a category.[19]

Just how far class analysis has fallen from favor is evident in the study of the French Revolution. Twenty years ago, Georges Lefebvre's ringing claim that "economic power, talent, and the perspective of the future passed [from the aristocracy] to the hands of the bourgeoisie" was the starting point for an enormous amount of research, even if it had to be accepted with reservations. Today, the leading voices in the field no longer expect to find class conflict among the causes of the Revolution. The literature is dominated by the study of political culture.[20] Of course, the irrelevance of class analysis could never be as complete for the history of the nineteenth century, if only because the language of class had entered political life. Nonetheless, one might question (as Reddy did) the centrality of class affiliation. In most countries, including France, the large majority of workers did not align themselves with workers' parties.[21]

Post-structuralism, with its attack on the positivistic epistemology of labor history (and of the discipline in general), has raised troubling questions and has even posed an alternate way of conceptualizing work in the field. Drawing on the philosophy of Michel Foucault and Jacques Derrida, it questions the experience-oriented analysis of conventional history by insisting on language (a system of signs) as a key to "reality."[22] The only way to arrive at issues that matter would be through an analysis of language. Post-structuralists want historians to recognize that there is no external referent for the concepts they use. Rather, meaning is socially constructed. There is always conflict over meaning, and any one meaning is inherently unstable because it arises from the suppression of other possibilities.

Post-structuralism imposes a radically new agenda on labor history, a "linguistic turn." The conventional scripting of labor studies, wherein socioeconomic forces created tensions that found expression in class-based protest, would disappear. Instead, scholars would focus on the discourses ("socially institutionalized modes of speech/writing with the effects of power and/or assistance") that defined workers as groups and constituted their experiences.[23] The agenda would include deconstructing the categories labor history has used, among them class, work, wages, markets, and skill. The exercise would reveal ways in which the terms have limited subjects, shaped conclusions, and even perpetuated oppression.[24]

Simply to explicate the post-structuralist agenda is to identify reasons why many historians might want to reject it out of hand. The claims threaten to discredit an enormous amount of scholarship. The call to read difficult and arcane philosophy in order to write history displeases many because the discipline has traditionally attracted students who have no taste to do so. Moreover, the "linguistic turn" leaves in doubt the traditionally close connection between labor history and labor politics. Responses to post-structuralism in history have been strong. Bryan Palmer's *Descent into Discourse* is the most ambitious attempt on the part of a Marxist to counter the challenge, and it is a ringing denunciation.[25] Even scholars who have broken with historical materialism are sometimes offended by aspects of the post-structuralist challenge. Reddy complains that its advocates have "launched into a heady kind of poetry that has divided their readers into the elect who understand and the frustrated, scoffing majority."[26]

Scoff as the majority might, post-structuralists have advanced some powerful critiques of the new labor history and some provocative claims for the value of discourse analysis. The work of Jacques Rancière has struck at a basic element of the new labor history, discovering the authentic voices of working people. His study of the pre-1848 worker-poets who helped invent the language of class showed they were not simply articulating the yearnings of skilled workmen like themselves. They were fashioning a myth about artisans bravely defending their culture and their way of life. Scholars have been all too ready to accept the writings at face value to root the labor movement in artisans' genuine concerns. Yet the discourse is not a direct reflection of the lived experience, nor could it be.[27]

In an article entitled "Work Identities for Men and Women," Joan Scott (breaking decisively with her earlier work) contested the assumption that artisans' protest during the first half of the nineteenth century was largely a response to proletarianization. Directing her attention to garment workers' discourses, she showed that occupational identities could not have arisen in a straightforward manner from capitalistic intrusion into the craft. Garment workers defined themselves in terms that were, at once, economic, sexual, and political. Representations of family and gender entered into their understandings of the organization of work. Scholars have tended to filter out these subjects and arbitrarily made an abstract notion of work the primary referent for the laborers' agenda, but it was not. Scott's analysis points to *interpreted* experience as the source of collective identities for tailors and seamstresses.[28]

Michael Sonenscher has reinforced the post-structuralist challenge with his acclaimed study of eighteenth-century wage earners. His findings cast doubt not only on the proletarianization thesis but also on a materialistic understanding of class conflict. Labor historians customarily account for the rise of a working class in the nineteenth century by referring to the disruptions artisans experienced as market forces penetrated into areas previously governed by custom and tradition. Sonenscher purports to show through exhaustive archival research that custom did not organize work even in the eighteenth century; the uncertainties of the marketplace were already a fact of everyday life. Proletarianization thus could not explain the emergence of class conflict a few decades after the Revolution. What did? The author looks to political discourses for the answer. After the Revolution destroyed the corporate structure of the Old Regime and made individualism the formal basis of the social order, workers had to find new ways to express their grievances and establish solidarities. A language of class arose from the effort. Sonenscher's claims, if they stand unchallenged, thus effectively uncouple structural economic transformation and the emergence of the working class.[29] If he is correct, most labor history of the last three decades is not.

Feminist theory, wielding the analytical tools of post-structuralism, has also contributed to an awareness of the inadequacies of the new labor history. For the first two decades of its existence, the field seemed to serve the intellectual agenda of the women's movement. Scholars illuminated the largely undocumented role of women engaged in the world of paid labor. They exposed the appalling levels of exploitation that plagued women wage earners. They gave a role to working women as agents of their own history. Yet labor history also provided feminists with grounds for dissatisfaction, for it was hard to avoid treating female workers as a special case, and the conceptualizations that seemed to apply to male workers pushed women to the margins of history. As Ava Baron has noted, labor history "elaborated upon rather than replaced a whole series of conceptual dualisms—capitalism/patriarchy, public/private, production/reproduction, men's work/women's work—which assume that class issues are integral to the first term in each pair and gender is important only to the second."[30] Above all, frustrations with labor history's inadequacies in dealing with gender inequality led to a questioning of the very categories used in the field. Joan Scott prepared the field for a revolution by arguing that it used and perpetuated a gendered concept of class. Notions of male and female were at the very core of the way laborers and their historians have understood their worlds. Deconstructing "class" would dethrone the male worker as the prototypical one and would open possibilities for writing a labor history that encompassed both genders equally.[31]

Under the impact of such challenges, the new labor history has entered the 1990s uncertain about the authority of earlier achievements and divided about basic methods and concepts. There is a widespread sense among an expanding circle of scholars that the shades have fallen from their eyes and that labor history will not be the same and should not be the same. The readiness to accept and build on fundamental, new insight is characteristic of labor history today. Yet there is much disagreement on how to do so and on how much of labor history's short past needs to be repudiated.

Readers who desire the immediate resolution of all uncertainties and divisions in labor history will not find comfort in this volume.

Instead, there is debate—respectful, but often sharp—about fundamentals. The essays make clear that the crisis of labor history is not simply a matter of post-structuralist and feminist attacks on Marxian-inspired history. Advocates of the latter concede mistakes and omissions but seek reform by returning to their ideological roots. In particular, they revive aspects of Marxian thought that allow for the autonomy of culture or politics. Revisions of that sort, they argue, constitute a sounder path for labor history than does a "linguistic turn." In this debate, the post-structuralists and feminists are setting the terms, but replies are coming from several directions.

The collection offers three different types of essays in the service of rethinking labor history. We begin with four theoretically oriented reflections on revisionism. The authors make evident, on one hand, the attractions of discourse analysis and, on the other hand, the promise of a renovated materialism. Although it was not intentionally planned this way, the theoretical statements fall into complementary pairs. William Sewell and Christopher Johnson propose sweeping conceptual overhaul, the first as a "post-materialist," the other as a materialist. Donald Reid and Ronald Aminzade bring theoretical concerns for their respective "sides" (the term, admittedly, is crude and downplays the shared interests among contributors) closer to concrete research designs by applying their arguments to their current projects. We then approach the crisis in labor history from a more immediate level. Case studies by Leora Auslander and Laura Lee Downs illustrate how scholars are responding to the opportunities and dilemmas inherent in the paradigmatic confusions. At question is how to apply discourse analysis to empirical research. The final two essays make an effort to sum up and focus the debate by commenting on the six preceding ones. Reflecting outstanding differences in the field today, Gay Gullickson and Michael Hanagan evaluate the state of the controversy from their respective positions.

William Sewell's essay continues his efforts to push labor history in a post-materialist direction.[32] He reasons with materialists, arguing that their categories do not withstand critical examination. He even shames them into rethinking their position by pointing out that their conventions do not have the most respectable origins. Sewell would like labor history to invent a new rhetoric that would make the divisions between post-structuralism and historical materialism obsolete.

Donald Reid's essay begins with an account of the author's own "linguistic turn." After a playful deconstruction of the language of resistance to post-structuralist approaches, he makes an attractive case for a linguistically informed labor history. Reid, like Sewell, seeks to capture the multiple dimensions of perceived reality and finds discourse analysis an admirable tool. He insists that such a reformed labor history need not neglect socioeconomic experience. Indeed, Reid's invitation to make the "linguistic turn" includes earnest reassurances for traditionalists.

Christopher Johnson's essay is equally personal, but in this instance the author writes from a materialist perspective. Johnson acknowledges regretfully that the current political and intellectual climate offers little ground for defending economic determinism. He accepts the criticisms post-structuralists have made of his own work on proletarianization.[33] He maintains, however, that the "linguistic turn" has its own pitfalls for labor history, above all, the inability to deal satisfactorily with change. He thus turns to Marxian thought for guidance and finds the work of Jürgen Habermas enormously stimulating. Johnson recommends a Habermasian perspective—already widespread among students of political culture—to labor historians as a convincing way to tie workers' culture to the processes that shape and change it.

Ronald Aminzade, a sociologist, offers a spirited defense of class analysis, but he seeks its renovation as much as its preservation. He admits that any attempt to connect structural position and class identity in a straightforward manner is likely to result in crude reductionism. The key to viable class analysis, he finds, lies in recognizing the complexities of the political process wherein workers form an identity and stake out their own programs. If Aminzade has his way, labor historians will bestow on formal political activity (especially the building of coalitions) the attention they formerly gave to shop-floor relations.

The case studies in the volume testify to a reorientation away from workplace and community and toward the issue of identity. Leora Auslander reexamines one of labor history's foundational interests, seeking workers' authentic voices. Like Rancière, she exposes the problems inherent in the quest and, still more, in connecting those voices to class-conscious labor movements. Auslander is concerned with how and why laborers produced diverse discourses. Using nineteenth-century furniture makers as her model, she demonstrates the need to place their discourses in context, for they were products of specific speech communities, each with constraints—among them linguistic ones—on what claims could be made. Auslander illuminates obstacles to discovering an authentic voice that would reveal the state of class consciousness. More positively, the essay shows how scholars might give meaning to the different voices through which workers defined themselves.

Laura Lee Downs's examination of strike activity on the part of female munitions workers during World War I explores the interplay between gender and class. The women's militancy did not so much baffle employers and trade union officials as lead them to a gendered interpretation of the strikes. Laborers, for their part, rejected the role of "apolitical" women and went on to construct an identity that brought them to the forefront of working-class protest. Downs's analysis should lead readers to reflect on workers' freedom to choose among political discourses.

Our two commentators arrive at conflicting conclusions about rethinking the field. Michael Hanagan stresses the costs. Though he would share Joan Scott's dual goals of interpreting society while trying to change it, he does not share Scott's definition of politics: "the process by which plays of power and knowledge constitute identity and experience."[34] Hanagan is concerned with maintaining the connections between labor history and national political movements. He worries that post-structuralist perspectives neglect the latter. Moreover, he contends that findings that are perfectly comprehensible in conventional political terms have been cast in linguistic terms. Hanagan is most comfortable with the reworking of class analysis that Aminzade proposes.

Gay Gullickson, on the other hand, believes that progress toward a better labor history—encompassing two genders—is at hand. The obstacle, as she sees it, has always been a bifurcation of perspectives: proletarianization was about males; female workers were covered by the theme of the sexual division of labor. She proposes that developing new subjects and broadening approaches to the formation of consciousness are keys to escaping the division. Gullickson identifies elements in each essay that can contribute to a two-gender history.

The volume concludes with a selected bibliography—unusual for a collection of essays but quite useful in view of our overriding purpose. Even a casual examination of the contributors' citations reveals that they point to something of a common reading list among scholars who are deeply engaged in the debate over the future of labor history. The selected bibliography that ends this book provides an excellent guide for further reading on the problem.[35]

Though the essays in this collection testify to the liveliness of the debate over fundamentals, it is crucial to note the narrowing of differences on many fronts. One side concedes qualifications to the literary representation of reality associated with post-structuralism.[36] The other side reconsiders privileging the workplace as the conduit to political ideas and consciousness. Both groups support autonomy of culture and politics over economic determinism. Identities that groups might assume, rather than appearing self-evident, now are taken as a problem for investigation. Finally, everyone is prepared to see in language more than a passive medium for expressing interests.

The possibilities for accommodation are worth celebrating, for they address the central dilemma in a field that is likely to be at a crossroad for a long while. The most redoubtable consequence of revisionism threatens to be the further compartmentalization of an already specialized field. Scholarship will surely suffer from a lasting division between those who examine discourse and those who examine experience.[37] The contributors do not want that to happen and do not think it has to. That is why they propose taking up new subjects and, in the long run, seeking a new rhetoric for labor history. They ask practitioners to be open-minded and ready to retool conceptually if need be. As with most calls for basic reform, they appeal more to a sense of courage than to a sense of comfort.

Notes

1. John E. Toews, "Intellectual History after the Linguistic Turn: The Autonomy of Meaning and the Irreducibility of Experience," *American Historical Review* 92 (1987): 879-907; Louise Newman, "Critical Theory and the History of Women: What Is at Stake in Deconstructing Women's History," *Journal of Women's History* 2 (1991): 58-68.

2. The *Bibliographie annuaire de l'histoire de la France* listed under the rubric "Workers" 84 entries in 1960 and 186 entries twenty years later.

3. For an excellent review of the connections between women's history and labor history, see Ava Baron, "Gender and Labor History: Learning from the Past, Looking to the Future," in *Work Engendered,* ed. Ava Baron (Ithaca, N.Y., 1991), pp. 1-46.

4. Joan Wallach Scott, *The Glassworkers of Carmaux: French Craftsmen and Political Action in a Nineteenth-Century City* (Cambridge, Mass., 1974).

5. Martin Jay, "Should Intellectual History Take a Linguistic Turn? Reflections on the Habermas-Godamer Debate," in *Modern European Intellectual History: Reappraisals and New Perspectives,* ed. Dominick LaCapra and Steven Kaplan (Ithaca, N.Y., 1982), pp. 86-110; George Marcus and Michael Fisher, *Anthropology as Cultural Critique* (Chicago, 1986).

6. Suzanne Desan, "Crowds, Community, and Ritual in the Work of E. P. Thompson and Natalie Davis," in *The New Cultural History,* ed. Lynn Hunt (Berkeley, 1989), pp. 46-61.

7. Lynn Hunt, "Charles Tilly's Collective Action," in *Vision and Method in Historical Sociology,* ed. Theda Skocpol (Cambridge, 1984), pp. 244-75. Tilly articulates his vision for social history in "Retrieving European Lives," in *Reliving the Past: The Worlds of Social History,* ed. Olivier Zunz (Chapel Hill, N.C., 1985), pp. 11-52, and in *The Contentious French* (Cambridge, Mass., 1986).

8. Charles Tilly, "Demographic Origins of the European Proletariat: A Proletarian World," in *Proletarianization and Family History,* ed. David Levine (Orlando, Fla., 1984), pp. 1-85.

9. Desan, "Crowds, Community, and Ritual," pp. 61-71; Natalie Zemon Davis, *Society and Culture in Early Modern France* (Stanford, Calif., 1975).

10. Michel Foucault's works that have had the greatest impact on social history are *Madness and Civilization: A History of Insanity in the Age of Reason,* trans. Richard Howard (New York, 1965); *Discipline and Punish: The Birth of the Prison,* trans. Alan Sheridan, (New York, 1977); *The History of Sexuality,* trans. Alan Sheridan, 3 vols. (New York, 1976-86). See Patrica O'Brien, "Michel Foucault's History of Culture," in *New Cultural History,* ed. Hunt, pp. 25-46; and Patrick Hutton, "The Foucault Phenomenon and Contemporary French Historiography," *Historical Reflections* 17 (1991): 77-102.

11. William Sewell, Jr., *Work and Revolution in France: The Language of Labor from the Old Regime to 1848* (Cambridge, 1980).

12. On Geertz's impact, see Aletta Biersack, "Local Knowledge, Local History: Geertz and Beyond," in *New Cultural History,* ed. Hunt, pp. 72-96.

13. Sewell, *Work and Revolution,* p. 11.

14. Gareth Stedman Jones, *Languages of Class: Studies in English Working Class History, 1832-1982* (Cambridge, 1983). In 1980, the History Workshop Group, with which Stedman Jones was closely associated, had held a conference on "Language and History."

15. For a critique of Stedman Jones, see Joan Wallach Scott, "On Language, Gender, and Working-Class History," *International Labor and Working-Class History,* no. 31 (1987): 1-13.

16. William Reddy, *The Rise of Market Culture: The Textile Trade and French Society, 1750-1900* (Cambridge, 1984).

17. E. P. Thompson, "The Moral Economy of the English Crowd in the Eighteenth Century," *Past and Present,* no. 50 (1971): 76-136; George Rudé, *The Crowd in History, 1830-1848* (New York, 1964); David Montgomery, *Workers' Control in America: Studies in the History of Work, Technology, and Labor Struggles* (Cambridge, 1979).

18. On this point, see Ira Katznelson, "Working-Class Formation: Constructing Cases and Comparisons," in *Working-Class Formation: Nineteenth-Century Patterns in Europe and America,* ed. Ira Katznelson and Aristide Zolberg (Princeton, N.J., 1986), pp. 3-41.

19. William M. Reddy, *Money and Liberty in Europe: A Critique of Historical Understanding* (Cambridge, 1987), p. 8.

20. Georges Lefebvre, *The Coming of the French Revolution,* trans. R. R. Palmer (Princeton, N.J., 1947), p. 2. On the revisionist interpretations, see Jack R. Censer, ed., *The French Revolution and Intellectual History* (Chicago, 1989); and the special issue of *French Historical Studies* 16 (1990) on François Furet's interpretation of the Revolution.

21. Aristide Zolberg, "How Many Exceptionalisms?" in *Working-Class Formation,* ed. Katznelson and Zolberg, pp. 397-455.

22. The most frequently cited philosophical writings are Michel Foucault, *The Order of Things: An Archeology of the Human Sciences* (New York, 1973); Foucault, *Power/Knowledge: Selected Interviews and Other Writings,* ed. Colin

Gordon (New York, 1980); and Jacques Derrida, *Of Grammatology*, trans. Gayatri Chakravorty Spivak (Baltimore, 1974).

23. Peter Schöttler, "Historians and Discourse Analysis," *History Workshop*, no. 27 (1989): 41. I have borrowed Schöttler's definition of *discourse*.

24. Joan Wallach Scott, *Gender and the Politics of History* (New York, 1988), pp. 15–90; Gabriel Speigel, "The Social Logic of the Text in the Middle Ages," *Speculum* 65 (1990): 59–86.

25. Bryan D. Palmer, *Descent into Discourse: The Reification of Language and the Writing of Social History* (Philadelphia, 1990).

26. Reddy, *Money and Liberty*, p. 4. At a recent visit to the University of Virginia, Lawrence Stone presented a paper on "The Future of History," which attacked post-structuralism on the grounds (unsustainable, in my view) that it dismisses empirical reality, offers no logic of cause and effect, and does not allow for distinctions between truth and fiction. The presentation suggests the gulf in communication that now exists within social history.

27. Jacques Rancière, *La nuit des prolétaires: Archives du rêve ouvrier* (Paris, 1981); Rancière, "The Myth of the Artisan: Critique of a Category of Social History," *International Labor and Working-Class History*, no. 24 (1983): 1–16. The book is now available in English as *The Nights of Labor: The Worker's Dream in Nineteenth-Century France*, trans. John Drury (Philadelphia, 1989).

28. Scott, *Gender*, chap. 5.

29. Michael Sonenscher, *Work and Wages: Natural Law, Politics, and the Eighteenth-Century French Trades* (Cambridge, 1989).

30. Baron, "Gender and Labor History," p. 17.

31. Scott, *Gender*, chaps. 2–3.

32. See William H. Sewell, Jr., "Uneven Development, the Autonomy of Politics, and the Dockworkers of Nineteenth-Century Marseille," *American Historical Review* 93 (1988): 604–37.

33. Christopher Johnson's influential work on proletarianization include "Economic Change and Artisan Discontent: The Tailors' History, 1800-1848," in *Revolution and Reaction*, ed. Roger Price (London, 1975), pp. 87–114, and "Patterns of Proletarianization: Parisian Tailors and Lodève Woolen Workers," in *Consciousness and Class Experience in Nineteenth-Century Europe*, ed. John Merriman (New York, 1979), pp. 75–84.

34. Scott, *Gender*, p. 5.

35. The selected bibliography excludes specialized works that relate primarily to the contributors' immediate subject.

36. William H. Sewell, Jr., has developed this qualification in his "Review of *Gender and the Politics of History*, by Joan Wallach Scott," *History and Theory* 29 (1990): 71–81.

37. Peter Novick notes that "the matter-of-fact, antitheoretical, and anti-philosophical objectivist empiricism which has always been the dominant stance of American historians continues to be enormously powerful." Novick, *That Noble Dream: The "Objectivity Question" and the American Historical Profession* (Cambridge, 1988), p. 593.

WILLIAM H. SEWELL, JR.

Toward a Post-materialist Rhetoric for Labor History

Labor history is not in crisis. Good work is being done not only by historians but by sociologists, economists, and political scientists as well. Such specialized journals as *International Labor and Working-Class History* and *Labor History* are thriving, and articles on labor history are featured prominently in major journals of the various fields. Yet it is hard to argue that labor history is a major site of historiographical innovation, as it unquestionably was in the 1960s or the 1970s. Here I think a comparison between labor history and women's history is revealing. Although both fields began their rapid expansion in the same historiographical and political era—labor history in the mid-1960s and the 1970s and women's history perhaps a half-decade behind—women's history has retained an intellectual vitality that labor history has lost.

The most obvious reason for this difference is that the political project of the women's movement, for all its setbacks and hesitations during the last decade, remains far more lively, self-confident, and aggressive than the contemporary labor movement. Because the organized working class seems less and less likely to perform the liberating role assigned to it in both revolutionary and reformist discourses about labor, the study of the history of the working class has lost some of its urgency.

There is also a difference of a more strictly intellectual kind. Women's history and feminist studies have been a major site of theoretical struggles in the human sciences. Advocates of cultural, neo-Freudian, deconstructionist, and materialist approaches are locked in intense and so far inconclusive battles in feminist studies. The intensity of the theoretical battles surely derives in part from the depth of the challenge that modern feminism poses to existing social identities and modes of thinking, both inside and outside the academy. Gender, as feminist scholars and critics have demonstrated, is everywhere—built into not only our families, churches, businesses, and public institutions but also the very language in which we discuss and evaluate our experiences, including the languages of philosophy, art, politics, science, and history. The intellectual project of feminism has consisted largely in bringing to consciousness a vast range of oppressive gender dynamics that existing modes of thought and speaking had rendered invisible. This work of exhuming, of bringing to light, has from the beginning required extensive and explicit theoretical work, a fundamental and ever-vigilant challenging, rethinking, or unthinking of conventional categories. Precisely because no theoretical discourse can be immune from feminist critique, virtually all theoretical perspectives have been drawn, in the very process of critique, into the orbit of feminist discussion.

At the same time, the personal stakes in feminist discussion are particularly high, since fundamental identities are at issue. Is the goal of feminism to reclaim and assert the superiority of genuinely feminine thinking, morality, feeling, or judgment, or is it to establish an essential similarity and equality between the sexes? Can men think and write in a feminist or a feminine mode? Are lesbian relationships by definition more feminist than heterosexual relationships? Does heterosexuality or participation in the masculinist academy necessarily recapitulate and reinforce male dominance? That feminist discussion raises such fundamental questions about personal identity adds a particular intensity to the theoretical debates.

In labor studies, by comparison, a broad and complacent materialist perspective dominates the field. There have been challenges—for example, Gareth Stedman Jones's and Joan Scott's mutually hostile arguments for the primacy of language over class in the determination of labor politics or Jacques Rancière's attempts to deconstruct the myth of the artisan—but Stedman Jones, Scott, and Rancière have so far recruited few followers among labor historians, who have tended to dismiss them for lapsing into "mere" intellectual history.[1] I believe labor history is destined to suffer from continuing intellectual doldrums unless its largely unexamined materialist common sense is more widely and vigorously contested. It would, of course, be chimerical to imagine that labor studies could, in the present situation, spawn a theoretical debate as intense and multiformed as that occurring in contemporary feminist studies. Yet the politics and the political economy of labor in the contemporary world hardly seem conducive to theoretical complacency. We are living through massive and fundamental changes in the nature, location, and meaning of work and in the fortunes of labor movements and socialist ideologies all over the globe. The world of work conjured up by labor history's materialist common sense—the production of heavy manufactured goods by union-ized male laborers in large factories—is in rapid decline in the advanced capitalist democracies. The most rapidly expanding forms of work and categories of workers in advanced capitalism tend to fall through the cracks of standard labor history—clerical and service work, information, consulting, flexible specialization, design, homework, and the like, much of it performed by ununionized women. Current developments in the world of work actually stand as an implicit theoretical challenge to labor history.

This essay does not offer concrete suggestions about new topics of empirical research that might more effectively address this challenge. Instead, it takes up the complementary and equally pressing task of theoretical critique and reformulation.

Theory and Rhetoric

What we usually call theory may be thought of as containing two complementary but distinguishable dimensions: the logical and the rhetorical. The logical task of theory is to elaborate and specify logical relations between theoretical propositions. The rhetorical task, on which I will concentrate in this essay, is to provide the figurative and linguistic frameworks or paradigms by means of which we select research prob-lems and evaluate the relevance, appropriateness, or completeness of researchers' truth-claims.[2] I would argue that most labor historians base their judgments on an implicit or explicit reductive materialist rhetorical paradigm. What this means in practice is that those features of the historical situation regarded as material are assumed to have greater causal power than features regarded as cultural or political or ideological. In my experience, labor historians are too easily satisfied by explanations that identify a material cause—say, declining control over the process of production—but are highly skeptical about explanations that identify cultural causes—say, shifts in political or religious discourse—no matter how well-documented or tightly argued the cultural explanation may be. The normal response of labor historians to cultural explanations is to argue that the supposed cultural cause is less important than some alternative material cause or that the proposed cultural cause is itself the effect of "deeper-lying" material factors. In this way the rhetorical common sense of labor history privileges material over cultural or political or ideological phenomena.

The extraordinary role played by the concept of proletarianization in recent labor history exemplifies the operation of this materialist common sense. Proletarianization, a preeminently material phenomenon, has tended to become a kind of omnibus, all-purpose causal force in labor history, at least for the nineteenth century. The term *proletarianization* actually combines under a single aegis a number of empirically distinct processes that have occurred in Europe and North America since the late eighteenth century: the movement of populations from agriculture to industry, the separation of producers from ownership of the means of production, a decline of producers' control over work processes, and the making obsolete of producers' skills. At least the first three of these processes underwent a global progression over the course of the nineteenth century. (The fourth, deskilling, had a more ambiguous history, since both deskilling and *re*skilling go on constantly and simultaneously in any society undergoing technological change. Labor historians have typically emphasized the deskilling and ignored the reskilling.)

The problem, as I see it, is that labor historians have tended to combine all these diverse processes under a single covering term, tending to see any example of, say, declining control of production or deskilling as evidence that the underlying master process of proletarianization is at work. A few well-documented examples of deskilling or declining control in a trade or a class are thus taken as evidence that the trade or the class as a whole is experiencing the underlying process and, consequently, that workers' actions, such as strikes, insurrections, or political movements, can be explained as responses to proletarianization. Labor historians' materialist predilections, I would argue, have made them willing to accept proletarianization as a sort of universally valid material explanation. As a consequence, they have paid insufficient attention to the profoundly uneven and contradictory character of changes in production relations, not to mention the role of discourse and politics in labor history.[3]

My goal in this essay is not to criticize the concept of proletarianization but to contest the materialist rhetorical common sense on which it depends. I do so in two steps. First, I attempt a historical deconstruction of the idea that the economy is material. My object will be to demonstrate not only that the equation of the economy with the material is arbitrary and misleading but that the genealogy of this idea is suspicious as well. Second, I attempt to provide a more appropriate figuration of the object of labor history, and of social history in general, than that offered by the reductive materialist model. I do so by pushing to their logical conclusions tendencies already present in contemporary labor studies—and in the contemporary human sciences more generally.

Is the Economy Material?

The founding metaphor of the materialist paradigm is the notion that the economy is material. On close examination, however, the idea that economic life is particularly or uniformly material is quite arbitrary. Much of what goes on in the sphere of production and exchange looks awfully ideal or cultural or symbolic to me.[4] Let me offer a few examples.

We should start from the top with money. In ordinary speech the *material* is more or less equated with *money-making*. Yet money is nothing if not a symbol system—and a very complicated symbol system at that. Money is not useful in itself but is only a conventional sign of value that is used to trade for commodities. As labor specialists from Karl Marx to William Reddy have argued, the fact that exchange relations are mediated by money commonly deludes people into thinking that such relations are free rather than coerced.[5] Like any symbol, in other words, money is defined by its relation to other symbols and has the power to fix the meanings, to shape the possible interpretations, of human action. Money, a symbol if ever there was one, stands at the center of and designates the very boundaries of that sphere of life that we designate as material in capitalist society.

A second aspect of economic activity that is hard to characterize as material is, of course, advertising. Since the late nineteenth century, a higher and higher proportion of the work and investment of capitalist firms has gone into advertising, that is, into symbolic representations of commodities to potential consumers. Advertising is the production of pictorial, musical, and verbal images for billboards, magazines, radio, television, and other media. These images are designed to incite potential consumers to desire specific symbolically marked commodities—to desire not bread or fountain pens but Wonder Bread and Parker pens. Moreover, the symbolic definition of commodities is not restricted to their packaging or their mediated imaging; it is also embodied in their production. Industrial designers must make sure that a Mont Blanc fountain pen is distinguishable in its actual material form from a Parker fountain pen, or a Braun electric coffee pot from a Mister Coffee. Armies of designers and advertisers, employed by major corporations and specialized agencies, engage in sculpting metal and plastic, composing tunes, and crafting evocative word sequences or photographic images. The actual work they do is not distinguishable in kind from the lofty creative activities of artists. But their activities are economic and are therefore assigned to the material sphere, while the empirically indistinguishable activities of painters, sculptors, musicians, or poets are not.

It might be objected that the seemingly immaterial aspects of economic life discussed thus far—money and advertising—concern only the circulation or exchange of commodities, not their production. In fact, the ideal or the symbolic also intrudes into production itself. The complex of machines that makes up an assembly line is not just a series of material objects but the result of an elaborately thought-out design—one that is developed on sketch-pads and blueprints, or nowadays on computers, long before it assumes a material form in the factory. Moreover, much production work is only ambiguously material. In contemporary production, workers may not actually manipulate the goods they are manufacturing; instead, they may program computerized tools and monitor their performance by means of computer-generated signals. The productivity of machines is not simply a function of their design and scientific efficiency; it also depends fundamentally on the knowledge and the morale of the labor force. Quality circles, in which workers develop means of improving the quality or efficiency of production through intensive discursive interchange, may have contributed more to the superiority of Japanese consumer goods than has any purely mechanical technique.[6] Nor is the intrusion of the ideal into production a peculiarity of very recent and highly technologized means of producing goods. Before the introduction of assembly lines, as David Montgomery (a materialist if ever there was one) reminds us, the manager's brains were "under the workman's cap"; it was the workers' skill and organizational know-how that made possible the sustained and effective production of high-quality goods.[7] To step back even further, guild apprentices were to be taught "the mysteries of the trade," the secret skills and formulas and the finesse and taste that would assure their ability to maintain the guild's reputation for quality and style. Aesthetic, symbolic, and organizational knowledge—all of which could be classified "ideal" as easily as "material"—have always been part and parcel of the production process.

When economic life is looked at closely, it turns out that a lot of what goes on in production and exchange ought to be classified as nonmaterial, according to conventional standards. Like activities that go on in other spheres—say, government, learning, religion, or warfare—production and exchange entail a complex mixture of what we would usually call the ideal and the material. The closer we look, the clearer it becomes that labeling economic activities "material" and distinguishing them from "nonmaterial" spheres is utterly arbitrary.

A Historical Deconstruction of
the "Materiality" of the Economy

Where did the bizarre notion that production and exchange were uniquely material come from? The answer, I think, is highly paradoxical. It derives from traditional European Christian and aristocratic metaphysics, which were subsequently stood on their head by the Enlightenment.

The notion of a distinct material realm comes from the Christian division of the cosmos into two radically different substances: spirit, which was lofty, orderly, and powerful; and matter, which was base, disorderly, and inert. The hierarchy of spirit and matter was also used metaphorically to make distinctions between different categories or orders of human beings. Although all premodern European countries had analogous distinctions, we might as well take the case of Old Regime France, where the population was divided into three estates. The clergy was, of course, the First Estate because its activities—spiritual affairs—were the loftiest. The nobles were the Second Estate because they magnanimously sacrificed their lives in defense of the realm. The Third Estate, by contrast, was vile and ignoble, soiled by its labor and its base pursuit of worldly material goods. So the clichés went. On close inspection, however, it is hard to see why the actual activities of commoners should be thought of as more material than those of nobles. The nobles normally spent their time either making war or practicing for it—riding horses, handling weapons, and developing their physical prowess through exercise. Peasants' activities were quite analogous—leading teams of oxen, handling plows, axes, and pitchforks, and pursuing an endless round of physical labor. Instead of the producers of goods being classified as base because their activity was uniquely material, the production of goods was classified as material because those who produced them were regarded as base. The characterization of production and exchange as material was thus logically arbitrary. It had nothing to do with the factual extent to which the different orders' or estates' activities involved the physical manipulation of material things. Rather, the designation of production and exchange as material was a metaphor; it resulted from an effort to align the hierarchies of social status in medieval and early modern Europe with contemporary cosmological theories.

The Enlightenment challenged both the cosmology and the assumptions about social status. The Enlightenment was inspired, of course, by the astonishing advances made in natural philosophy in the seventeenth century. The discoveries of Newton and others had demonstrated that the world of matter, far from being gross and disorderly, was ordered by sublime and invariant natural laws. Simultaneously, the realm of spirit, at least as manifested in the various versions of the Christian religion, had proved in the seventeenth century to be an endless source of tumult, warfare, slaughter, and discord. Enlightenment thinkers therefore eschewed theological disputation and attempted to apply the methods of science—or, more exactly, its rhetoric—to the study of human society.

The philosophy of the Enlightenment was, broadly speaking, materialist. This materialism was manifested, for example, in Montesquieu's climatic determinism or in Lockean epistemology, which held that the mind was furnished with ideas by sense impressions taken directly from the material world. In this intellectual climate, the conventional metaphorical operation that coded production and exchange as material represented an inviting opportunity, one that was seized by the economic thinkers of the Enlightenment, both the French Physiocrats and the Scottish moralists. If production and exchange were material, they should be governed by invariant laws analogous to those that governed physical matter. Over the course of the eighteenth century the economists duly discovered such laws. It is highly significant that the first coherent school of economic thinkers actually dubbed themselves the Physiocrats. The title "physiocracy," which of course means "the rule of the physical," makes clear the overall thrust of the economists' project: to find the essential ordering principles of human life in the material sphere of production and exchange, the very sphere that had for so long been disdained by philosophers, theologians, and rulers as vile and lowly. That the activities they saw as determining the wealth, power, and happiness of nations could be characterized as material or physical, and therefore as analogous to the physical nature studied by the natural philosophers, subtly but powerfully fortified their claim to have discovered a genuine science of human government. The early economists, in other words, took over intact the traditional equation of production and exchange with the material, but they inverted the traditional valuation of the material, which for them implied order and reason rather than vileness and turpitude.

Both the materialist bias of the Enlightenment and the conventional coding of production and exchange as material were carried over into the nineteenth century by the political economists, and they were appropriated by Marx in his famous attempt to turn Hegel's idealism on its head. Since Marx, they have saturated the discourse of the left and have become the unquestioned conventions of labor history. Notice the irony, however: Marxists proudly proclaim their radicalism by employing an arbitrary identification of the economic as material, never realizing that they have inherited this idea intact and uncriticized from traditional Christian and aristocratic discourse. Would-be friends of the proletariat hence believe they are being progressive when they denounce as "idealists" historians who actually take seriously what past proletarians thought. The claim that the economy is uniquely "material" always was arbitrary, misleading, and tendentious; that it continues to be clung to by purportedly leftist scholars is an embarrassing anachronism.

Beyond the Ideal and the Material

It is Marxist scholars who most explicitly embrace the label of materialism. It is important to note, however, that the materialist common sense I am attacking in this essay is by no means limited to Marxists. It is shared by a wide spectrum of liberals, populist radicals, and free-market conservatives as well. An identification of Marxism as the problem might have the effect of rendering this broader materialist common sense more smug than ever. In fact, economic reductionism, which is the central analytical procedure associated with the materialist trope, has come under increasing, and increasingly sophisticated, attack from within the Marxian tradition over the past three decades. From E. P. Thompson and Louis Althusser in the 1960s through Ernesto Laclau and Chantal Mouffe or Samuel Bowles and Herbert Gintis in the 1980s, a central theme of Western Marxism—a theme most forcefully symbolized by endless evocations of Antonio Gramsci—has been a deepening critique of economic reductionism.[8] For Laclau, Mouffe, Bowles, and Gintis, this critique had gone so far by the mid-1980s that they no longer considered themselves Marxists. They had entered the terrain of post-Marxism, but with Laclau and Mouffe's apt proviso that "if our intellectual project . . . is *post*-Marxist, it is also post-*Marxist.*" Rather than abandon the achievements of Marxian scholarship, they have attempted to go beyond Marxism by developing "certain intuitions and discursive forms constituted within Marxism," while eliminating certain others.[9] The post-materialist rhetoric I advocate is as much a continuation of developments within Marxism as it is an attack on Marxism.

Whether my argument is seen as coming from within or outside Marxism, it is intended as a radical and irreversible step beyond all materialisms. I want to make it clear that this emphatically does not imply an antimaterialist position. Quite the contrary: an antimaterialist perspective would merely reembrace from the opposite side the same archaic and sterile opposition between ideal and material that caused the trouble in the first place. We need, to paraphrase Laclau and Mouffe, a rhetoric that is both *post*-materialist and post-*materialist.* It should be *post*-materialist in the sense of going beyond the constraining conventions and dichotomies of materialist common sense, but it must also be post-*materialist* in the sense of building on, instead of simply rejecting, the vast and productive scholarly enterprise carried on for so long under the banner of materialism. In my opinion, the only way to accomplish this is to obliterate, to deny as nonsensical, the opposition between ideal and material on which materialist common sense has been built.

A denial of the opposition between ideal and material might begin with some reflections on human biology. Like other living things, humans are composed of organic molecules arranged into cells and organs; they metabolize nutrients and are subject to laws of growth and decay. What makes them different from other forms of life is that their behavior is controlled to a remarkable extent by what Clifford Geertz calls "extrinsic" as opposed to "intrinsic" information.[10] Unlike other animals' responses to stimuli, which are substantially determined by the innate "hard-wired" neural patterns we usually call "instincts," human responses are shaped primarily by the publicly available, learned symbolic patterns we usually call "culture" or "ideas." Human neural responses to stimuli are extremely generalized; it is not neural patterns but cultural information that tells humans what to do when threatened, hungry, or sexually aroused.

It is the extraordinary role of culture in human behavior that makes the distinction between the ideal and the material a plausible way of talking about humans.[11] According to Christian metaphysics, humans occupied a unique position in the cosmos. In a universe divided into the two utterly distinct substances spirit and matter, only humans had a dual or compound nature. They were composed of both a material body and a spiritual soul bound to the body by God and released only by the body's death. It was the dual character of the human person that made human lives battlegrounds between the lofty desires of the spirit and the base desires of the flesh and that consequently gave them the unique but terrible freedom to choose between good and evil. Within the dualist cosmology of Christianity, the notion that human actions could be under-stood by classifying their sources as ideal or material made sense. But in a post-theological framework, a dualist theory of human action loses its raison d'être.

From the standpoint of contemporary human biology, what is striking is not the categorical contrast between cultural and physiological, or extrinsic and intrinsic constraints on behavior, but their inextricable organic and phylogenetic connection. The connection is phylogenetic because the development of the human brain was rendered possible only by the simultaneous development of culture. The highly general and flexible character of human neural functioning, which makes the organ-ism capable of a vastly greater range and complexity of response to stimuli than in other animals, could have evolved only in conjunction with the cultural information that gives the neural responses their specificity and efficacity. In the absence of extrinsic, symbolically constructed, cultural information, the human being would be radically incomplete, a confused and probably unviable site of powerful but unfocused emotions, perceptions, and urges. "A cultureless human being," as Geertz puts it, "would probably turn out to be not an intrinsically talented though unfulfilled ape, but a wholly mindless and consequently unworkable monstrosity."[12] Homo sapiens would be a *physiological* impossibility in the absence of ideas or culture. In human biology, the ideal and the material, or the mind and the body, are not opposed substances but a consubstantial evolving system.

A philosophical reflection on human action gives rise to a parallel conclusion. Any action undertaken by a human is simultaneously physical and ideational. The physical efficacy of humans' bodies—say, in work, athletics, or warfare—is always inextricably intertwined with their thoughts, knowledge, fears, desires, intentions, and memories. Ideation is always a bodily process that works in physical media. Oratory and writing burn calories, require the development of bodily gestures and muscular prowess, and involve the manipulation of physical substances—paper, ink, or computer keyboards; vibrating columns of air, lecterns, pulpits, or soapboxes; lecture halls, churches, studies, or libraries. The material being of human bodies can only be separated from processes of ideation or symbol manipulation in the exceptional case that proves the rule: the brain-dead body that is kept alive artificially by a machine. For human beings, the action of physical bodies is always symbolically governed, and thought is always a physically mediated process. To categorize human actions as ideal or material is philosophically absurd, since they are always and inextricably both.

A post-materialist labor history—or for that matter a post-materialist social science—must study human action in the world. Human action, the preceding arguments imply, must always be understood as the intelligible action of physically constrained and culturally trained thinking bodies. Such action takes place in a world consisting of physical things, including persons, that are located in space and time but are made meaningful and efficacious because they are defined and activated by culture or ideas. The study of the physical features of the world—the spatial configuration of cities, the layout and mechanical fittings of factories, the shape and fertility of fields, the relations of bacteria or parasites to their human hosts—is always also a study of the culturally informed actions that created, sustained, adapted to, and transformed the world's physical features.[13] The study of culture or meaning must always also be the study of the use of symbols or ideas by embodied minds that communicate through physical media and inhabit and act on a world whose physical features are culturally shaped.

Developing an explicitly post-materialist rhetoric will require both theoretical and literary invention, but the work of invention is already well underway, often in the work of avowed materialists. My own strategy of invention in the remainder of this essay is to show how certain existing trends in labor studies and in the human sciences more broadly might be appropriated or accentuated to create a more effective and theoretically alert figuration for labor history.

Reflections on Oxymoronic Book Titles

My starting point is an observation that might seem tangential to my project: oxymorons have been proliferating recently in the titles of books in labor studies. Let me offer five examples: *Manufacturing Consent* and *The Politics of Production,* both by the avowedly materialist Berkeley sociologist Michael Burawoy; *The Managed Heart,* by his colleague Arlie Hochschild; *The Rise of Market Culture,* by William Reddy; and my own *The Language of Labor.*[14] These oxymoronic titles, properly understood, point toward a new rhetorical paradigm for labor history.

What makes these titles oxymoronic? Oxymorons are figures of speech whose evocative power arises from their uniting of opposites, as in "murky brilliance," "gentle terrors," "deep play," or the unintentional classic "military intelligence." The labor studies titles cited are all oxymoronic because they unite realms conventionally regarded as not only *distinct* but *opposing*—the realms of politics, the economy, and culture. "Language of labor," "market culture," "managed heart," and "manufacturing consent" all unite the realm of culture (language, culture, heart, consent) with the realm of economy (labor, market, managed, manufacturing); similarly, "politics of production" unites the realms of economy and politics. The titles are all tantalizing, and they tantalize because they suggest that the supposedly distinct and material sphere of production and exchange is in fact interlaced with culture and politics.

The books deliver more or less what they promise. All of them challenge, explicitly or implicitly, the notion that production and exchange constitute a distinct sphere of material relations. They show how labor movements arise from semantic transformations, how market culture predates and shapes the formation of market institutions, how emotion can be managed to create profits, how ideological consent is as important a product of factories as physical goods are, and how relations of production arise less out of technology than out of "factory regimes." All the books demonstrate that relations of production are not only affected but actually constituted by politics and culture. They do this by applying to the supposedly material realm theoretical approaches and methods originally developed to study other realms; thus, Burawoy develops a formal political typology of what he calls "factory regimes," and Reddy elaborates a semantic history of the crucial term *grève* (strike).

The oxymoronic titles, then, point toward a rhetorical paradigm for labor history quite different from the standard reductive materialism. They refuse, by implication, to recognize a distinct material realm. They insist that production and exchange be understood as no less susceptible to shaping by politics and culture than are the art world, religion, and the state. They also sustain powerful and empirically rich nonreductive accounts of the political and cultural constitution of labor relations. I think these books are valuable examples and are on the right rhetorical track, even though none of them attempts to spell out explicitly an appropriate paradigm to replace the materialist reductionism that both their titles and their arguments have effectively dissolved. The message of the oxymoronic titles is there for all to read, but it clearly needs both exegesis and publicity.

Blurred Genres, Interdisciplinarity, and Imperialist Claims in the Human Sciences

Clifford Geertz observed a decade ago that the genres of the human sciences have become increasingly "blurred."[15] Although his observations came principally from a particular territory—the ambiguous borderlands between the social sciences and the humanities—I think the condition he describes is quite general and has become more general over the ensuing decade. The pervasive use of oxymoronic titles, both inside and outside of labor studies, is in fact one marker of the blurring of genres. (It might be pointed out in passing that Geertz is something of a virtuoso in the oxymoronic genre, having contributed "thick description," "deep play," "the theater state," and "local knowledge.")[16] One sign of generalized genre blurring is the growing rage for interdisciplinarity. The proliferation of interdisciplinary scholarly journals, which has been going on for some time, shows no signs of slackening. It is probably now the case that more genuinely path-breaking articles are published in such journals as *Comparative Studies in Society and History, Critical Inquiry, Signs, Politics and Society,* or *Representations* than in the leading disciplinary journals—for example, *American Political Science Review, Journal of Modern History,* or *American Anthropologist.* A particularly striking contemporary development is the proliferation of interdisciplinary programs and research centers in major universities—for example, the Committee on Historical Studies at the New School for Social Research, the Program on Rhetoric of Inquiry at the University of Iowa, the History and Society Program at the University of Minnesota, the Center for Social Theory and Comparative History at UCLA, and the Program on the Comparative Study of Social Transformations at the University of Michigan.

Although disciplines continue to control graduate training, hiring, and promotions, they have effectively ceased to control the intellectual life of the human sciences in leading American universities. The intellectual map is now characterized not by distinct disciplinary territories with heavily fortified boundaries but by amorphous disciplines with porous and distended boundaries that are crisscrossed by overlapping interdisciplinary projects. I think we should welcome this ill-defined landscape because it inspires much greater intellectual variety than the old discipline-dominated landscape did. Yet it could be argued that the very indefiniteness of intellectual boundaries also endangers variety by making possible the formulation of grand imperial schemes—ambitious attempts to sweep across the whole of the human sciences and impose a new and uniform order on all branches of knowledge.

The classical map of the human sciences regarded culture, the economy, and politics as distinct institutional spheres, each of which was governed by principles elaborated in a distinct analytical vocabulary and assigned to a distinct discipline: the economy to economics departments, politics to political science, and culture to anthropology and literature. In the post–World War II American academy, all these disciplines were essentially atemporal; the past and questions of change over time were consigned to history departments, with the proviso that historians eschew theory. The massive advent of social history (including labor history) that began in the 1960s was actually a significant force for boundary dissolution. Social historians accepted the entire past as their object of study, but they were determined to make sense of it through theoretical and methodological borrowings (or appropriations) from the various social sciences. Like the French historians of the Annales school before them, they produced a history "without frontiers," a "total history" that transgressed and blurred the conventional boundaries of the social science disciplines.

In the past decade or so, interdisciplinary explorations of the sort pioneered by social historians have been generalized to the human sciences at large. The explosion of interdisciplinary projects has liberated analytical vocabularies from disciplinary enclosures and from exclusive concern with any narrowly defined institutional sphere. In the open and amorphous landscape of the contemporary human sciences, economic theories, cultural theories, and political theories have all claimed the capacity to encompass by themselves the full range of social relations.

The process by which these imperialist claims arose is itself revealingly interdisciplinary. For the most part, it was not a matter of economists, political scientists, anthropologists, or literary critics aggrandizing their disciplines by increasing the range of phenomena to be subjected to their standard intellectual procedures—although there certainly was some of this. The expansive theoretical movements in the contemporary human sciences resulted at least as much from independent invention, poaching by outsiders, or incursions from the margins as from disciplinary aggrandizement.

The claim that all social relations are economic, or, more precisely, are determined by choice under conditions of scarcity, has been advanced most forcefully by the "rational choice" movement. This movement, which is probably the most coherent and best organized of the imperialist currents, also comes closer than any of the others to disciplinary imperialism. Much of its analytical framework not only arose out of neoclassical microeconomics but was elaborated by economists, such as Gary Becker and Mancur Olson.[17] But the contemporary conceptual vocabulary of rational choice theory has also been influenced decisively by the development of game theory, which, for reasons mysterious to me, developed most impressively in departments of political science.[18] The coalescence of microeconomics and game theory has made rational choice a distinct multidisciplinary enterprise, one that has made significant inroads in sociology as well as in economics and political science.[19]

Rational choice theorists insist that choices among alternative means to attain scarce ends beset not only entrepreneurs concerned with how best to produce goods, or workers concerned with enhancing wages and working conditions, or merchants concerned with what to sell and what to buy, but all sorts of people faced with all sorts of decisions, from major policy issues to the conduct of daily life. Economic reasoning, they claim, characterizes behavior not only in economies but also in the full range of institutional spheres that make up societies. For example, Gary Becker's "new home economics" shows that decisions to have a baby or to get married can plausibly be treated as instances of investment, consumption, or the formation of commercial contracts.[20] Most labor historians would belittle Becker's claims, in part because he is a conservative neoclassical economist of the Chicago school. In practice, however, we ourselves commonly and quite properly treat workers' decisions as results of calculations about advantage, personal or collective. Human action is pervasively shaped by ends-means considerations under conditions of scarcity. Rational actor theorists are attempting to clarify and systematize these considerations and to extend them formally to situations outside the sphere of production and exchange.

Theories claiming that all social relations are cultural or discursive have probably spread even more widely in the contemporary academy. Here one might speak of initially independent movements, each of them profoundly interdisciplinary, that have increasingly converged over the past decade. One of these was symbolic anthropology, represented most notably by Clifford Geertz, whose perspectives were taken up and developed outside anthropology as much as within it—most rapidly and avidly by historians but also by philosophers, literary critics, sociologists, and political scientists.[21] A second locus of innovative work about culture was in literary theory, where the ideas of the French philosopher Jacques Derrida were championed by American professors of literature and have become increasingly influential across the humanities and social sciences.[22] A third point of innovation was in the English cultural studies movement, initially launched by Birmingham University's Centre for Contemporary Cultural Studies and represented most prominently by the writings of Stuart Hall.[23] Work in this style has been centered more in sociology than in anthropology; it has focused above all on media and the subcultures of youth and ethnic communities in contemporary Britain. It is now attracting attention in a variety of humanities and social science disciplines in the United States as well as in Britain.

All three of these approaches, which increasingly blend into each other at the edges, tend to claim that all of human existence, from the most elaborate to the simplest of our activities, from the most abstract learned disquisitions to the most concrete bodily functions, are shaped by linguistic and paralinguistic processes of meaning formation, by symbols and their manipulation, by discourse, in the very broad sense in which this term is used by Joan Scott or Ernesto Laclau and Chantal Mouffe.[24] This implies there is no sphere of human life that cannot be analyzed profitably by means of literary, semiotic, or rhetorical techniques to discover and interrelate the meanings it instantiates and displays.

Theories claiming that all of social life is political are harder to characterize in terms of distinct and organized intellectual movements. What can be said is that over the last decade or two notions of "politics," "the political," and "power" have been extended far beyond the traditional realms of the state and official politics to all corners of social life. It seems fair to say that very little of this extension of the conceptual boundaries of politics has come from the discipline of political science, whose practitioners, with rare exceptions, have maintained a focus on state politics in the conventional sense.

As I see it, expansion of the category of the political has come from three different transdisciplinary or extradisciplinary sources. The first is the feminist movement, with its powerful insight that "the personal is political." Feminists have demonstrated that such areas of life as sexuality, education, the family, clothing styles, or art, which are represented in social science and in pre-feminist common sense as apolitical arenas of personal expression, are in fact shot through with power, domination, authority, oppression, and struggle. There is a sexual politics as real and as important in its effects as state politics is; patriarchy is as much a form of domination as aristocracy or imperialism is, and it can only be over-come by conscious political struggle. A feminist perspective demonstrates that political categories cannot be limited to questions of struggle for state power but must be extended to the analysis of (potentially) all social relations.

A second source of an expanded sense of the political is the later work of Michel Foucault, especially *Discipline and Punish* and *The History of Sexuality*.[25] In these books Foucault argues that arenas regarded by liberal society as outside of or antithetical to power—sexuality and scien-tific knowledge—are in fact among the major loci of power in the modern world. To see this, we need to reconceptualize power and its operation, looking not so much at formal domination through the use or threat of force as at subtler and "gentler" but paradoxically more constraining and more pervasive forms of power—at disciplinary complexes and modes of self-knowledge that invest the body with power relations. The forms of power Foucault examines are not concentrated but dispersed or "capillary." They constitute not a mode of command but a "microphysics." Above all, they are all inseparable from the production of knowledge—from the procedures and discourses of the human sciences. The elaboration of the human sciences, from the Enlightenment to the present, has simultaneously been the elaboration of new, subtler, and more potent forms of power. Foucault's work, which has had a wide impact in the social sciences and the humanities, implies that power and politics are to be sought not just in relations with the state but in social relations of all kinds, diffused throughout the social body.

The third source of an expanded concept of the political has been the explosive development of a Gramscian current in recent Marxism. From his cell in a Fascist prison, Gramsci developed a Marxist reflection on the means by which dominant classes hold subordinate classes in subordina-tion without the direct exercise of physical force and on the means by which Communists might struggle against such domination in periods when violent confrontations were doomed to failure—when class struggle had to take the form of what he dubbed a "war of position" rather than a "war of movement." Gramsci's crucial concept was hegemony, which he used to denote the taken-for-granted practices and presuppositions that made subordination seem natural and inevitable to the dominant and subordinate alike.[26] In the 1960s and 1970s, Marxists impatient with the economism and determinism of Stalinist discourse used the concept of hegemony to validate cultural and artistic forms of political struggle and to investigate the role of language and culture in sociopolitical processes. One result of this effort was a heightened awareness of the political significance of social relations outside the sphere of formal politics—an insistence that literature, art, ritual, custom, and everyday practices of all kinds established and reinforced relations of power. Like feminist and Foucauldian perspectives, Gramscian analyses have suggested that politics is not confined to supposedly "political" institutions but is constitutive of social relations of all kinds.

These three "imperialist" tendencies are not altogether parallel. The rational choice movement is clearly more unified and better organized than the others, and proponents of both economic and cultural theories normally are more explicitly imperialist in their claims than are advocates of political theories. Indeed, both the Foucauldian and Gramscian tendencies are notable for their *conflation* of culture and politics rather than for any attempt to *reduce* culture to politics. Foucault and his followers speak of "power/knowledge" as a single category, and "hegemony" is a political term used to denote a relationship that is simultaneously cultural and political. In spite of these differences, all three tendencies represent striking expansions of previously "regional" categories over the whole of social life. They are powerful attempts to impose a unitary interpretive order on social phenomena in general.

Toward a New Rhetoric

I would argue that we must accept all of these imperialist claims—cultural, economic, and political. But from this it also follows that the imperialism of each claim systematically undermines the imperialism of the others. The imperialist discourses are right to insist that their analytical vocabularies—whether economic, cultural, or political—cannot be limited to any "home" institutional domain. Although we may still wish to distinguish between what are conventionally called economic, cultural, and political institutions, such distinctions are purely matters of convenience. They do not designate "natural kinds" of institutions subject to distinct forms of causality. Instead, all human institutions belong to the same kind, and all are shaped by the same range of human constraints and capabilities. Questions of meaning, scarcity, and power are universal, not sectoral, in scope. For this reason, it is entirely proper that the "imperialist" theorists have extended their political, economic, and cultural theories to all areas of social life.

The "imperialists" have been wrong, however, to believe that because their theories hold in all institutional sectors, they are by themselves adequate to explain social relations in all those sectors, or for that matter in any sector. This presumption is actually a holdover from the old disciplinary division of labor, where economic theories employed by economists were assumed to hold universal sway in the economic realm, political theories employed by political scientists to hold comparable sway in the realm of politics, and cultural theories employed by anthropologists to hold sway in the realm of culture. The same breaching of disciplinary boundaries that made possible the spread of any given theoretical perspective into new institutional territory also enabled rival disciplines to infiltrate that same theory's previously secure institutional redoubt. The recent spread of imperialist discourses implies not only that no discourse can become universally sovereign but also that none can claim an uncontested sovereignty anywhere. Paradoxically, the price of universal reach is the loss of even local claims to full causal or interpretive sufficiency.

The simultaneous flourishing of multiple imperialisms implies that the social world must be fundamentally refigured. The classical disciplinary map of society as constituted by more or less autonomous spheres of politics, culture, and economics clearly is no longer viable. Nor can we accept the "imperialist" picture of the world as constituted by a range of diverse institutions and practices, all of which can be explained sufficiently either by meaning, or by power, or by scarcity. Instead, I would argue that we must imagine a world in which every social relationship is simultaneously constituted by meaning, by scarcity, and by power. This would imply, for example, that all social relations are discursive but that social relations are never exhausted by their discursivity. It also implies something much more radical: the discursive features of the social relationship are themselves always constitutively shaped by power relations and conditions of choice under scarcity. It further implies that this constitutive shaping is reciprocal—just as meanings are always shaped by scarcity and power, so scarcity is always shaped by power and meaning, and power is always shaped by meaning and scarcity.

To see what this formula of mutual constitutive shaping might mean in practice, we could consider one of the most striking patterns uncovered by labor historians: the large and persistent gap between male and female wage rates. How is this gap to be understood? A simple if rather naive explanation in terms of scarcities would be that women had fewer marketable skills than men. But this scarcity itself resulted from power discrepancies (men controlled the apprenticeship programs that taught skills) and meanings (gender ideologies defined women as incapable of or unsuited for skilled work). The power discrepancies in turn were consequences of scarcities (men controlled unions in part because so few women worked in the trade) and meanings (union organizing was a public activity and therefore coded male). Moreover, meanings resulted from power discrepancies (men's control of their wives, sisters, and daughters made it difficult for women to express views that challenged male superiority, let alone to get them accepted) and scarcities (few women had access to the public spaces and the media in which meanings were communicated). The meanings, scarcities, and power relations are analytically distinct dimensions of the complex that produced the male-female wage gap. Each dimension had its own effectivity and internal logic. For example, cultural definitions of women as lacking skill were tied to a wider body of gender distinctions that coded women as private rather than public, emotional rather than rational, weak rather than strong, dependent rather than independent, and so on. But the logically tied sets of scarcities, power differences, and meanings never exist in a pure state—or do so only when abstracted onto the pages of academics' books. In real social relations, they are always mutually constitutive dimensions of a complex.

A theoretical figuration of the social world as mutually constitutive complexes of meanings, scarcities, and power relations does not by itself dictate the rhetorical form of our labor histories, but it opens up certain possibilities and closes off others. It is predicated on abandoning not only the base and superstructure model that has been under attack in labor history ever since E. P. Thompson published *The Making of the English Working Class* but also the more fundamental rhetorical assumption that production and exchange can legitimately be characterized as material—a notion still espoused in practice by most professed Thompsonians.[27] It is compatible with the implicit message of the oxymoronic book titles—that the economic realm is also a realm of power and meaning—and with the "imperialist" efforts to extend the reach of political, economic, and cultural analyses to every sphere of social relations. It would certainly have a place for the Foucauldian, rational choice, or Derridaian labor studies that are now beginning to appear.[28] But it might also urge oxymoronic or imperialist scholars to recognize the limitations of those particular rhetorical modes. It might induce oxymoronists to enlarge their interpretive schemes beyond the redescription of economic institutions in terms of meanings or power by making them recognize that such a redescription could itself always be redescribed from yet another angle. Moreover, it might alert imperialists anxious to demonstrate the universal applicability of power analytics to the possibility that the very institutions so triumphantly claimed for politics can just as plausibly be claimed by enthusiasts for meaning or scarcity. It points toward a labor history more multiple in its theoretical strategies, more ironic in its rhetorical stance, and more open in its search for understanding.[29]

Of course, this call for openness and multiplicity is itself a particular rhetorical strategy—the sudden imposition of a comic narrative trope that brings apparently conflicting and dissonant forces into harmony at the end.[30] It is not the only conclusion that might be drawn from the story I have told up to this point, and it is not without potential dangers. If all labor historians were to heed this advice, arguments for the interpretive power of any particular perspective might be blunted by awareness of the counterclaims of other perspectives and therefore might not be pushed to their most radical conclusions. The result might even be a descent into a cozy consensus, where all labor historians become so multisided that they suffer paralysis of the will. Currently, however, I see little practical danger of consensus, other than the old materialist consensus that so badly needs to be superseded. My prediction is that the imperialist projects now sweeping the human sciences will ensure diversity in labor history, as elsewhere, for some time. My "comic" conclusion represents an effort—however personal—to retain the bracing energy of contemporary intellectual projects without succumbing to any narrow imperialism.

Notes

I would like to thank Keith Baker, Larry Griffin, Sherry Ortner, Lou Roberts, and Donald Herzog for their comments on this essay. I presented earlier versions at the 1990 meeting of the Society for French Historical Studies in Columbus, Ohio; at a brownbag at the Center for Research on Social Organization at the University of Michigan; at a fellows' seminar at the Center for Advanced Study in the Behavioral Sciences in Stanford, California; at a meeting of the Seminar in Comparative Studies at the University of California, Berkeley; and at the Workshop on European History at Stanford University. I am grateful for the critiques and suggestions I received on all of these occasions. This essay was completed while I was a fellow at the Center for Advanced Study in the Behavioral Sciences. I am grateful for support provided by the National Science Foundation, grant number BNS-870064, and by a fellowship from the John Simon Guggenheim Memorial Foundation.

1. Gareth Stedman Jones, *Languages of Class: Studies in English Working Class History, 1832-1982* (Cambridge, 1983); Joan Wallach Scott, "On Gender, Language, and Working-Class History," in *Gender and the Politics of History* (New York, 1988), pp. 53-67; Jacques Rancière, "The Myth of the Artisan: Critique of a Category of Social History," *International Labor and Working-Class History*, no. 24 (1983): 1-16, and *La nuit des prolétaires* (Paris, 1981). See also

Donald Reid's discussion of Rancière in "The Night of the Proletarians: Deconstruction and Social History," *Radical History Review,* nos. 28-30 (1984): 444-63.
The majority reaction of labor historians to such work is perhaps exemplified by
the published comments on the Scott article by Brian Palmer and Christine
Stansell, *International Labor and Working-Class History,* no. 31 (1987): 14-23
and 24-29, respectively. The initial version of Scott's article was published in
International Labor and Working-Class History, no. 31 (1987): 1-13.

2. See, for example, John S. Nelson, Allan Megill, and Donald N. McCloskey,
eds., *The Rhetoric of the Human Sciences: Language and Argument in Scholarship and Public Affairs* (Madison, Wis., 1987); and Donald N. McCloskey, *The
Rhetoric of Economics* (Madison, Wis., 1985).

3. As correctives to the homogenizing history of *proletarianization,* I would
suggest Raphael Samuel, "Workshop of the World: Steam Power and Hand
Technology in Mid-Victorian Britain," *History Workshop,* no. 3 (1977): 6-72;
Charles Sabel and Jonathan Zeitlin, "Historical Alternatives to Mass Production:
Politics, Markets, and Technology in Nineteenth-Century Industrialization," *Past
and Present,* no. 108 (1985): 133-74; and William H. Sewell, Jr., "Uneven
Development, the Autonomy of Politics, and the Dockworkers of Nineteenth-
Century Marseille," *American Historical Review* 93 (1988): 604-37.

4. For a particularly illuminating argument on this line, see Marshall Sahlins,
Culture and Practical Reason (Chicago, 1976), esp. chap. 4, entitled "La Pensée
Bourgeoise," pp. 166-204.

5. William M. Reddy, *Money and Liberty in Europe: A Critique of Historical
Understanding* (Cambridge, 1987).

6. Robert E. Cole, *Strategies for Learning: Small-Group Activities in American,
Japanese, and Swedish Industry* (Berkeley, Calif., 1989); Paul Lillrank and
Noriaki Kano, *Continuous Improvement: Quality Control Circles in Japanese
Industry* (Ann Arbor, Mich., 1989).

7. David Montgomery, *Workers' Control in America: Studies in the History of
Work, Technology, and Labor Struggles* (Cambridge, 1979), p. 9.

8. E. P. Thompson, *The Making of the English Working Class* (London,
1963); Louis Althusser, *Lenin and Philosophy, and Other Essays* (New York,
1971); Ernesto Laclau and Chantal Mouffe, *Hegemony and Socialist Strategy:
Towards a Radical Democratic Politics* (London, 1975); Samuel Bowles and
Herbert Gintis, *Democracy and Capitalism: Property, Community, and the Contradictions of Modern Social Thought* (New York, 1986). The question of how
Gramsci, whose own critique of economism is so tentative and incomplete,
became the pervasive tutelary spirit of the far more vigorous and explosive
antireductionist strain of Marxism in the 1970s and 1980s strikes me as a
fascinating topic for intellectual history.

9. Laclau and Mouffe, *Hegemony and Socialist Strategy,* p. 4.

10. Geertz's discussion of extrinsic and intrinsic information is in "Religion
as a Cultural System," in *The Interpretation of Cultures* (New York, 1973),
pp. 92-93. The conception of human nature and of human biological evolution
from which this distinction derives is discussed more fully in the immediately

preceding essay, "The Growth of Culture and the Evolution of Mind," pp. 55-83.

11. It must be emphasized that distinguishing ideal from material or spirit from matter is merely *plausible*. Such a distinction is certainly not a human universal. Anyone desiring a proof need not stray beyond the Western tradition. In his *Confessions*, Saint Augustine indicates that one of the principal sticking points in his conversion to Christianity was that he could not imagine an incorporeal god who inhabited a realm of pure spirit instead of occupying space. It was only after he succeeded in breaking through this barrier of Christian metaphysics that his conversion could be complete. *The Confessions of Saint Augustine*, trans. John K. Ryan (Garden City, N.Y., 1960), pp. 127-28, 157-59.

12. Geertz, *The Interpretation of Cultures*, p. 68.

13. No historical work I have seen does this more effectively or movingly than Marc Bloch's discussion of the history of the rural landscape in his book originally published in 1931, *French Rural History: An Essay on Its Basic Characteristics*, trans. Janet Sondheimer (Berkeley, Calif., 1970).

14. Michael Burawoy, *Manufacturing Consent: Changes in the Labor Process under Monopoly Capitalism* (Chicago, 1979) and *The Politics of Production: Factory Regimes under Capitalism and Socialism* (London, 1985); Arlie Hochschild, *The Managed Heart: Commercialization of Human Feeling* (Berkeley, Calif., 1983); William Reddy, *The Rise of Market Culture: The Textile Trade and French Society, 1750-1900* (Cambridge, 1984); William H. Sewell, Jr., *Work and Revolution in France: The Language of Labor from the Old Regime to 1848* (Cambridge, 1980).

15. Clifford Geertz, "Blurred Genres: The Reconfiguration of Social Thought," in *Local Knowledge: Further Essays in Interpretive Anthropology* (New York, 1983), pp. 19-35.

16. Clifford Geertz, "Thick Description: Toward an Interpretive Theory of Culture" and "Deep Play: Notes on the Balinese Cockfight," in *The Interpretation of Cultures*, pp. 3-30, 412-53, respectively; *Negara: The Theater State in Nineteenth-Century Bali* (Princeton, N.J., 1980); *Local Knowledge*.

17. Gary S. Becker, *A Treatise on the Family* (Cambridge, Mass., 1981); Mancur Olson, *The Logic of Collective Action* (Cambridge, Mass., 1963).

18. See, for example, Russell Hardin, *Collective Action* (Baltimore, 1982); Robert Axelrod, *The Evolution of Cooperation* (New York, 1984); and the many works of Jon Elster, including *Sour Grapes* (Cambridge, 1983), *Ulysses and the Sirens*, rev. ed. (Cambridge, 1984), *Solomonic Judgements* (Cambridge, 1989), and *Cement of Society* (Cambridge, 1989).

19. Important books in the rational choice mode by sociologists include James S. Coleman, *Foundations of Social Theory* (Cambridge, Mass., 1989); and Michael Hechter, *Principles of Group Solidarity* (Berkeley, Calif., 1987). For lucid introductions to rational choice theory, see Jon Elster, *Rational Choice* (Oxford, 1986), pp. 1-33; and Jon Elster, *Nuts and Bolts for the Social Sciences* (Cambridge, 1989).

20. Becker, *A Treatise on the Family*.

21. Geertz, *The Interpretation of Cultures*, is the central text. Two historians

influenced by symbolic anthropology are Robert Darnton, *The Great Cat Massacre and Other Episodes in French Cultural History* (New York, 1984); and Natalie Zemon Davis, *Society and Culture in Early Modern France* (Stanford, Calif., 1975).

22. An ingenious study of Derrida's influence is Michèle Lamont, "How to Become a Dominant French Philosopher: The Case of Jacques Derrida," *American Journal of Sociology* 93 (1987): 584-622.

23. Stuart Hall and Tony Jefferson, eds., *Resistance through Rituals: Youth Subcultures in Post-War Britain* (London, 1976); Stuart Hall, ed., *Culture, Media, Language: Working Papers in Cultural Studies, 1972-79* (London, 1980).

24. Scott, *Gender and the Politics of History;* Laclau and Mouffe, *Hegemony and Socialist Strategy.*

25. Michel Foucault, *Discipline and Punish: The Birth of the Prison,* trans. Alan Sheridan (New York, 1977), and *The History of Sexuality,* trans. Alan Sheridan: vol. 1, *An Introduction* (New York, 1978); vol. 2, *The Use of Pleasure* (New York, 1985); and vol. 3, *The Care of the Self* (New York, 1986).

26. Antonio Gramsci, *Selections from the Prison Notebooks,* trans. Quintin Hoare and Geoffrey Nowell Smith (New York, 1972).

27. Thompson, *The Making of the English Working Class.*

28. Examples are David Levine, "Punctuated Equilibrium: The Modernization of the Proletarian Family in the Age of Ascendant Capitalism," *International Labor and Working-Class History,* no. 39 (1991): 3-20 (Foucauldian history); Adam Przeworski, *Capitalism and Social Democracy* (Cambridge, 1985) (rational choice history); and Scott, *Gender and the Politics of History* (Derridaian history).

29. In keeping with this note of openness, I should point out that I do not regard meaning, scarcity, and power as a holy trinity. These three dimensions certainly do not exhaust the complexity of social relations. I give them priority here not because they are intrinsically more important than other dimensions but because they have been pushed forward by current theoretical movements in the human sciences. To fortify this point, I propose another three dimensions that could also be said to constitute (mutually) all social relations: the demographic-ecological, the social, and the geographic. Let me briefly justify these. First, the demographic-ecological: all social relations are subject to the entry and exit of persons and organizations through time, and the dynamics of such exits and entries both affect and are affected by power relations, relative scarcities, and the generation of meanings. Second, the social: all social relations are composed of more or less sustained face-to-face encounters whose informal patterns and norms are influenced by but distinct from questions of scarcity, power, demography-ecology, and meaning. Third, the geographic: all social relations take place within spatial constraints that are profoundly shaped by but not reducible to questions of demography-ecology, scarcity, sociality, meaning, or power. The relevant dimensions of social complexity constitute an open rather than a closed set, as do the consequent possibilities for imperialist or oxymoronic rhetorical strategies.

30. See Hayden White, *Metahistory: The Historical Imagination in Nineteenth-Century Europe* (Baltimore, 1973).

DONALD REID

Reflections on Labor History and Language

When I first read Jacques Rancière's *La nuit des prolétaires* in Paris in 1981, I was disoriented.[1] Maurice Agulhon, Christopher Johnson, William Sewell, none had quite prepared me for Rancière's book. What he talked about and especially the ways he talked about it were alien to me. Clearly, Rancière knew and wrote about history; he had spent years in the archives. What bothered me was that Rancière did not introduce workers' writings to illuminate insights derived from studying their activities in the community or the workplace. On the contrary, it was precisely the distance between the workplace and the accounts of those who wrote of it that interested him. Nor did Rancière use workers' pronouncements to reproduce familiar narratives of class formation and class consciousness. (I was particularly aware of this because I had just had my first article accepted. Feeling insecure about its significance, I had inserted the phrase "the development of working-class consciousness" into the title, although this was questionably related to the content of the essay.[2]) What Rancière spoke about instead was a kind of suffering and longing among workers for the opportunity to do unproductive labor, such as writing poetry and philosophizing, which had little place in most studies of the working class. Even the works of labor history I found lyrical, like E. P. Thompson's *Making of the English Working Class,* seemed ultimately to circumscribe workers in a historical narrative and a habitus of community and workshop. Thompson and his alter ego William Blake were the poets; Thompson's subjects were on the whole sober-minded workers and politicians.

To say what he wanted to say, Rancière had developed a style that made me feel I was entering in the middle of things and leaving before they were fully resolved. The familiar forms of the American monograph and the French thesis were lacking. Only later did I come to see that *La nuit des prolétaires* resembled classical philosophical texts, like the dialogues of Plato in which conversations and stories are pieced together in such a way as to question the orderings of social life. In Rancière's work, these orderings include the nineteenth-century bourgeois radicals' and working-class spokesmen's representations of the nature of labor and cultural activity, the contemporary sociologist's assumptions about the relationship between threats to skills and militancy, the Leninist's interpretation of the transformative effects of the encounter of radical bourgeois and worker, and the anthropologist's affirmation of the radical difference between workers' culture and that of the rest of society. In sum, Rancière had crafted a literary form that could convey his dialogue with both nineteenth-century workers and intellectuals and contemporary critical traditions.

In *The Making of the English Working Class,* Thompson had sought to rescue his subjects from "the enormous condescension of posterity" embodied in the liberal, capitalist narrative of progress by explaining and justifying their actions in the political, social, and moral counternarrative of class formation and consciousness.[3] Would a history that did not see meaning as necessarily reducible to such dichotomous narratives threaten Thompson's rescue effort? Or, I started to wonder, do we accord historical figures even more respect when we see that the "independence" or "honor" they speak of may contain a kernel of indecipherability that makes them human—even though this defies our own categories or explanations of their actions?

Reading *La nuit des prolétaires,* I found myself moved, like the workers Rancière describes, whose lives were changed in ways they never totally understood by their chance meetings with Saint-Simonians and Fourierists. Thinking about *La nuit des prolétaires* was a liberating experience, in the way that the generation from whom I learned labor history felt liberated by its encounter with *The Making of the English Working Class.* Rancière suggested new questions for labor historians, new ways of reading texts, and new ways of writing history. Yet responding to his challenge proved difficult. I voiced inner doubts about the kind of sociological labor history I was doing in a title, subtitling my first book *A Genealogy of Deindustrialization,* an oblique and undeveloped reference to the idea that we begin with effects and move to causes but construct our narratives inversely.[4] About the same time I used the term *discourse* in another title—but loosely enough to win the approbation of Bryan Palmer, the sharpest critic of the new interest in language among social historians.[5]

In my second book, a study of the sewermen of Paris, I returned to some of the questions raised by my reading of Rancière.[6] The methods that had served me well in my first book were inadequate to explain the two things that had led me to this project: the laudatory nature of accounts that bourgeois observers like the great early nineteenth-century public health expert A.-J.-B. Parent-Duchâtelet gave of sewermen; and Belle Epoque sewermen's creation of an agricultural settlement outside of Paris, where invalid and retired sewermen and sewermen's orphans and widows lived as a "big family." The former pointed toward the ways in which language helps give meaning to human experience; the latter led me to think about how language works to constitute rather than simply reflect social groupings.

Unease, excitement, the desire to reconcile admiration and respect for a historiography of the working class and the labor movement with a parricidal wish to *épater le prolétariat* of books and its creators—I have many reasons to welcome the current debate over whether labor history should take a "linguistic turn." This is a contest over epistemology and politics, but such conflicts are never limited to these arenas. The identities each side constructs of itself and the representations it proposes of the other are crucial factors in how the debate is understood and what its outcomes will be.

Bryan Palmer, a distinguished historian of Canadian labor, has produced the most developed critique of the linguistic turn in social history. Although Palmer represents only one response of those hostile to linguistically informed history—just as Sewell, Rancière, Gareth Stedman Jones, and Joan Scott present only a few possibilities of such a history—his thought-provoking analysis is well worth our attention. In the first chapter of *Descent into Discourse,* Palmer succinctly summarizes the history of the linguistic turn in linguistics, philosophy, and literary criticism. According to Palmer's account, proponents of the linguistic turn see language as a system of signs that derive their meaning from relations to (and differences from) one another rather than from a determining material context or reality outside of language.[7] Once this is understood, he thinks it should be clear that the linguistic turn has little to offer social history. His general critique of works by social historians addressing language in ways with which he disagrees is that their authors have failed to see the nihilist abyss, in the form of the loss of a stable, knowable material reality, opening up at the end of their projects.

Palmer then turns to the new social history of the 1960s and 1970s to argue that its practitioners had long been interested in the ways in which social groups had come to consciousness of their social identity through the development of languages expressing the particularity of their social experience. Social historians often celebrated the linguistic creativity of the speakers but attributed the meanings of what they said to some fundamental social, cultural, or political reality. Palmer devotes much of the rest of *Descent into Discourse* to an examination of recent work in history that addresses questions of language. Palmer is a Marxist and finds the most to praise in Marxist histories. His aim, however, is to develop a materialist popular front against the potentially fascist implications of the linguistic turn (revealed in Paul de Man's wartime writings). Palmer tries to rally as wide a range of supporters as he can. The criterion he uses in constructing his coalition in the field of labor history is an acceptance of some form of class analysis. Sewell's *Work and Revolution in France,* which situates the origins of class in the explosive interaction of corporate discourse and the revolutionary language of liberty, is therefore included;[8] William Reddy's *Money and Liberty* is not.[9]

Palmer's concern with drawing boundaries ultimately obscures an understanding of language that could serve as the basis of a linguistically informed social history. I would like to see labor historians take up the linguistic challenge offered by other disciplines and use it as an opportunity to clarify and rethink our own ideas about language. Unlike Palmer, I think we can see language as consisting of signs that derive meaning from their relations to (and differences from) one another *as well as* from reference to contexts or social and material realities, with the understanding that accounts of the human experience of these contexts or realities are themselves given meaning through language. Language and the interpretation of experience are inseparable; the historian has no choice except to develop techniques to study them together.

In the place of a single interpretive narrative, such as the Marxism grounding Palmer's critique, Joan Scott, a practitioner of a linguistically informed history, proposes a method that questions the apparent coherence of such narratives. This is at the heart of her use of the analytical category of gender to challenge such canonical labor histories as *The Making of the English Working Class.*[10] For Scott, narratives of class formation cannot adequately incorporate the complexity of the languages that shape conceptions of gender; if women workers are marginal in our sources and our histories, for example, we can study the production of that marginality as an expression of prefiguring linguistic categories.[11]

The goal of linguistically informed history is to open up material reality to a multiplicity of meanings and to understand history as involving contests over these meanings. This is the source of the "terrifying relativism" to which Scott refers.[12] Power is revealed in the ways in which linguistic structures define social relations as they describe, incorporate, and give meaning to social reality. This is an activity that can be studied through analysis of contestation in all its forms, including social and political movements and institutions. All parties are themselves linguistically defined, and in every social conflict they use language (broadly defined) to represent and contest power. Not surprisingly then, linguistically informed historians are suspicious of accounts predicated on social actors who simply know their interests, class or otherwise, and act on them. Interests are constructed through both unconscious and conscious uses of language, and the meanings of specific actions take shape in relation to these constructions.

Scott was a leading practitioner of the "new labor history" of the 1960s and 1970s. Palmer accuses her of failing to undertake an adequate reconsideration of her past work in light of her present concerns.[13] What is needed, however, is not autocritique but an understanding of the relationship of the construction through language of the "self" of the historical narrative (class, women, and so forth) and that of the historical narrator. Traversing the epistemological break separating Scott's early work from her recent essays helps explain the particular challenge that new work in language offers to the understandings, rules, and practices by which labor historians produce their books and their identities. The new labor history of the 1960s and 1970s developed in reaction to extensive bodies of literature on economic history and on socialist, communist, and workerist leaders, organizations, and ideas. The discipline posited as its primary objects of study the workplace and community organization and culture of workers, instead of a determinist economics or a congeries of ideologies and parties. While new labor historians disagreed on much, they saw in both their own political practice and the lives of the workers they studied a moral and political dynamic that earlier forms of labor history had obscured. The dialectic embedded in the new labor history's goal of uncovering the essence of the working class through careful reconstruction of its social and cultural existence, on the one hand, and economists' and ideologues' inadequate representations of labor, on the other, has made it particularly difficult for new labor historians to accept the sacrifice the linguistic turn would demand: recognition that the labor historians' account of social reality and the political and moral narrative it supports or reflects also ultimately rely on linguistic constructs.

New labor historians developed their identities and their narratives through a complex process of differentiation from their historiographic forebearers and association with the experiences and cultures of the world of labor they were simultaneously uncovering and constructing. Asked about her graduate career, Scott responded that when she went to the University of Wisconsin in 1962, it was "a vast factory turning out Ph.D.s."[14] The individual staffing the departmental graduate personnel office accorded her a five-minute interview and placed her in French history. She worked with the preeminent historian and socialist intellectual Harvey Goldberg, whose project of assigning each student a famous socialist brought together the old historiography of leaders and the standardized assembly line of topics; this in turn assured the power of the *patron* Goldberg, since he had already produced the definitive biography of the greatest of French socialists, Jean Jaurès.[15] Scott rebelled. Evoking the motif of the pre–assembly line apprentice, she depicted herself as "like a young glassworker" in writing her acclaimed study of the Carmaux glassworkers.[16] Skilled workers take center stage in Scott's book, displacing their deputy Jaurès, her dissertation director's historiographic tradition, and for some, Marxism itself.[17]

In embedding the history of socialism in specific experiences or examples of labor history, historians as diverse as Thompson, Scott, and Sewell challenged histories that stressed importing class or socialist consciousness into the working class. Yet their very success helped further a labor history based on the dominant narrative structure of the development of class consciousness. It is the exclusionary nature of such a unitary narrative that Scott now critiques. She suggests that in responding to challenges to this narrative, labor historians have ironically adopted the tactics of socialist politicians whose histories they had previously questioned, ignoring gender except when, "acting on a kind of popular-front mentality," they recite the litany of race, class, and gender as a cover for their study of class.[18]

Labor historians' identification with their subjects and their affirmation of the morally and politically uplifting narrative in which workers' history is embedded reinforce their resistance to linguistically informed history. As Scott tells labor historians, "It is threatening because it requires a critical stance . . . to one's own self-concept as a member of the 'fraternal' order"; "difficult, for it requires the mastery of philosophically complex, often abstruse, theories."[19] Labor historians will be no happier than skilled glassworkers to hear that their investments in work culture (tramping to obscure archives) and technical skills (regression analysis) have apparently been devalued. Some will be reminded of the conclusion to *The Glassworkers of Carmaux:* the socialism of skilled workers generated a new class of managers—caricatures of *la nouvelle* Scott?—former workers whose power flowed from mastery of the pen rather than the blowing pipe and who flouted union rules, asserting that capitalism had been banished from the cooperative glassworks.[20]

Faced with linguistically informed history's challenge to their identity and ways of doing things, not a few labor historians have responded by coding it as the foreign "other": flighty, modish, and irrational; in a word, French. "The critics sport about in the fields of cosmopolitan debate, tossing glamourous French names to and fro, plying intellectual arabesques," declared one historian.[21] A French organism, the linguistic turn is made doubly dangerous when propagated in the United States, away from its natural predators.[22] Labor historians' suspicions about the instability and alien nature of linguistically informed history reveal the guild's mentality. They frequently entertain a disquieting dialectic between their own past (as individuals and as a community) and that which they study. The resulting fear of vertigo has helped enforce a certain moral code among labor historians: particular sobriety is required among those whose duty is to chronicle the hardships, injustices, and exploitations of working women and men and to recover their efforts to do something about them.

I see this at work in the "tongue in cheek" scenario of a demonstration in 1842 in Halifax with which Palmer begins a rejoinder to Scott in a 1987 essay in *International Labor and Working-Class History*. "Consumed by the gnawing desire to know what these men and women are all about," Palmer "become[s] one with the throng" in order "to interrogate a marcher." He is "captivated" and "on the verge of entering into [the] ensemble of meanings" in her speech, when he is knocked down by a soldier's horse. "Looking up into the flared nostrils of the state's steed reminds me of a similar view I 'experienced' fifteen years ago at a May Day anti-imperialist rally in Washington. As my mind wanders to that event I catch a glimpse of the woman . . . beating a hasty retreat. No discourse today! The class struggle has intervened, and somewhat rudely at that."[23] Palmer does not see that the meanings of events in 1842 are linguistically constructed in his text in relation to the meanings conveyed by memories of much later events. Instead, the lesson he draws is that workers and historians have experienced contusions, whose evident meaning requires no recourse to linguistic constructions—and that the iron heel of the oppressor will fall on those who lose themselves in the land of language. The memory of Washington thus performs a policing function, wrenching Palmer at the point of consummation from a world where desire and captivation have threatened to lead him astray.

What can we conclude from my incomplete and idiosyncratic rendering of a labor history infiltrated by the reconstituted languages, cultures, and experiences of those it studies and who study it? Labor history today is a field settled with established monographic routines and, as the increasing diversity of recent studies in labor history suggests, ripe for a mid-life crisis.[24] Like anyone in such straits, it is torn between affirmation of past successes and ways of doing things and the desire to cut loose, to be different, to achieve at least temporarily the distance necessary to assess its past and future. What is most disturbing about such situations is the inability to be in two places at once. Questioning the old life involves living the new, with its attendant accusations of immorality and infidelity. It is in the nature of things that each side will claim there is no looking back to the old life, but this very insistence should raise suspicions.

The radical embrace of heterogeneity implicit in the linguistic turn and the contestatory nature of an approach that reveals a multiplicity of meanings frustrate those who want to see in linguistically informed history a single-minded attack on the project of labor history (except to the extent that labor history limits itself to a singular project and way of carrying it out). By rejecting a single counterparadigm, the linguistic turn can extend as well as challenge other explanatory systems. Its attention to the processes of inclusion and exclusion common to the histories and disciplinary delineations of all areas of the new social history offers ways of conceptualizing relationships among them other than the popular front.

Linguistically informed labor history is inextricable from other forms of labor history. It explores terrain uncovered by historians writing in diverse traditions. Scott's essays, for instance, constantly beckon to diverse methodologies and their findings, often concluding with evocations of the utility of her insights to established problematics in labor history. Although accounts of social experience necessarily come to us coded in language, it can also be said that language always comes to us referring to experience. The new interest in language can therefore be seen as an invitation to reinterpret rather than to rebuff the world of agency and experience.[25] Put bluntly, a linguistically informed history never ceases to ask who speaks, who listens, who acts, when, where, why, how often, and to what effect; it simply reveals that efforts to understand the meanings of these activities are inseparable from the languages available to both historical actors and historian analysts.

With this in mind, we can appreciate Scott's contention that uncovering information on which women did or did not participate in a certain movement and explaining this in terms of social background and similar variables—the kind of problematic social historians have generally posed—would be enriched by an approach that seeks to reveal how the

languages in which source materials and models of contemporary historical scholarship are coded help determine both our queries and our
answers to them. Histories limited to assessing either the presence or
absence of women in a movement or the ways in which that movement
and its history were constructed through the languages of specific historical and historiographic cultures are insufficient; a linguistically informed
labor history would reject this dichotomization.

Decoding "a double historical document"[26]—a work of history that
interprets historical texts—offers particular opportunities and challenges
to linguistically informed history. It is important that we not immediately
conflate the construction of categories in the work of history (or our own
historical period) with those of the period the text reconstructs. Keeping
this in mind ensures that linguistically informed history will remain
radically historical rather than ahistorical, as critics often charge. Discovering, for instance, that contemporary commentary on a movement in
the past was constructed around categories with significance to us as
well, like masculinity and femininity, does not on its own reveal how men
and women of the time might have consciously or unconsciously interpreted
the movement. Categories like public/private and masculine/feminine
may have generated different meanings in the languages of the society
under examination than they would in the languages of the societies of
later interpreters (even if these interpreters can be seen to have appropriated elements of earlier languages). Meanings are determined in relation
to both contemporary and current languages, although reference to these
can never assign a single meaning to a text. In other words, questioning
interpretive systems in the past always involves questioning our own.

Proponents of linguistically informed history suggest the constant
relation of historical reality to linguistic meanings for the histories that
historians construct and the actors whom they describe. No category of
analysis is without consequence for the object under analysis. Study of
the conflicts over meaning in the actions and cultural products among
members of a seemingly coherent collectivity—a class, an occupation, or
a sex-specific group, for instance—may reveal mechanisms of identification and differentiation marginalized in models or narratives that move
from social conditions and social experience to social consciousness. A
linguistically informed analysis can suggest ways in which language constructs rather than reflects identity, interests, intentions, and actions.

Significant work has been done in this vein. Arguing for the autonomy
of politics from socioeconomic explanations, Sewell has referred to the
"(as yet insufficiently recognized) crisis of labor history's reigning explanatory strategy."[27] Reddy criticizes Marx for what he sees as Marx's incom-

plete critique of liberal economists, while simultaneously proposing a
labor history that challenges the liberal languages of market and class.[28]
From a different perspective, Anson Rabinbach has recently contended
that "the ways in which scientific ideas, epistemological frameworks, and
reform strategies redefined labor (and its practical consequences) [in the
late nineteenth and early twentieth centuries] eluded most social historians because they did not emerge directly from class conflict."[29]

Much labor history in the past has been marked by a slippage in the
movement from narratives of exploitation and class formation to constructions of identity and interests under the rubric of class consciousness. In
fact, one of the compelling things about class has been the way it
functions to smooth over frictions at points where the constituent elements of studies (demography, culture, politics, and so forth), each with
its own internal logic and narratives, come together. How, in such accounts,
has class acted to include, exclude, and structure? Some insights into this
problem can be derived from recent work on the concept of the lumpenproletariat and the ways in which it operates to construct linguistically
the proletariat in Marx's texts.[30]

Class analysis has rewarded labor historians for interpreting texts in
terms of contexts. They usually read sources in the light of the presumed
political, social, and economic interests of their authors or use them as
local color—confirmation of what is already known. For example, where
Michael Hanagan cites Armand Audiganne's 1854 description of Loire
coal miners as illustrative of the findings of his valuable reconstruction of
miners' lives in *Nascent Proletarians,*[31] others might examine the meanings revealed in Audiganne's presentation of miners as carefree, happy
men as long as their wages and work were ensured. Audiganne's comments could be read not as a fortuitous reflection of social reality but as
part of a contest over the meaning of workplace life, a discussion fed by
reflection on the strikes and protests in the Loire Basin during the
previous decade. Such an analysis would in turn allow us to question the
ways in which our own narratives privilege certain ideas of what is
natural and what constitutes causality. Labor historians may thus come to
read texts as sites for the production of meaning rather than solely as sites
to be mined for information.[32]

A related project for labor historians is to learn to interpret representations—systematic linguistic encodings of material reality and social
experience—as something other than pale or distorted echoes of social
reality. As an analytical concept, the working class has been structured
by contesting representations of labor—including those produced by labor
historians—which draw their meanings from the relationships they form
with one another as well as from the processes through which language

constitutes the interpretive frameworks for understanding material conditions and social and cultural contexts and experiences. In examining how representatons of labor attempt to fix meaning, we may come to see labor, like gender, as what Scott terms a "useful category of historical analysis."[33] Labor historians can learn much from the efforts of feminist historians to understand the ways society is ordered and the social order given meaning by examining the interpretations offered of specific groups of women in society (prostitutes, mothers, etc.) and the ways in which discourses are coded in gendered terms. Certainly, binary oppositions of manual and mental labor or producer and image-maker are among the most widespread means used to establish seemingly evident social and (often inverse) moral hierarchies.

My own recent foray into Paris sewage is in part an effort to understand how a society reveals itself in the process of endowing with value and values what it excludes and those charged with its exclusion. Maybe I should not admit it, but I have known for a while now that *my* workers are linguistically constructed—that is to say, characterized by identities and differences that work to structure and explain their actions. I do not doubt that the workers I write about are (or were) real or that their sufferings and exultations were any less real. I talked with some and went to work with them, to their houses for dinner, and to their children's weddings. My belief in their reality (and that of workers in the past) does not, however, mean that they came to me free of interpretive systems that act to produce and secure the meanings of who they are and what they do. Workers with their hardships and aspirations enter and emerge from labor newspapers and my word processer enmeshed in these systems of meaning.

Let me suggest how such ideas might aid in the interpretation of the texts I used in my study of Paris sewermen. The account Parent-Duchâtelet gave of sewermen is one of the clearest examples of workers represented as what I have termed "moral proletarians," laborers whose individual and collective moral practices allow them to triumph over potentially degrading labor and penury. Variants of the moral proletarian went on to play a major role in nineteenth-century social thought, and they have not vanished from social histories written today, my own included.

It was through a linguistically informed interpretation of Parent-Duchâtelet's writings that I was able to transcend a reading of them as one individual's personal reflections. There is an irony in this since Parent-Duchâtelet strove to achieve true knowledge of sewermen free of the filter of language by means of keen observation of their bodies in what he saw as the particularly revelatory world of the underground. Yet while Parent-Duchâtelet's texts refer, often very graphically, to human experience and material conditions, it is because these writings draw upon and comment on languages as diverse as Jansenism and Jacobinism and are structured in linguistic constellations laden with meaning for his culture (and ours), like high and low, clean and filthy, true and false, moral and immoral, worker and bourgeois, that they work through identification and differentiation to produce new meanings. Language refers to experience and materiality, while deriving meaning from linguistic referents; this property of language makes possible the concept of the moral proletarian and explains its discursive dissemination and inherent contestability.

But what of sewermen themselves? Must our labor history become primarily an analysis of the linguistic construction of experience in the texts of outside observers, whether those of nineteenth-century bourgeois or contemporary historians? If so, we would lose a lot. One of the achievements of the new labor history of the 1960s and 1970s was to recover and take seriously the experience and thought of people in the past who had previously received only cursory attention. Among other things, a linguistically informed history can offer this project an appreciation of the ways in which the identity and actions of social groups rely on linguistic constructs.

As I reflected on the sewermen, I came to feel that narratives of their material conditions and social life, however invaluable, took me only so far in accounting for the unusual burst of communal enthusiasm necessary for sewermen to build and operate their settlement. It was, I decided, the intended and unintended consequences of the construction of the sewermen's identity and interests through the meaning-laden metaphor of the family, encompassing sewermen and their families, past and present, that helped differentiate them from other communities of laborers. This familial metaphor gave unity and continuity to a group faced with the perpetual threat of disintegration through death, disease, injury, and the effects of state social welfare policies. Although the Third Republic conceived of welfare benefits as individual in nature, to be used collectively only in state, municipal, or church-sanctioned institutional settings, the sewermen's familial language grounded and gave meaning to an innovative set of social practices that drew on the patriarchal meanings of the language of the family (sewermen look after their families even after death) to suggest an alternative to the welfare bureaucracies of the day.

Linguistically informed history encourages readings that recognize the multiple voices and forces at work in texts, including the production and echoing of our own voices in the course of the deciphering and ordering required to enter into and sustain historical debate. Attention to this play of language and meaning may suggest to labor historians differ-ent ways of writing. Some may discover vocabularies that allow them to express ambiguity or irony, not as signs of a failure of intelligence or will but as means to develop more revealing representations of the past. In keeping with the questioning of unitary narratives, the essay collection, which allows for greater play and contestation within the book, may challenge the hegemony of the monograph. In pursuing such avenues, labor historians need not produce works that look like Derrida's or read like Foucault's (or Rancière's); they have their own rich traditions and ways of saying things upon which to draw—and to react.

Perhaps we ought to take Scott at her word when she employs the not so terrifying adjective *useful* in proposing the linguistic turn (via gender in that instance) to historians. I like this particular formulation because it emphasizes the practicality of linguistically informed history rather than a forbidding theoretical rectitude. The linguistic turn is no more an excuse to turn away from the problems that have absorbed labor history than entering analysis is an excuse for avoiding the business of living. First, linguistically informed history does not question the existence or experience of material reality; it offers a more complex model of reality in which language and experience are always linked. Neither ever come to us in isolation. Second, linguistically informed history does not deny power relations or social contestation; it simply stresses that the exercise of power and the challenge to power always rely on symbols and linguis-tic systems, codes, and the like, which are partially conscious and par-tially unconscious. Linguistically informed labor history is therefore not apolitical. On the contrary, it reveals that the possibility of a workers' politics is bound up with the languages that create, contest, or deny their existence as a group. Third, the new appreciation of language does not take labor historians away from narratives of exploitation and injustice; instead, it directs them toward new understandings of why certain narra-tives have functioned better than others and why material experiences can lead to a variety of actions or interpretations. In sum, the linguistic turn does not deny the legitimacy of what labor historians do. Rather, it builds on the critical traditions of labor history to launch a new and fruitful appraisal of its sources, its literature, and its goals.

Notes

I owe an especially large debt to friends who commented on earlier drafts of this paper: Judith Bennett, Herrick Chapman, Leon Fink, Jacquelyn Hall, Lynn Hunt, Michael Kazin, Sarah Maza, William Reddy, Holly Russell, and Steve Vincent. All will see the fruits of their labors in this version. My greatest thanks go to Lloyd Kramer. He read this piece twice, and it incorporates his suggestions, emendations, and caveats throughout.

1. Jacques Rancière, *La nuit des prolétaires: Archives du rêve ouvrier* (Paris, 1981).

2. Donald Reid, "The Role of Mine Safety in the Development of Working-Class Consciousness and Organization," *French Historical Studies* 12 (1981): 98-119.

3. E. P. Thompson, *The Making of the English Working Class* (New York, 1966), p. 12.

4. Donald Reid, *The Miners of Decazeville: A Genealogy of Deindustrialization* (Cambridge, Mass., 1985).

5. Donald Reid, "Industrial Paternalism: Discourse and Practice in Nineteenth-Century French Mining and Metallurgy," *Comparative Studies in Society and History* 27 (1985): 579-607. For an approving reference to my use of *discourse* in this article, see Bryan Palmer, *Descent into Discourse: The Reification of Language and the Writing of Social History* (Philadelphia, 1990), p. 220n9. For a critique, see Peter Schöttler, "Historians and Discourse Analysis," *History Workshop*, no. 27 (1989): 62n79.

6. Donald Reid, *Paris Sewers and Sewermen: Realities and Representations* (Cambridge, Mass., 1991).

7. Palmer, *Descent into Discourse,* pp. 3-4.

8. William H. Sewell, Jr., *Work and Revolution in France: The Language Of Labor from the Old Regime to 1848* (Cambridge, 1980).

9. William M. Reddy, *Money and Liberty in Europe: A Critique of Historical Understanding* (Cambridge, 1987).

10. Joan Wallach Scott, *Gender and the Politics of History* (New York, 1988), pp. 68-90. See also William H. Sewell, Jr., "Review of *Gender and the Politics of History,* by Joan Wallach Scott," *History and Theory* 29 (1990): 71-81.

11. Elaine Abelson, David Abraham, and Marjorie Murphy, "Interview with Joan Scott," *Radical History Review,* no. 45 (1989): 47; Scott, *Gender,* pp. 72, 163.

12. Scott, *Gender,* p. 54.

13. Palmer, *Descent into Discourse,* p. 79. Palmer's ad hominum attacks reach their nadir in his comments on Michael Kazin (pp. 122-24).

14. Abelson, Abraham, and Murphy, "Interview," p. 44.

15. I mean no disrespect to the memory of Goldberg, whose work I greatly admire.

16. Joan Wallach Scott, *The Glassworkers of Carmaux: French Craftsmen and Political Action in a Nineteenth-Century City.* (Cambridge, Mass., 1974), p. ix. Scott is referring in metaphoric terms to her apprenticeship with Charles Tilly.

17. At least this is what prominent Marxists in the field of French history held. Sanford Elwitt, "Politics and Ideology in the French Labor Movement," *Journal of Modern History* 49 (1977): 468-80; Tony Judt, "A Clown in Regal Purple: Social History and the Historians," *History Workshop*, no. 7 (1979): 84.

18. Scott, *Gender,* p. 54. Historians of women with very different outlooks make the same charge. See, for example, Judith Bennett, "Feminism and History," *Gender and History* 1 (1989): 257-58.

19. Scott, *Gender,* p. 67.

20. Scott, *The Glassworkers,* pp. 182-87.

21. Christine Stansell, "A Response to Joan Scott," *International Labor and Working-Class History,* no. 31 (1987): 24. Stansell, a first-rate historian of women and labor, tries to be as sympathetic as possible to Scott's project.

22. "For class to be read as a text in a post-structural manner demanded French input." Palmer, *Descent into Discourse,* p. 125. See especially Palmer's characterization of Jacques Derrida as a French nobody, whose irrational world view flourished only after admission into "that bastion of liberty, the American university." Ibid., p. 33. Note also Stewart Weaver's snide comment on Scott and the "Parisian experts" in "The Political Ideology of Short Time: England, 1820-1850," in *Worktime and Industrialization,* ed. Gary Cross (Philadelphia, 1988), p. 82. This wariness of things French can affect American historians of France as well: "the new cultural history, with its signature French passport." Steven Zdatny, review of Palmer's *Descent,* in *French Politics and Society* 8 (Fall 1990): 109.

There is, of course, a tradition in Anglo–North American labor history of defense against French theorizing and especially native exponents of French heresies. As Michael Kazin pointed out to me, Palmer's *Descent into Discourse* is modeled on Thompson's attack on English Althusserians in *The Poverty of Theory and Other Essays* (New York, 1978).

23. Bryan Palmer, "Response to Joan Scott," *International Labor and Working-Class History,* no. 31 (1987): 14-15. Scott has pointed to the place of gender in Palmer's musing and to his problematic use of the term *language.* Scott, "Reply to Criticism," *International Labor and Working-Class History,* no. 32 (1987): 39-40.

24. My reference to a mid-life crisis alludes to Scott's evaluation of the gendered nature of labor history, though I am cognizant of the imposition of unity involved in evoking the biographical metaphor. Scott, *Gender,* p. 72.

25. Joan Scott raises an important challenge to social historians' use of experience in "The Evidence of Experience," *Critical Inquiry* 17 (1991): 773-97.

26. Scott, *Gender,* p. 71.

27. William H. Sewell, Jr., "Uneven Development, the Autonomy of Politics, and the Dockworkers of Nineteenth-Century Marseille," *American Historical Review* 93 (1988): 637.

28. William Reddy, *The Rise of Market Culture: The Textile Trade and French Society, 1750-1900* (Cambridge, 1984); Reddy, *Money and Liberty.*

29. Anson Rabinbach, *The Human Motor: Energy, Fatigue, and the Origins of Modernity* (New York, 1990), p. 15.

30. See Dominick LaCapra, *Rethinking Intellectual History: Texts, Contexts, Language* (Ithaca, N.Y., 1983), pp. 268-90; Jeffrey Mehlman, *Revolution and Repetition: Marx/Hugo/Balzac* (Berkeley, Calif., 1977), pp. 5-41; Jacques Rancière, *Le philosophe et ses pauvres* (Paris, 1983), pp. 143-47 and passim; and Peter

Stallybrass, "Marx and Heterogeneity: Thinking the Lumpenproletariat," *Repre-sentations* 31 (1990): 69-95.

31. Michael Hanagan, *Nascent Proletarians: Class Formation in Post-Revolutionary France* (Oxford, 1989), p. 110.

32. LaCapra, *Rethinking Intellectual History,* pp. 33-34.

33. Scott, *Gender,* pp. 28-50.

CHRISTOPHER H. JOHNSON

Lifeworld, System, and Communicative Action: The Habermasian Alternative in Social History

This essay was conceived in the context of a debate between discourse theory and Marxism as they have been applied in French working-class history. As it turned out, I was reading the recent work of Jürgen Habermas and discovering a perspective on politics and history that clarified in coherent theoretical form my reservations about both. More important, Habermas stimulates a way of looking at history that not only suggests modes of theoretical integration of recently articulated historical problematics—above all, the encounter of class with gender—but also charts new pathways of empirical research. This essay will not, therefore, be a defense of historical materialism against discursive-rhetorical methodology or its enfant terrible, deconstruction, or Geertzian cultural anthropology, for I have no essential quarrel with the usefulness of these approaches. Many of our colleagues are inclined to regard the discourse phenomenon as a kind of virus invading our communicative machinery that must be purged or all is lost. This is the spirit of Bryan Palmer's *Descent into Discourse: The Reification of Language and the Writing of Social History.*[1] It is a great romp, marvelous polemic, and certainly reminds us of some of the dangers of deconstruction gone berserk.

Moreover, he reminds us that a great deal of the new cultural history sets up a Marxist bogeyman that does not exist and never has (save for a few years in the pages of *Die Neue Zeit*). In his enthusiasm to nail such "apostates" as Jacques Rancière, Gareth Stedman Jones, and Joan Scott, however, he undervalues the deeply radical agendas underlying much of this work (indeed, *Dissent through Discourse* would be a viable title for a counter-Palmer piece), especially in the deconstruction of the language of patriarchy through the attentive search for the "absent other" or in Michel Foucault's and Jacques Donzelot's dissection of power with the analytic tools of "marginalization" and "normalization" in contemporary society.

The Limitations of Lifeworld Analysis

In Jacques Rancière's work, discourse analysis takes us to the heart of labor history—the historical study of the working class, class relations, and the concept of class—and has shown us how amorphous such categories and the imputed behavior attached to them are by underscoring the instability of the lives and the ambiguity of the thought of nineteenth-century workers. Although he himself succumbs to the sin he warns against, trying to find the "essence" of the working class, Rancière nevertheless is closer to the truth than most "social historians" are when he writes of his worker-intellectuals after a review of their checkered histories, "This aleatory population . . . represents less the army of the marginal or the declassed than the proletariat in its very essence that is concealed under the wretched or glorious images of the factory damned or the pioneers of mechanics. They represent very accurately the aleatory history and geography that bring together those individuals who live, each and every one, in the absolute precariousness of having no trump to play but the availability of their arms and suffering from the day-to-day uncertainty of their employment more than from the exploitation of their product."[2] Rancière's image of the early working class is confirmed in numerous empirical studies. Legions of workers throughout France (and Europe and the United States) went from job to job, place to place, struggling to make their way under circumstances that go far beyond those cited by Rancière: women, married or unmarried, whose families needed their income contributions or who had to support themselves; the hordes of men and fewer women and children across the face of Europe who tramped far and wide to find work or to sell goods on consignment—the temporary migrants whom Abel Chatelain estimates at something like a third of the French working population at its high point in the mid-nineteenth century; the hundreds of thousands of truly redundant workers whose lack of place in the current structural/technological order of things threw them (or their children) into competition with workers in less affected crafts; those workers whose skills were in demand and who therefore did not fit the profile of poverty but whose ability to exit created a similar kind of labor-market uncertainty; and, more generally, workers who popped in and out of work by choice, even if their skills were not great or in demand, who "made do" and rather seemed to enjoy the contest. Michael Sonenscher wants to extend this picture of flux well back into the eighteenth century, and his magnificent new study amply demonstrates how ineffective and constantly contested the guild system was in containing and regulating it.[3]

It is also abundantly clear that, as is true with Rancière's worker-intellectuals, the first thought in the minds of many workers when they realized they were in something called *la classe ouvrière* was to get out of it. This sentiment was recorded in other epochs—as Sheila Fitzpatrick has shown in the recruitment of Communist party cadres under Stalin and as American sociologists of work demonstrated in their interviews with "happy workers" in the booming auto industry in the 1950s, who sought the American road to success in small-business ownership. The urge to autonomy, though naturally structured by one's social environment, cannot be surpressed.[4] Certainly another way workers knocked about was to go back and forth among waged work, subcontracting, independent production or sales, and shop-ownership with employees of their own.[5] Clearly, there were ambiguities all over the cultural and social landscape; clearly, workers were torn in various directions; clearly, a vision of a unitary working class was then and is now (but maybe less so in the mass-production era in between) a Marxist pipe dream.[6]

Among the questions ignored by Rancière as he so fruitfully explores an aspect of cultural reproduction (with implications for the character of social integration and personality formation) in the Parisian working-class lifeworld is this quite simple one: What is the source of the flux? Proletarianization under the impact of capitalism beckons. Obviously, the nature of the Parisian labor market, the product market, and the structure of production, along with the legal-administrative system that regulated them, are factors, although abstract and therefore not immediately "readable," that must be addressed. To address them, however, requires a paradigm shift, a shift, using the terminology of Jürgen Habermas, from a conception of society as lifeworld, the lived day-to-day human experience of communicative interaction, to a conception of society as a self-regulating system, in which "actions are coordinated through functional interconnections of action consequences." As we shall see, Habermas's way of conceptualizing "the integration problems of society" as both social integration in the lifeworld and system integration will inform much of the analysis in this essay.[7]

For now, we must remind ourselves of the long and deep, systemically induced process of proletarianization that has been so elaborately mapped by our economic and social historians. That process is perhaps best described in Charles Tilly's essay, subtitled "A Proletarian World," in which he asserted that "proletarianization was arguably the most far-reaching change in the quality of everyday life to occur in the modern era. It had a more profound impact than did urbanization, secularization, bureaucratization, or any of the other 'izations' that occurred in its company. The growth of wage labor at expropriated means of production transformed family life, altered the structure of local communities, created whole new varieties of politics, and overturned the conditions determining the life chances of individuals and households." Tilly goes on here and elsewhere to analyze the interactive dynamics between demographic changes and economic change, to emphasize the centrality of rural proletarianization, and to chart the place of proletarianization in patterns of collective behavior and conflict.[8]

The myriad studies of rural industry and the demographic consequences and causes of "proto-industrialization" emanating from the research centers of Zurich, Madison, Ann Arbor, Göttingen, Toronto, Warwick, Cambridge, Lille, Lyon, Bologna/Fiesole, and Chapel Hill (to name a few) exposed the pervasive growth of out-working (though not always waged work to be sure) in a European textile industry responding to worldwide markets created, shaped, structured, and often guided in their production orientations by states, large and small, themselves clearly understanding that "profit and power ought jointly to be considered," as Sir Josiah Child so eloquently put it in 1672. To this was added eighteenth-century *urban* proto-industry and attendant proletarianization, largely in the form of extra-corporative subcontracting arrangements not only in textiles but also in other apparel, such as hats, metalwares, instruments of all sorts, and finally, in one form or another, in virtually all the basic trades. Maurice Garden and Carlo Poni pioneered such study, followed by dozens of others. Simultaneously, large-scale manufacturing, often sponsored or carefully regulated by states, blossomed in the eighteenth century, especially in textiles and papermaking. In France, royal manufactures provided models for vertically integrated manufacturing, and plenty of entrepreneurs took the challenge. The stimulus of what we would today call defense spending or military provisioning also cannot be overlooked, particularly in developing technical and structural measures enhancing productivity—and proletarianization. This brief tour through the literature reminds us of the enormous investment that social historians have made in pursuing the problem of proletarianization as a systemic phenomenon arising before the advent of the factory, with the assumption—as in the Tilly quote—that lifeworld patterns simply followed suit. The big arguments were over which of three systems was the most important: demography, production and exchange mediated by money, or the internal and external systems of states mediated by power.[9]

As a researcher at the University of Wisconsin, I latched onto a social-historical systems approach that privileged the second element—the "economic factor"—and through my research on Cabet's Icarians found myself in the midst of Karl Marx's world and thought that he had made much sense of it. My major discovery, I thought, could be summed up in a fairly simple proposition: the primary determinent in the creation of working-class turbulence was to be found in economic change. By inference, so was the embrace of a vision of a radically different existence as well as the willingness to reject the existing constitution of France with violence. The problematic at that point, of course, had to do with Marx's alleged technological determinism: no factories, no industrial capitalism. The *nature* of the economic change, then, was the issue. Tailoring was just about the least mechanized and "factoryized" industry there was. What had happened in their system of production that might account for tailors' (both journeymen and masters) turbulence? What appeared to be occurring was a massive change in the structure of the industry that accompanied the rise of large-scale merchant tailors and the growth, on a broad scale, of *confectionnement,* the manufacturing of ready-made clothes and the subcontracting of much of the sewing work to tailors working full or part-time in their own dwellings (though also in subcontractors' shops), many of whom were women—in a trade in its traditional made-to-order mode where women worked only exceptionally.

I thus argued that this was very much the "rise of capitalism in one of the purest artisan [understood simply as handwork] crafts of the age." The central fact was that to compete effectively in an expanding product market where ordinary men, especially urban workers, increasingly viewed a Sunday-best suit as a need, clothing manufacturers effectuated cost-price savings through decreased supply costs (large-scale cloth purchase, often on credit—most *confectionneurs* began after all not as tailors but as substantial cloth merchants); lowered labor costs by operating through subcontractors, who tapped the long-standing fringes of an overcrowded male labor market where journeyman regulations and apprenticeship practices were no longer part of public law (whatever pre-1791 enforcement might have been like); employed women workers, whose wage levels had nothing to do with their worth; and finally, as time went by, exploited the labor of bespoke worker-tailors made redundant by the competition from ready-made. Many small masters fell by the wayside for the same reason, but they were also driven out of business by the ongoing concentration in the bespoke trade as well. Many of these small masters had nowhere to go except to become subcontractors for both sides of the trade, but especially for ready-made manufacturers. Lastly, broad retailing networks for ready-made goods developed: department stores to be sure, but also traveling salesmen working for manufacturers who spread throughout France to sell those Sunday suits at the weekly markets and occasionally had their stocks trashed and their persons abused by irate tailors—masters and men together. Capital and hence capitalism were thus very much involved in creating the flux of proletarian existence, continuing proletarianization, and protest of a political sort.[10]

Michael Sonenscher, in his recent book, *Work and Wages: Natural Law, Politics, and the Eighteenth-century French Trades,* has criticized this explanation. Most of the book studies the stable cores and especially the anarchic peripheries in many trades, with journeymen "bobbing like corks" from one job to another and experiencing long and precarious periods of unemployment. Many of their institutions, particularly the journeymen's associations, sought to mitigate such problems and conflicts. The peripheral spheres, where unregulated hiring practices abounded, gave rise to numerous legal suits under the terms of the public law on corporations. Sonenscher has made splendid use of these documents to reconstruct the most accurate picture we have to date of the work life of eighteenth-century artisans. It is one that certainly gives pause to those of us who thought that the nineteenth-century environment was something new. Sonenscher then drives home a more general point:

> Modernity, at least in France, is very much less easy to identify than appearances suggest. Arguably, much of what was modern in France was already there, many generations before Marx wrote the *Eighteenth Brumaire of Louis Bonaparte.* Much of what has been associated with the dissolution of craft-communities—generalised sub-contracting, marchandage, the elimination of customary practices, the dilution of skill—were either the subject of intermittant conflict between employers and workers throughout the eighteenth century, or like skill, wage-systems, or customary practices, existed in conditions that were so radically different from those usually associated with artisans that it is impossible to assimilate them into the linear process of material change that, putatively, led from craft production to factory production.[11]

But, it should be asked, what is wrong with the concept of *craft* capitalism, or rather merchant capitalism rooted in craft production? That is exactly what existed in the nineteenth century, before it led to the clothing factory—to the extent that it did.

"What changed in France between 1748 and 1848," Sonenscher continues, "was not so much the relationship between workers and employers, or the immediate circumstances in which production was carried out, as the identity of the public to which actors in conflicts appealed and the manner in which those appeals were couched. Instead of lawyers and magistrates, nineteenth-century workers and their employers addressed other workers and employers and, increasingly, their own political intermediaries or representatives. The identity of modernity cannot be found, in other words, by extrapolating from the labor process, or productive relations as such, towards political action or institutional procedures."

Sonenscher goes further and in a lyrical conclusion argues that in breaking with a "capitalism-did-it" perspective, we open up vast areas for thinking about history and ourselves anew: "Fuller understanding of their many different constituent parts may reveal more about the diversity and indeterminate character of past societies than it has been usual to assume and, at the same time, may also suggest a wider variety of future possibilities than it has been customary to assume." This sentiment, with its stress on agency, is quite appealing, but the world of his artisans seems somehow insulated from the wider market forces that surely existed in the eighteenth century and just as surely accelerated in the nineteenth. It would appear that Sonenscher is trapped within roughly the same paradigm as Rancière, although he does not interrogate workers struggling to liberate themselves from their station but interprets the voices of real workers in legal conflict. He offers a level of authenticity that does not exist in Rancière's work. His goals, however, are quite similar, namely to "go beyond" the words to the "conditions and circumstances that were left unsaid and undescribed because they were so banal," to "understand an economy and a political culture that in the eighteenth century, were effortlessly taken for granted." Rather incredibly, he succeeds, creating the picture described above. The workers' political culture, their political action largely took place in the civil courts; this was their parliament, though the term is anachronistic. The economy, in Sonenscher's view, was not a capitalist one but the "economy of the bazaar," comparable to Clifford Geertz's bazaar at Suq. In short, just as in Rancière, we have the unearthing of the lifeworld of the trades with a rather Husserlian commitment to get down not only to the "day-to-day" but to the "taken-for-granted," the world where knowledge is intuition.

The two lifeworlds are thus similar. What has changed from the eighteenth to the nineteenth century, argues Sonenscher, is the law that articulates the political communication (or "legitimately ordered interpersonal relations" in Habermas's terms) within this lifeworld. In the first, it is the positive public law of the absolute state and in the second, the natural law (that is, law guaranteeing the private rights of individual persons), or what Habermas would call "bourgeois private law." The legal bases for capitalism thus enter the economy of the trades, if not the thing itself, and the bazaar economy is apparently retained well into the nineteenth century. The *meaning* of labor relations is transformed, having lost its context of mutually accepted authority. Its new context is the "liberty of private persons"—exemplified in the labor arbitration courts, where Alain Cottereau has shown the law was for the most part neutral. This same liberty of private persons also allowed artisans to form, voluntarily, associations that under the Old Regime had been obligatory, though they were now compelled to justify their existence to governmental authorities and "potential constituents." Thus, says Sonenscher, they draw on the "resources" of the "advantages of fraternal association" and the "moral benefits of social cooperation" to do so—in effect mutual aid is taken on its own terms. Then he goes on to see socialism arising out of this context of unregulated liberty (the "absence of any formal injunctions compelling artisans to associate as they had before the revolution") rather than from the impact of "unregulated markets and capitalist development." The argument really breaks down here, for in trying to stay within the lifeworld (culture, social interaction, which includes politics, socialization), he ends up with a polarized, unrealistic, and, despite his disclaimers, quite ideological explanation. A few lines later he alludes to an economic reality that is well documented: "the growth in the size and the depth of the internal and external [product] markets." Their impact, however, was not to disrupt the trades, says Sonenscher, but to stabilize them. This takes place only in the late nineteenth century.[12] To claim that market forces did not have a disruptive effect on craft production is as "one-sided" as an unqualified economist Marxism is. Sonenscher's argument that the interactive politics in the trades, transformed in and by the larger transformation of the political culture effectuated by the politically driven contingencies of the French Revolution, alone account for the upheaval in the trades over the intervening century as well as the origins of socialism is only part of the story.

Sonenscher's and Rancière's preoccupation with the inner world of their protagonists and the laudable desire to get behind their words to the realm of their assumptions, their intuitive knowledge, their nightmares, and their dreams seems to obscure for them the impact of the systems within which they are forced to function. This "lifeworld approach," taken by itself, writes Thomas McCarthy in his admirable summary of Habermas's perspective on the problem, "runs the risk of a 'hermeneutic idealism' that conceptualizes society from the perspective of participants and remains blind to causes, connections, and consequences that lie beyond the horizon of everyday practice. It implicitly relies on such idealizing fictions as the autonomy of actors, the independence of culture, and the transparency of communicative interaction—that is the absence of systematic distortions."[13]

On the other hand, lifeworld analysis, or the analysis of symbolic representations expressed in discourses, not only has vastly enriched our understanding of context and the internal processes of cultural (intellectual), social (political), and personality (developmental) production and reproduction but also has provided historians with sharp critical tools to expose the inadequacies of the systems approach, of the functionalist analysis of society as practiced by Rancière's "social historians." Moreover, the post-structuralists (as opposed to, say, Geertzian cultural anthropologists) would argue that they cannot be tarred with the brush of hermeneutic idealism because they reject the egocentric subjectivism and the concept of a coming to consciousness through the rational understanding of the world that has marked the Western project of enlightenment since Descartes and Kant. Language conceals as much as it reveals and in its very nature is disorderly, fraught with contradictions—indeed built on contradictions. What pass for rules, criteria, and products in rational speech are really conventions and contingencies determined socially in a multiplicity of historically differentiated lifeworlds: "Subjectivity and intentionality are not prior to, but a function of, forms of life and systems of language; they do not 'constitute' the world but are themselves elements of a linguistically disclosed world."[14]

How does this relate to historical method? Joan Scott has phrased it eloquently in describing why post-structionalist critics have been so important for her: "They point to the importance of textuality, to the ways arguments are structured and presented as well as to what is literally said. And they draw attention to the need carefully to tease out what Barbara Johnson calls 'the warring forces of signification within the text itself.' This approach rests on the assumption that meaning is conveyed through implicit or explicit contrast, through internal differentiations."[15] If historians can bring such attitudes to the reading of our sources, be they printed or manuscript, graphic, oral, notational, or statistical renderings of human actions (including gestures), ideas, or natural phenomena, we will write more critical, less preconceived history.

If this were its only agenda, discourse theory could be regarded as a major, welcome addition to our methodology, though not one that should *replace* systems analysis. Unfortunately, many of its practitioners seem to want the whole cake. This is Bryan Palmer's chief concern, but what he does is to attack from the "other side," from a Marxist perspective, thus posing the problem as a confrontation between two opposites. He is naturally galled, as am I, that much discourse history is little more than Marx-bashing, as if the big point to be made is that "economics" did not determine this or that, or that "class" interest does not work in one case or the "market" in another case, and "Marxism" is therefore dead. As we shall see shortly, I have my own deep reservations about the validity of Marx's philosophy of history, but I will not abandon the usefulness of many of his social-theoretical contributions. To return to the grander claims of post-structuralism, Michel Foucault and Jacques Derrida, while both radical critics of power, in rejecting Marxism also abandoned all forms of the philosophy of modernity—subjectivism and consciousness, functionalism and structuralism. They thus enter the free-floating worlds of Martin Heidigger and Friedrich Nietzsche. They reject all totalizing ideologies—indeed "philosophy" itself—and seem at peace with a mental universe bounded only by language, the analysis of which fuels a radical critique of power, whatever its form, whatever its source. In literary theory, this has invited often savage attacks on the power of the "canon" and allowed, in the manner encouraged by the literary critic Paul de Man, texts to become an endless series of playrooms for the critic. It is the critic's ultimate revenge against the artist, in which the artist's creativity, intentions, and own critical projects are swallowed up by the critic—and by the thousands thereafter who can always read the text in a different way. Does truth—which is always relative anyway—or what might have caused the text to be the way it is really matter? The play's the thing.[16]

Perhaps literary critics can abide such an open-ended methodology. Can historians? It makes me quite anxious when I see François Furet, the "new dean" (according to *Le Monde* and the *New York Times*) of French Revolutionary studies, say that the study of the internal dynamics of the revolutionary process, the dramatic text of the revolution, 1789–93, is far more significant than the search for its causes. He says this in the same *Annales* bicentennial issue that gives thirty pages to throwing doubt on Ernest Labrousse's studies of economic cycles. Something is up. Or when, in his seven-hundred-page textbook stretching from the earlier eighteenth to the later nineteenth century, Furet devotes twenty-six pages to economic history as if it has no meaning for the "political culture" of France. It is but a small step from here to the Revolution as pure contingency, "mud and blood" (as John Merriman has put it), an update of the *Tale of Two Cities,* that is, Simon Schama's *Citizens.*[17] Although it is illegitimate to throw Sonenscher's sophisticated and deeply researched analysis into the same pot, the general resonances between his work and the profoundly ideological agenda of Furet cannot be overlooked.

Lifeworld analysis can come unhinged if it fails to address seriously questions of causality. Even if it does (and certainly Sonenscher grapples with them), it becomes ensnared in an amalgam of internally generated cultural, social, and psychological construction of readable symbolic practice, while ignoring the systemic constraints and stimuli that have influenced the way in which that practice occurs and thus subsuming the latter phenomena into the universe of discourse and analyzing change and causation in terms of "politics." Let me again quote Joan Scott: "Instead of attributing transparent and shared meaning to cultural concepts, post-structuralists insist that meanings are not fixed in a culture's lexicon but are rather dynamic, always potentially in flux. Their study therefore calls for attention to the conflictional processes that establish meanings, to the ways in which such concepts as gender acquire the appearance of fixity, to the challenges posed for normative social definitions, and to the ways these challenges are met—in other words to the play of force involved in any society's construction and implementation of meanings: to politics." And then: "The mention of politics inevitably raises the question of causality." One thus moves to "conflicting interests."[18]

Her next paragraph summarizes a perspective on interest and political interaction that provides a simple but acute critique of the Marxist view on the issue as well as a way of looking at the crystallization of political action that is at once profound and incomplete. I also wonder whether it is, in fact, "post-structuralist." In whose interest is it to control or contest meanings? What is the nature of that interest, what is its origin? There are two ways to answer those questions. One, in terms of an objectively determined, absolute, and universal interest (economics or sexual domination, for example); the other, in terms of a discursively produced, relative, and contextual concept of interest. The second is not the reverse of the first; rather, it refuses the opposition between objective determination and subjective effects. In both cases we grant the effects of interest in creating social groups (classes or genders, for example). In the first case, however, there is a separation assumed between material conditions and human thoughts and actions they are said to generate. In the second case, no such separation is possible since "interest" does not inhere in actors or their structural positions but is "discursively produced." In other words, we have the perfectly reasonable point that individuals conceptualize what their interests are in light of a process of mutual understanding. It is arrived at through communication with other individuals, based on their cultural matrix (what is regarded as valid knowledge), their social space (the range of contact they have within and outside their several social groupings), and their own experience (their personal history). There is no automatic connection between objective conditions—similar relation to the means of production, similar positioning in a political, ethnic, or religious hierarchy, similar place within the sexual or age divisions of society—and what people will construe their interests to be and act on them.

Now this may make politics what it is, but it does not account for the systemic constraints, what Habermas calls the boundaries of the lifeworld, the "horizons" (always different depending on time and place and always changing), within which that action can take place. The economic subsystem does give shape to what is possible. The state through its power mechanisms, its administration, does the same. "Politics," however, can alter, diminish, and (in Habermas's vision) obliterate those boundaries. It can also submit—and has submitted—to them. Perhaps Joan Scott would not disagree with this. If she does not, then it seems to me that she should explore the world of Jürgen Habermas. This would mean, however, a repudiation of the philosophical underpinnings of Derrida and Foucault as they stretch back through Heidigger and Bataille, respectively, to Nietzsche, if not the critical insights that their methodologies bring to historical study.[19]

The Dangers of Systems Analysis

On the other hand, "the other side," the Marxist paradigm, which sees such constraints and stimuli—rooted in material reproduction—as "ultimately" determinative and the entire historical process as a "totality" that has its own complete internal logic, has lost much of its salience. Certainly the critique of historians, whatever their motivation, has had an impact: for instance, the Marxist-Leninist interpretation of the French Revolution is dead.[20] Although there still remains much to be said for the Marxist way of looking at history and certainly for the Marxist utopia of a humane society wherein autonomous individuals actually do control their own destiny, the whole construct that links the two—the philosophy of consciousness that ordains purposive action by a self-actualizing historical subject (and none other)—is indefensible. Obviously space does not permit anything like a thorough defense of the following propositions, so please bear with me.

Let us begin at the end. In his speech before the U.S. Congress on February 22, 1990, Vaclav Havel captured our sense of awe over the meaning of the revolutions of 1989: "The human face of the world is changing so rapidly that none of the familiar political speedometers are adequate. We playwrights, who have to cram a whole human life or an entire historical era into a two-hour play, can scarcely understand this rapidity ourselves." We historians have a little more leeway, perhaps, but there is no question that what has unfolded in the last two years in the Communist world forces us to reflect seriously on our practice. This is especially true for those of us who work on the 1848 era, not only because of the obvious parallels but also because of the direct—and disastrously overinflated—significance of the revolutionary experiences of that age in the formulation of the political theory that has now been decisively refuted (at last) by these events: the Leninist theory of the state and the Party and, more fundamental, the teleological heart of historical materialism, Marx's Hegelian metasubjectivist idea of working-class predestination inherent in his labor theory of value.

The Party, as the journalists all-too-cutely put it, is over. On the one hand, we have the total, overwhelming rejection of its role and rule by ordinary citizens throughout the former Soviet orbit; on the other, we witness the reconsideration of the possibility of combining parliamentary, "bourgeois" democracy with movement (or council) "socialist" democracy in liberation struggles in the Third World (so brilliantly outlined in Nelson Mandela's first speech after his release). Together, these events point us toward a fundamental inventorying of the place and force of the concept of the vanguard party, of the "smashing of the bourgeois state," and of the dictatorship of the proletariat in Marxist thought and experience. From there, the way is opened to an examination of the idealist under-growth in Karl Marx's philosophy of consciousness.

For a long while, the easy answer to "the problem of the Party" was "Stalinist aberration," whether justified or not by "capitalist encirclement." Specifically, this entails the fundamental error of "socialism in one country" and the Barthesian mythologizing of the Party and the Leader as History incarnate, followed by the tragic and brutal deformation of the genuine social-revolutionary impulses in Eastern Europe by militarily grounded Communist party coup d'etats, themselves impelled by the imperative of bipolar realpolitik. These events were matched at home by the final triumph of bureaucratization under the "Zhdanovshina." This perspective sustained Trotskyists, most Gramscians, and more than a few "Western Marxists" in the belief that there was nothing fundamentally wrong with the vanguard party idea. After all, the very nub of the problem of building a counterhegemonic culture (using Antonio Gramsci's terminology) reduced to this question: from whence would the elements of that culture derive, how would, could, workers' alienated experience (or reified existence) translate into a revolutionary consciousness without the guidance of an historical understanding of their proper role and destiny that only intellectuals—albeit themselves constantly intermeshing theory and practice—could impart? Georg Lukács had seen the Party as the bearer of an "imputed consciousness," and through the organizational medium of grass-roots revolutionary organizations, soviets, the necessary interaction would occur. Gramsci, writing later, implicitly criticized the whole Leninist project in distinguishing between what happened in Russia and his own projected "war of position" in the West that would progressively liberate workers from the cultural shackles of bourgeois hegemony, thus creating a democratic foundation for the revolutionary advent of socialism. This still meant there was a "true consciousness" that would overcome the false, and only fully when the internal contradictions of capitalism led to economic collapse. Economic collapse had occurred in Russia in a context, Gramsci argued, where "civil society was primordial and gelatinous," where bourgeois power, such as it was, came in the form of *dominio*, mere coercion through the state, and could thus be overwhelmed by a "war of movement." Consciousness thus had to be built after the revolutionary fact, a prospect with which the outwardly loyal Leninist Gramsci had no problem.[21]

In such a context, however, the dictatorship of the proletariat could not help but be the dictatorship of its vanguard, the Party, first, because the proletariat was obviously riven with false consciousness in the forms of anarchism, syndicalism, and Menshevism, as well liberalism, nationalism, and anti-Semitism and, second, because it made up a small minority of the nation, even if one counted agricultural proletarians, whose numbers were rapidly declining in any case, given the wholesale seizure of land and the resuscitation of anticollectivist *mir* concepts of redistributive individual tenure. Thus it was that Lenin, albeit with operational democratic centralism, undertook to dissolve the National Assembly; to dismantle the power of the Soviets and hence "revolutionary democracy," as Carmen Sirianni has shown, even before the Civil War began and Allied troops invaded; to crush non-Bolshevik working-class political formations; to smash the Workers' Opposition within the Party; and, finally, to extirpate the last gasp of Russia's workers' revolution, the Kronstadt uprising. What is often forgotten in this now familiar story is that Lenin also took full and outright responsibility for this entire process, even declaring, in the wake of Kronstadt, that the working class of Russia was so decimated and emaciated that it had virtually ceased to exist. The organ bearing the "imputed" consciousness and will of the proletariat thus floated ghostlike above a denuded terrain.[22]

It then became incumbent on the Party not only to create a socialist consciousness but also to re-create the working class, the self-actualizing subject of history. The inherent absurdity of this last combination of words need not be elaborated. But in fact, first through NEP (New Economic Policy) and then, with a vengeance, through collectivization, the Party did create a large industrial proletariat, and the Party became proletarianized. Stalinism had a working-class base, but it was a manufactured proletariat, some of whose members gradually came to dominate Party positions as the old Bolsheviks, those intellectual imputers, were liquidated. The whole relationship between the Party and the proletariat was thus inverted—in a really quite concrete way—and in the process the Party became the avenue for social mobility, finally embodying a new class that looked suspiciously like a bourgeoisie in most "really existing socialist" countries, though more like a mafia in Romania and a new scholar-gentry class in China.[23]

Meanwhile, in the capitalist West—whose domination of world markets and military might created the boundaries within which the tragic evolution of "socialism" in the East occurred—Marxists valiantly tried to comprehend it all. Typical of what they conceived Marxism to be, they really did try to comprehend it *all*, that is, to keep alive the concept of totality. I will not even begin to discuss the vicissitudes of a process that has produced thousands of books; instead, I refer the reader to Perry Anderson, Martin Jay, and Andrew Arato, among its many competent chroniclers.[24] Let me emphasize two threads, though.

First, to return to Gramsci. He took on the daring task of trying to understand how *consent* was forged in capitalist society, stressing that it was not based simply on the imposition of capitalist values by the hegemonic bourgeois culture through the integuments of civil society but arose from ongoing conflict in which workers pursued what they construed to be their interests (discursively arrived at, indeed) and made compromises, not "collaborations." With his strong emphasis on agency, in his mind arising largely out of the "contested terrain" at the point of production, Gramsci contributed to the "fighting back" school of Marxist labor history, spearheaded in this country by David Montgomery. Gramsci also deeply influenced a more functionalist thread of Marxist history, which, although emphasizing resistance, gave greater attention to the institutional and ideological bases sustaining the power of the dominant class, as seen in the work of, for instance, Eugene Genovese or Sanford Elwitt. Whatever the orientation, however, the Gramscian perspective, whether in scholarship or politics, assumes that the capitalist system remains beset by internal contradictions creating crises that undermine the gains made through compromise and ultimately will provide the context of a socialist revolution, whether violent or, more likely, via the ballot box à la Chile. This brings up again the question of the Party, for the problem in Chile was the lack of postelectoral revolutionary resolve, which allegedly Gramscian Euro-Communist parties will allegedly possess. The agent of revolution will be the working class, defined—an objectively accurate assessment—as the vast majority of the population in any advanced capitalist country that are wage earners.

The second grand thread of Marxist theory in the West is associated with the Frankfurt school and its derivatives. It is characterized above all by its pessimism, born as it was facing the twin totalitarianisms of Fascism and Stalinism. Its principal theoretical contribution arose from trying to cope, as had Lukács, with Max Weber's theory of rationalization, which posited that the technical achievement of enlightenment had created in science and bureaucracy monster blacksmiths who had forged the "iron cage" of modern society. Max Horkheimer, for many years the key figure at the Institute for Social Research, stayed with Lukács, seeing "rationalization as reification." The essential contributions were, first, to elevate the state and its technical, administrative, and police capabilities to a level equal to the productive system as a force shaping the processes of negative social integration through domination (Franz Neumann still optimistically saw the authoritarian state as a special form that "represented only the totalitarian husk of a [dying] monopoly capitalism") and, second, to focus attention on the reified consciousness of the individual personality and the mechanisms by which the state-capitalist "culture industry" maintained this emptiness and thus submissiveness. Though Horkheimer and Theodor Adorno were largely responsible for developing these ideas, they were best summarized, with a slightly less pessimistic twist, by Herbert Marcuse, who fully updated the perspective to include and condemn the Keynesian welfare state. Revolt against it must ultimately be a spiritual one, for the internal cohesion of state and economy as systems promised little self-generating potential. The jump from here, perhaps through Louis Althusser, to Foucault was a short one.[25]

The most obvious consequence of this thread is the de-centering of economic change and the role of the working class in understanding contemporary society. The state can keep the economy in repair by a thousand manipulations, and, if need be, states can coordinate their economic activity to adjust and restabilize at will, through diplomacy and force but increasingly through international organizations created for the purpose. Moreover, the capitalist club constantly expands, thereby enhancing the potential for capital mobility. No longer simply extracting resources from the wider world in the hope of reexporting manufactured goods, multinationals happily invest in plants in low-wage areas, but even more happily they buy cheap parts or totally finished products from indigenous manufacturers to whom the banks and governments of the advanced states have loaned money. This process does have detrimental effects on the working classes of the advanced states—deindustrialization has been going on since the late nineteenth century at least, constantly creating pockets of severe economic distress, usually in the midst of a more general downturn. The relative selectiveness of distress, directly related to capital mobility, has left and leaves in its wake regionalized and sectionalized protest potential. Only the depression of the 1930s came close to creating the general crisis that Marx thought might do the trick. What happened instead, of course, was that states coped—often in extreme fashions, to be sure—and created the foundations of the modern welfare state and in the wake of the war, the international mechanisms, GATT, IMF, World Bank, and, of course, the EEC, already alluded to.[26]

What happens to workers as the hopscotch of international capitalist development presses forward, leaving the holes behind? To start with, coordinated action is difficult on the face of it because of regional and temporal differentiation. Broad sectoral collapse can generate a much greater threat, as the British miners' strike of the mid-1980s demonstrated. But the usual, copiously documented impact—and my own work on deindustrialization in Languedoc amply demonstrates it—is quiet acquiescence in an atmosphere of despair and *sauve qui peut*. The adjustments in the household economy, the stairstep withdrawal of relief, the loss of self-esteem, the self-abuse through stimulants/depressants, the abuse of family, the breakup of friendships, and the disdain shown one by those still employed and in particular by their unions that desperately bargain to defend paying members all add up to withdrawal, not engagement. Neighborhood organization for protest activities, as Eve Rosenhaft has shown in her book on the unemployed in early 1930s Berlin, can make some headway; and the unemployed councils in the United States proved to be a training ground for CIO organization later on. But the protean catalyst of the revolution, world economic collapse, did not fulfill its function. Moreover, the splintered and segmented world of waged work that grows with the new economies of the post-Fordist era, as Andre Gorz and dozens of others have argued, has today made the thought of looking to the "industrial working class" as the source of societal transformation ludicrous. Its percentage of the active population in the advanced capitalist world is no higher than a quarter anywhere and is falling rapidly. Objectively, there may be the bases for new ties, but they will have to breach sectoral, social, sexual, and ethnic/racial boundaries that have heretofore been durable. This does not mean, of course, that other social configurations, otherwise defined, cannot emerge from the ongoing contradictions of modern societies to act as agents of change—and indeed side-by-side (and substantially overlapping) with the working class.[27] Obviously, however, the subject of history has not answered the call, and no Party is going to make it do so.

The problem is not simply that the wrong subject has been chosen.

The problem is subjectiv*ism*. According to Habermas, both Hegel and Marx, in rejecting the individual knowing subject of Descartes and Kant, substituted a metasubject with which they "overtrumped" individual subjectivism in the form of Absolute Knowledge. For Hegel, it was to realize itself in the world in the state. For Marx, absolute labor was to realize itself in the world in the proletariat. In Marx's philosophy of praxis, however, self-realization occurs in the real world of material objects in which the motor is the inherently human and aesthetic quality of creativity, which is "short-circuited" by the "private appropriation of socially-produced wealth." Labor in the process is abstracted into labor power and asymmetrically exchanged for wages, while surplus value is transformed into capital, which is "dead labor." This alienated labor then becomes "systematically autonomous," that is, operates as the foundation of the capitalist system. Alienated labor thus deviates both from an aesthetic model, self-satisfying creativity, and from a "natural-rights model of an exchange of equivalents." In this light, alienated labor is abnormal and unjust, psychologically devastating and socially immoral. This is the foundation of arguments for Marxism as a humanism. Habermas then delivers the coup:

> Lastly, however, the concept of praxis is also supposed to include "critical-revolutionary activity," that is to say, the self-conscious political action by which associated laborers break the capitalist spell of dead labor over living labor and appropriate their fetishistically alienated essential powers. If, then, the ruptured ethical totality is thought of as alienated labor, and if the latter is supposed to overcome the alienation from itself, then the emancipating praxis can proceed from labor itself. Here Marx is entangled in basic conceptual difficulties similar to Hegel's. Praxis philosophy does not afford the means for thinking [of] dead labor as mediatized and *paralyzed intersubjectivity*. It remains a varient of the philosophy of the subject that locates reason in the purposive [self-fulfilling] rationality of the acting subject instead of the reflection of the knowing subject. But in the relations between an agent in the world and the world of perceptible and manipulable objects, only cognitive-instrumental rationality can come into its own. The unifying power of reason, which is now presented as emancipatory praxis, is not exhausted by this purposive rationality.[28]

The instrumentalism inherent in Marx's philosophy helps us understand the confusions and manifest contradictions that exist in his political theory and the multiple "interpretations" that have been made of it. Why workers will act to change society and to fulfill their subjective role becomes a matter that simply "follows" from the objective conditions of their existence and will be stimulated by the realization that "capital" is an illusion; this will somehow "give back to a lifeworld rigidified under the dictates of the law of value its sponteneity." The question of whether the exposure of the illusory character of other possible subsystems (e.g., administrative necessity, gender as nature, kin systems as god-given) might stimulate revolutionary will is "not even posed."[29]

This is Habermas's basis for rejecting Marx's philosophy, for it *is* a philosophy and as such stands or falls on its basic assumptions. These were established by Marx in his dialogue with Hegel in his early writings and were never abandoned—indeed, they were only strengthened by his lifework in the economic analysis of capitalism. The essential divide between the internal contradictions of the system in creating the bases for its own demise, on one hand, and the process of how the gravediggers would bury and at the same time reappropriate "dead labor" and thus participate in "making their own history," on the other hand, was never bridged by Marx or any of his followers who remained faithful to those assumptions because it was unbridgeable.[30]

Does this mean that economic forces are not important in history, do not distort and orient the lifeworlds of people? Of course not. What is at stake, however, is the abandonment of a teleology in which the end of history, viewed as a totality, is immanent in its development and in which certain categories of "being," such as class consciousness, if not realized or on the track to realization, are "false" by the measure of the putative "end." It also demands a different assessment of the nature of society and its evolution, one not governed by a transcendent force.

In his own praxis, of course, Marx himself ranged very far from his philosophical core, which permitted virtually any interpretation of his work. Thus, for example, he comes quite close on many occasions to allowing virtual autonomy to the state. Jon Elster has identified at least three theories of the bourgeois state in Marx: (1) the instrumentalist theory, which appears prominently in the *Communist Manifesto,* wherein the state is the direct political instrument of the dominant class, the "ruling class"; (2) the abdication theory, "government by proxy," wherein the bourgeoisie benefits from not controlling the state directly, depending on circumstances, for five different reasons: incompetence (e.g., Napoléon I), "pre-emption of detronement" (e.g., Napoléon III), the "poisoned gift" (let the workers share power, thereby coopting them), the "costs of power" (we can spend our time more usefully making money), and "defusing opposition" (let the aristocracy or "the politicians" take the heat); and (3) the "class-balance theory of the state," in which the state, as an entity with its own interests (or rather a group of people with their own interests), specifically power, "can indeed exploit conflict between classes in the social arena," an explanation Marx offered for understanding both the absolutist state and various nineteenth-century states; it is also the foundation of neocorportist concepts of the state in the twentieth century and, viewed positively, figures prominently in social-democratic political theory today. Elster then concludes that "what in Marxist theory is supposed to be the 'normal case'—the subservience of the state to the interests of the bourgeoisie—is only exceptionally realized."[31]

This does not at all deny the interest that Marx's analysis of the various forms the state holds for historians and political theorists. They amount to "middle-level theories" and, if they are disengaged from Marx's teleology, can be empirically investigated, fine-tuned, or rejected in their own right, without the sense of pasting another star on the helmets of the team in red or the team in white. To shift the metaphor, with the passing of the age of the canonized Marx, the wars of religion that have underlain much intellectual confrontation, especially in our field, should wind down, and truer scholarship should result.[32]

The same may be said for Marx's theories of revolution, which arose, quite concretely, in the context of his lived experience, his practical engagement with the great events of his own time and his attempt to understand their roots in history. Unless they are embedded in this experience, their use can be enormously misleading. It was above all in the only revolutions in which Marx ever participated directly—those of 1848 and their aftermath—that he formulated various analyses and programs that came to embody later Marxist theoretical arguments. Marx himself, however, never attempted to systematize them. Elster, again, is very good in showing the variety of theories Marx suggested in multiple nontheoretical writings. Besides the minority and majority "theories" of revolution, there were the reformist "competing systems" (workers control) and the potential parliamentary road to socialism in England and the United States. What became "canon," however, were the decontextualized minority and majority revolution arguments that separated the Bolsheviks from the rest of the Second International. Marx himself, I think it is fair to say, held to the latter, after expressing the former in the first chapters of *Class Struggles in France* and, of course, the famous "Address to the Communist League," in which he adumbrates ideas of prerevolutionary class alliance with the petty bourgeoisie only for the purpose of dominating it; stage-skipping; the sham of "bourgeois democracy"; the working class as the only true revolutionary force; revolutionary workers' councils; dual government; the vanguard role of the Central Committee of the Communist League; the dictatorship of the proletariat under the "strictest centralization" of the Jacobin model; immediate uncompensated take-over of the "productive forces" by the workers' state; exposure of the petit bourgeois character of all merely reformist proposals; and even the precept that the German revolutionaries will spark the revolution in more advanced France. "Their battle-cry," said Marx, "must be: Revolution in Permanence." Franz Mehring, George Lichtheim, Richard Hunt, and David McLellan have all demonstrated that this core of Leninism was for Marx in all likelihood a passing fancy rooted in a compromise with some of his conspiratorial Blanquist associates in the Communist League. It was rejected six months later, as McLellan says, after Marx read some economics in the British Museum. All elements, of course, did not entirely disappear in Marx's thought—in particular the postrevolutionary dictatorship of the proletariat—but the minority revolution, on which twentieth-century Marxism-in-practice was built, was a speck in the text of Karl Marx—or perhaps we should say a "trace"—which Lenin used to deconstruct his master.[33]

Karl Marx lacked a coherent theory of politics, not because he did not have the time but because his teleological philosophy of the metasubject stood in the way. The proletariat would somehow (*any*how) make the revolution and redeem its, and therefore humankind's, humanity, impelled forward by the inevitable final phase of capitalism, when the relations of production would come into full contradiction with the forces of production.

Along the way, Marx was the most acute and original social critic of his age. Specifically, his analysis of what happened as rationalism and capitalism exploded simultaneously in the eighteenth and nineteenth centuries must continue to engage our attention. Still, although the "laws of motion" derived from the theory of value explained a great deal about the dynamics of nineteenth-century "liberal" capitalism, their expected effects on the social relations of production have been rendered increasingly suspect under the "organized" capitalism of our time.[34] On the other hand, the theory of value loses none of its explanatory significance in revealing the economic bases of the social and psychological alienation of wage workers and the unfairness of the wage bargain and thus conflict at the point of production, the foundation of worker resistance and trade unionism. Moreover, as a guide to understanding the elemental structure of capital formation by means of the extraction and reinvestment of surplus value, Marx's analysis, especially as ramified in volume three of *Capital* and in the *Grundrisse,* remains quite convincing. The labor theory of value, however, stood in the way of Marx's comprehension of markets, their dynamics, and the multiple ways they could be deformed, resisted, manipulated, forestalled, and monopolized. Although the pressure on profit and thus on capital formation remains an endemic reality of the system, productivity through the consequent enhancement of constant capital has far exceeded anything Marx dreamed of. There are unquestionably environmental and international limits to this process, but the direct impact of these potential crises is not specific to the world of industrial workers or necessarily generative of conflict at the point of production. Indeed, in the light of the eminently rational negative responses of most workers and certainly of their organizations to the calls to contain ecological devastation and advanced capitalist imperialism, it becomes obvious that one must look beyond the working class to envisage the potential for protest in these looming contemporary crises.[35]

What happened historically, of course, was that industrial workers *participated* in the alteration of markets. The successes of resistance, specifically strikes, trade unionism, and collective bargaining, have themselves deeply altered the structure of demand and consumption patterns. The leisure benefit of technological development and the organized labor movement's drive to reduce hours demand that we gain a clearer understanding of consumption and the place of demand in the capitalist economy. Furthermore, Marx's assumptions of an undifferentiated labor market and the perfect mobility of labor, along with disregard for the skill factor, turned out to be critical simplifications because cultural and gender differences, ties to community and family, and different opportunities for training and education among workers allowed employers to exploit these factors to their profit, while at the same time they also functioned as sources of intermittent unity for protest activity. Collectively, what occurred was what Marx did not think possible: in crudest terms, the buyout of the industrial working class, which through unions and class politics had forced capitalists and such economic theorists as John Maynard Keynes to rethink their own ideology and to recognize that accommodation was not only safe but profitable. What was lost for workers was the quest for power; the manifestations of alientation lived on, though deflected by consumerism. Simultaneously, the state, responding to pressure now from the organized working class, then from the old-fashioned capitalist and conservative lower-middle-class backlash, passed through proto-welfare-state and authoritarian phases and finally emerged as a seemingly effective regulator of economic life.

Habermas and History

Understanding this process, barely outlined here, has engaged the energies of this century's greatest social thinkers, most of whom, unless simply apologists for capitalism, have ended with grim visions of what rationalism and capitalism have wrought beyond a degree of still unequally divided material wealth; the project of enlightenment, the "ideology" of modernity, has ironically led to reification, meaninglessness, anomie, alienation, and authoritarian personalities, and the list goes on and on.[36] Even the linchpin, the buyout, seems threatened by the very expansion of capitalism itself on a worldwide scale, not only because of its impact on the middling "good jobs" of Fordism but also because of the threat to resources, especially energy, and the threat of more general ecological disaster.

It is against the voices of antimodernism—not only the thread from Nietzsche to Derrida but also that of Habermas's own tradition, which culminated in Horkheimer and Adorno's *Dialectic of Enlightenment* —that Habermas has turned his formidable intellectual powers. Two recent books, *The Philosophical Discourse of Modernity* and the two-volume *Theory of Communicative Action,* are the latest, and by no means final, installments in what he describes as an extension of the project of enlightenment by means of a thoroughgoing critique of it. This involves three elements of analysis. The first is to build a concept of rationality that would be an alternative to that of the Cartesian tradition, in which the individual thinking subject interprets the objective world and the understanding gained thereby progressively reveals a rationally ordered universe and creates the basis for a rationally ordered society in which individuals, left free to act, pursue their self-interests according to discoverable "natural" laws of society. To this "cognitive-instrumental" reasoning, Habermas opposes a concept of reason grounded in communicative interaction. He posits the "pure speech act" as an "ideal" and makes the simple point that understanding is a mutually arrived at process in which competing validity claims grounded in the speakers' lifeworlds are tested. It is only when this understanding is acted on, however, that it actually meets the test. This is an ongoing process of clarification. "Translated into social terms, this rational validity testing can take place only between or among equal subjects in non-hierarchical relationships. But because such social arrangements have rarely prevailed, the linguistic telos of undistorted communication has not been hitherto generally realized in history."[37] This ideal, however, serves as the basis for his emancipatory project, for in political terms it forms the bedrock for a theory of democracy that merges parliamentary and movement politics and may be described as rational-critical debate in the public sphere.

Habermas's first book, *The Structural Transformation of the Public Sphere,* is of great interest to historians of the French Revolutionary Age because it examines the *bürgerlich* (which in German means both bourgeois as a class and civic and civil) world of public interaction in the literary and the political realm, the opening up of a politics rooted in natural law in which individual rights are respected and individual claims and interests compete through representative structures. This was the politics of the Enlightenment and a political world in which capitalism could flourish. The ideal of rational-critical communication as a means of achieving social integration was thus presented, and the likes of François

Guizot and John Stuart Mill wrestled with the failure of the bourgeoisie to take up its responsibility, on one hand, and the inability of the public sphere, so conceived, to absorb the masses, on the other. This public sphere thus unraveled, under the pressure of the working class to join it, in 1848 and beyond, increasingly captured by the "propagandistic-manipulative" public sphere orchestrated by states and the dominant class in their pursuit of their (not always identical) interests.[38]

This was Habermas's first articulation of the central problem in his social theory: how was it that the promise of rationality was deformed and retracked into structures of dominance? He has since developed an approach of considering societies as "lifeworlds" and as "systems" simultaneously, posing as the ideal the rational-critical communicative action in the public sphere that would implement the power of a rational-ized lifeworld to limit and indeed eliminate the functional imperatives of social systems, specifically state administration and the market. The second objective of *The Theory of Communicative Action*—the better part of volume two—is to describe the structure of the lifeworld, under-stand the disturbances that occur in it, and connect the latter up with the growing systemic constraints. The lifeworld is the world of language and culture: beyond Edmund Husserl's "taken-for-granted," we can think of the lifeworld as "represented by a culturally transmitted and linguistically organized stock of interpretive patterns," those givens that are "always already familiar." The lifeworld then is a "transcendental site where speaker and hearer meet, where they can reciprocally raise claims that their utterances fit the world (objective, social, or subjective) and where they can criticize or confirm those validity claims, settle their disagreements, and arrive at agreements." Language and culture make communication possible, or, as Paul Ricoeur puts it, "language is only the locus for the articulation of an experience which supports it.... Everything consequently, does not arrive *in* language, but only comes *to* language."[39] In communicative interaction, actors thus draw on their personal experience (their subjective world rooted in socialization and education), facts (their objective world), and norms (from their social world) to construct their mutual understanding. Then: "Action, the mastery of situations, presents itself as a circular process where the actor is at once both the initiator of his accountable actions and the product of the traditions in which he stands, the solidary group to which he belongs, of the socialization and learning processes to which he is exposed."[40] Cultural reproduction, social integration, and socialization in their turn are built and altered by communicative action. Habermas does not privilege any one of these areas, avoiding the biases that he sees in the sociologists Alfred Schutz, Émile Durkheim, and George Herbert

Mead, all of whom, however, were enormously influential in formulating his perspective.[41]

Lifeworlds, taken as a whole, were gradually rationalized over a long historical period, fundamentally grounded—here following Durkheim and Mead—in the "linguistification of the sacred," meaning the establishment of a human language of norms in the form of law, particularly in the regulation and protection of property. More broadly, it means that "the prejudgmental power of the lifeworld over the communicative practice of everyday life diminishes" and that actors increasingly reach understanding by "their own interpretive accomplishments." As this process, which culminates in the Enlightenment, unfolds, the components of the lifeworld become more differentiated. Culture, social space (classes and class relations), and socialization processes become more autonomous and lose the integrated character typical of tribal societies. As a model for anthropological investigation, the lifeworld approach, in which material reproduction appears subsumed under all three elements and is also mediated through language, is useful indeed.[42]

This approach, however, is "one-sided" and cannot explain historical dynamics, except insofar as one can say that the sacred lost its explanatory power in the face of rationalism. Habermas thus insists "(1) that we conceive of societies simultaneously as systems and lifeworlds. This concept proves itself in (2) a theory of social evolution that separates rationalization of the lifeworld from the growing complexity of social systems so as to make the connection Durkheim envisaged between forms of social integration and stages of system differentiation tangible, that is susceptible to empirical analysis."[43]

Habermas then proceeds to the heart of his theory, which is a reformulation of Weber's paradox of rationalization and of Horkheimer and Adorno's reification. While in no way does it have a necessarily happy ending, thus maintaining strong elements of their pessimism, it does underline the emancipatory potential of communicative rationality. What it does not do is argue for some inevitable path. Although the origins of the process are not clear, with the advent of capitalism the economy became a "functionally specified subsystem by the institutionalization of money in civil law, particularly contract and private law." Monetarization invaded noneconomic environments in the form of wage labor, thus connecting up the social environment with the functioning of the system and therefore responding to its vicissitudes, namely the market. The state was integrally connected in a process where power and profit coincided and was then increasingly drawn into a cooperative relationship with the economic subsystem. "The economy can be constituted as a monetarily steered subsystem only to the extent that it regulates its

exchange with its social environments via the medium of money. Complementary environments take shape as the production process is converted
over to wage labor and the state apparatus is connected up with production via the yield from the taxes on those employed. The state apparatus
becomes dependent on the media-steered subsystem of the economy;
this forces it to reorganize and leads, among other things, to an assimila-
tion of power to the structure of a steering medium: power becomes
assimilated to money."[44]

There is no reason that the relation between system and lifeworld
should be a one-way street, and by implication, most of the great popular
struggles in the early modern period and well into the nineteenth century
may be seen as resistances from the lifeworld threatened by "mediatization,"
the press to turn human beings into functional servants of the economy
and state. The revolutions of 1848 can be viewed as the heart of the
process. The promise that citizenship could operate to reclaim lifeworld
autonomy was posed—and had grown from within the ideology of
rationalism—but was first negated by the violent rejection of proletarian
access to the public sphere, then "neutralized" by the administrative
capacities of the state in the form of a buyout through welfare measures,
creating *clients* instead of citizens. Mass political parties served as agents
of material redistribution. Meanwhile, and integrally connected, the
economy continued to grow as its technical accomplishments burgeoned.
Worker resistance became increasingly formalized and lifeworld problems receded into the background as, again, unions, increasingly separated
from community, family, or gender issues, bureaucratized and provided
material services, thus shifting the focus of workers to consumption. All
of this Habermas sees as the "colonization of the lifeworld," paradoxically made possible by its rationalization. "The burdens that result from
institutionalizing an alienated mode of political participation are shifted
to the role of client, just as the burdens of normalizing [or pacifying]
alienated labor are shifted fully to that of consumer."[45] In effect, the
material bases of overt expression of discontent have receded, though
they have not disappeared. Even the language sounds a bit Foucauldian,
and if one stopped at this point, the essense of Habermas would get lost,
which leads us to the third element of his project.

Our historiography has focused on the central drama of conflict at the
point of production and on the formation of those mass parties that did
after all create an improved material life for a majority of the society.
What we are seeing today—and in fact have been seeing throughout
modern history—is another kind of protest, which is nonmaterial, at least
in the direct sense of the word, even at the point of production. It has to
do with the quality of life: "these new conflicts [how new is a key

question for historians] arise in areas of cultural reproduction, of social integration, and of socialization." They arise outside (or if inside, rejecting the bureaucracies) the existing political or economic-benefit institutions as movements, along the "seams between system and lifeworld." Habermas wisely points out that such movements arise with both left-wing and right-wing agendas (such as pro-choice or pro-"life" movements in the United States), but they include the feminist, ecology, minority rights, gay rights, and welfare rights movements, conflicts over regional and cultural autonomy, religious fundamentalism and sectarianism, grass-roots politics in general, communalism, and I would add such things as the people's struggles against the devastation of drugs and alcohol and the whole range of dissident union activity stressing noneconomic as well as economic inequities.[46]

What makes these phenomena happen? In general, "crises of legitimation" in the functional subsystems; injustice and irrationality cannot always be plastered over with ideology. The current U.S. battle over gays' rights to be in the military is an excellent example. A hitherto submerged normative argument arising from rational-critical communicative interaction in the private lifeworld is being brought into the public sphere to challenge a systemically induced and system-maintaining norm, though as yet the arbiters of the state and its law have resisted. Will they be able to buy these men and women out? This is the crucial question upon which Habermas's hope for democracy hinges. He thinks not, because that ideal of communicative rationality, the testing of validity claims intersubjectively for the purpose of reaching mutual understanding—that reshaped vestige of the Enlightenment—stands as a utopian impulse in the human mind because it *is* the core of what makes us human. Many cultural imperatives undergirding the capitalist and administrative systems' colonial occupation of the lifeworld stand in the way, to be sure, but their functionality to the material purposes of dominance can be shown to be increasingly at odds with the nonmaterial (as well as material) needs of the wonderfully heterogeneous human species that modernity has produced. For Habermas, this multifaceted resistance arises from the unresolved contradictions inherent in system maintenance, but in no way is it inevitable. It is, however, rational, most fundamentally in the (marxist) sense that alienation from one's "species-being" (defined as intersubjective problem-solving—first in the material realm, ultimately in all others) is an unbearable psychic condition. This is what most fundamentally divides him and his marxism from Foucault and post-modernists generally, for they accept schizophrenia, fragmentation, and flux as essential to the definition of the human condition. Resistance must therefore be understood as an endless series of resistances to endless structures of power, without hope for mutual understanding. Finally, history in this view becomes an archeological dig in the search for artifacts to be "assembled, side by side in the museum of modern knowledge"[47] and deployed as discrete weapons in the guerrilla war against power. For Habermas, as for Marx, history is the means for comprehending the possibilities of human liberation.

Habermas in History

Jürgen Habermas is probably the key figure in what we might call supra-Marxist socialist thought. Although his path was more arduous and disciplined, he takes a place alongside André Gorz, Chantal Mouffe, and Ernesto Laclau, among others, who expose the injustices, irrationalities, and domination inherent in the contemporary welfare state but keep their eyes fixed on the potentialities of democracy, though more on movement politics than parliamentary. This "fin-de-siècle socialism" is prudent and chastened before the collapse of great dreams. Martin Jay, the historian of Marxist "totality," captures the mood in his book by that title. It is largely about Habermas.[48]

What does Habermas have to say to those of us interested in labor history? Until recently, little work in French or English has indicated much debt to him. Joan Landes's *Women and the Public Sphere in the Age of the French Revolution* is a pioneering attempt to employ and engage Habermasian categories in meaningful history. She exposes the masculinity that inhered in the thought and practice of the classical bourgeois public sphere and Habermas's failure to consider this in emphasizing its "utopian" potential. Nevertheless, he could only applaud her further demonstration of the ideological character of much Enlightenment thought, despite its universalist claims, for, in his view, it is precisely that tension between the utopian (universalist) claims and the ideological (interested) outcome of Enlightenment thought that gives it its ongoing force. I should also mention that William Reddy's *Money and Liberty* seems to owe something to Habermas, especially his concept of the "ideal speech situation" and his goal of approaching societies as both lifeworld and system.[49]

In general, however, Habermas has not been employed much in our field, outside the intellectual history of the Enlightenment.[50] One of the main problems, or so it seems, is the level of generalization at which he writes. Still, it seems to me that he invites empirical work of all sorts (and rethinking much that has been done), for he sees his whole oeuvre as an hypothesis always subject to change—and indeed it already has been considerably recast. It is obvious that a "Habermas for historians" of any depth will have to await another essay, but perhaps I can make a few comments about the kind of research he suggests.

The relevance of his work for the Revolutionary Age, especially the middle decades of the nineteenth century when the bourgeois public sphere failed the test and a plebeian public sphere arose only to be smashed, distorted, *and* absorbed, is great, as it is to broad aspects of modern history. Our focus here, however, is labor history. I shall therefore limit myself to the labor movement as it evolved from the later nineteenth century. I am hardly the first to say it, but we must stop thinking about what might have been. The reality is the triumph of bureaucracy rooted in the practical trade unionism of male workers in major industrial sectors of the economy. It was not all reformism and false consciousness. The struggle at the point of production was violent, indeed revolutionary—most strikes went beyond the law until they were "normalized" in the twentieth century. Mass parties claiming workers' support took the same direction—with the same history of militance that went beyond rhetoric and the same history of pacification and integration into the system of state administration in more recent times. Both unions and parties achieved enormous material advances for their members, but that was largely the extent of their accomplishments.[51]

How this actually happened, how these great movements were "systematized," uncoupled from the lifeworlds of their members to become agencies serving them for a fee (dues and votes), not unlike insurance companies, has not been the serious topic of historical analysis that it should be. Charles Maier's *Recasting Bourgeois Europe* is an outstanding example of the kind of global analysis that can be done,[52] but the main focus needs to be on how the institutions disengaged from their members in specific unions and communities, where detailed study can proceed. Here are "the seams between lifeworld and system" that Habermas is talking about. Here, too, we can see the kinds of lifeworld problems that unions and parties did not take up seriously because they were seen as so much less relevant than problems of work and struggles for material distribution. These "other" problems had to do with family (for example, questions about the intervention of the state in family affairs, or child care facilities, or contraception, or marriage laws, or divorce rights, or teen pregnancy, or abortion, the list is endless), with health, with the environment where people lived, with impediments to sociability, with education, and above all with the multiple unaddressed claims of women for equality not only in the workplace and the state but in all the multiple dimensions of the lifeworld, the historic rationalization of which made the inequality of women increasingly irrational. All these lifeworld problems were posed and movements around them developed in the heyday of union and mass party formation. We are beginning to understand how poorly they were drawn into these key institutions by which workers haltingly and tangentially penetrated the public sphere, but we know less about why. We know, however, that the material buyout was being extracted, however slowly, and that capitalists, bureaucrats, and most ideologically aware militants, overwhelmingly men (as was the idealized worker of *L'Humanité* or *The New Masses*), all adhered, if from different perspectives, to a materialist interpretation of history, so the likelihood of lifeworld problems' making much headway in these domains was slim. A great deal of research is now going on about these matters, but only in Germany, especially among the "everyday life" historians, do we see the impact of Habermasian theory.[53] There is something there for us all.

Notes

1. Bryan Palmer, *Descent into Discourse: The Reification of Language and the Writing of Social History* (Philadelphia, 1990).

2. Jacques Rancière, *The Nights of Labor: The Worker's Dream in Nineteenth-Century France,* trans. John Drury (Philadelphia, 1989), p. 147.

3. For whatever reason (though it undoubtedly has something to do with his deconstructionist approach—see Donald Reid's excellent introduction), Rancière largely ignores the vast secondary literature on the early French working class. To cite several that shaped the foregoing list: Abel Chatelain, *Les migrants temporaires en France de 1800 à 1914,* 2 vols. (Lille, 1977); Alain Corbin, *Archaïsme et modernité en Limousin au XIXe siècle,* 2 vols. (Paris, 1975); Louise A. Tilly and Joan W. Scott, *Women, Work, and Family* (New York, 1978); Gay Gullickson, *Spinners and Weavers of Auffay* (Cambridge, 1986); Elinor Accampo, *Industrialization, Family Life, and Class Relations in Saint Chamond, 1815-1914* (Berkeley, Calif., 1989); Laurence Fontaine, *Le voyage et la mémoire: Colporteurs de l'Oisans au XIXe siècle* (Lyon, 1984); Duncan Bythell, *The Handloom Weavers* (Cambridge, 1969) and *The Sweated Trades: Outwork in Nineteenth-Century Britain* (Cambridge, 1985); Christopher Clarke, *The Roots of Rural Capitalism: Western Massachusetts, 1780-1860* (Ithaca, N.Y., 1990); Jonathan Prude, *The Coming of Industrial Order: A Study of Town and Factory Life in Rural Massachusetts* (Cambridge, 1986); Alain Cottereau, "The Distinctiveness of Working-Class Cultures in France, 1848-1900," in *Working-Class Formation: Nineteenth-Century Patterns in Western Europe and the United States,* ed. Ira Katznelson and Aristide Zolberg (Princeton, N.J., 1986), pp. 111-54; Michelle Perrot, "A Nineteenth-Century Work Experience as Related in a Worker's Autobiography: Norbert Truquin," in *Work in France: Representations, Meanings, Organization, and Practice,* ed. Steven Kaplan and Cynthia Koepp (Ithaca, N.Y., 1986), pp. 297-316; Michael Sonenscher, *Work and Wages: Natural Law, Politics, and the Eighteenth-Century French Trades* (Cambridge, 1989). The problem of work careers is one of the most interesting on our current agenda. It is obviously hard to

research, for it requires intensive, virtually biographical reconstructions of obscure lives about which little information exists. Gullickson, Accampo, and Clarke have made some suggestive inroads. In my own work on Lodève, I have been able to follow some workers though *état civil* indicators over their lifetimes and witnessed the impact of deindustrialization on job opportunities and labor market competition. Cottereau's research is the best we have on firm-to-firm movement of workers not changing occupations.

4. Sheila Fitzpatrick, *Education and Social Mobility in the Soviet Union, 1921-1934* (Cambridge, 1979) and "Stalin and the Making of a New Elite, 1928-1939," *Slavic Review* 38 (1979): 377-402; Daniel Bell, "Work and Its Discontents: The Cult of Efficiency in America," in *The End of Ideology* (New York, 1961); U.S. Department of Health, Education and Welfare, *Work in America* (Cambridge, Mass., 1973); Georges Friedmann, *Où va le travail humain?* (Paris, 1963). Rancière tells the tale of the four last-makers hanging around the National Workshop chantiers in 1848 who buy a log with their last two francs—they obviously had not hocked their tools—and go on to develop a wooden-form business that had seventy employees and was worth 80,000F a year.

5. William Reddy's *Rise of Market Culture: The Textile Trade and French Society, 1750-1900* (Cambridge, 1984) has already stimulated considerable thought on this subject, and Tessie Liu's *Weaver's Knot* (Ithaca, N.Y., 1992) provides irrefutable evidence of the range of waged, contracted, and entrepreneurial work that a single individual might be engaged in, not just in a lifetime but at the same time.

6. For perspectives, see David Gordon, Richard Edwards, and Michael Reich, *Segmented Work, Divided Workers: The Historical Transformation of Labor in the United States* (Cambridge, 1982); Charles Sabel and Michael Piore, *The Second Industrial Divide: Possibilities for Prosperity* (New York, 1984); and Charles Sabel and Jonathan Zeitlin, "Historical Alternatives to Mass Production: Politics, Markets, and Technology in Nineteenth-Century Industrialization," *Past and Present*, no. 108 (1985): 133-74.

7. Jürgen Habermas, *The Theory of Communicative Action*, 2 vols., trans. Thomas McCarthy (Boston, 1987). On Habermas, see Thomas McCarthy, *The Critical Theory of Jürgen Habermas* (Cambridge, Mass., 1978); Richard Bernstein, ed., *Habermas and Modernity* (Cambridge, Mass., 1985); Peter Dews, "Editor's Introduction," *Habermas: Autonomy and Solidarity—Interviews with Jürgen Habermas* (London, 1986); Steven K. White, *The Recent Work of Jürgen Habermas: Reason, Justice, and Modernity* (Cambridge, 1988); Dominick LaCapra, "Habermas and the Grounding of Critical Theory," in his *Rethinking Intellectual History: Texts, Contexts, Language* (Ithaca, N.Y., 1983); and Martin Jay, *Fin-de-siècle Socialism* (New York, 1988).

8. Charles Tilly, "Demographic Origins of the European Proletariat: A Proletarian World" in *Proletarianization and Family History*, ed. David Levine (Orlando, Fla., 1984), pp. 1-2.

9. There is no need to rehearse the vast literature engendered by Rudolf Braun's ground-breaking study of the effects of rural industry in the Zurich highlands (*Industrialisierung und Volksleben*, 2 vols. [Zurich, 1960]) and Frank-

lin Mendels's theoretical hypothesis ("Protoindustrialization: The First Phase of the Industrializing Process," *Journal of Economic History* 32 [1972]: 241-61). The central debates concerned the demographic consequences (David Levine, *Family Formation in the Age of Nascent Capitalism* [New York, 1977] and Gullickson, *Auffay,* are representative), the nature of structural transformations internally and globally (e.g., Peter Kriedte, Hans Medick, and Jürgen Schlumbohm, *Industrialisierung vor der Industrialisierung* [Göttingen, 1977]; Immanual Wallerstein, *The Modern World System: Mercantilism and the Consolidation of the European Economy* [New York, 1980]), and whether or not protoindustrialization should be viewed as a "stage" of capitalist development (D. C. Coleman, "Protoindustrialization: A Concept Too Many," *Economic History Review,* 2d. series, 36 [1983]: 435-48, provides the key counterargument). The range of the debate may be seen best in Pierre Deyon and Franklin Mendels, eds., *Section A2: La protoindustrialisation: Théorie et réalité,* VIIIe Congrès international d'histoire économique (Budapest, 1982). The complexity of the problem can be seen in the subregional variations in lower Languedoc. See James K. J. Thomson, *Clermont-de-Lodève, 1633-1789* (Cambridge, 1983) versus Christopher H. Johnson, *The Life and Death of Industrial Languedoc, 1700-1920* (Oxford, forthcoming). On urban proletarianization before industrialization, see especially Maurice Garden, *Lyon et les lyonnais au XVIIIe siècle* (Paris, 1970); and Sonenscher, *Work and Wages.* Serge Chassagne's thesis, "La naissance de l'industrie cotonnière en France, 1760-1840" (Ecole des hautes études en sciences sociales, 1986), will soon be in print.

10. Christopher Johnson, "Economic Change and Artisan Discontent: The Tailors' History, 1800-1848," in *Revolution and Reaction,* ed. Roger Price (London, 1975), pp. 87-114. Provincial reactions to ready-made clothes merchants are registered in several of the reponses to the "Enquête sur le travail agriculturel et industriel of 1848" (Archives Nationales, C 944-965).

11. All quotations from Sonenscher, *Work and Wages,* pp. 367-76. For Husserl's discussion of the lifeworld, see *The Crisis of European Sciences and Transcendental Phenomenology,* trans. David Carr (Evanston, 1970), pp. 123ff.

12. Sonenscher, *Work and Wages,* p. 374; Alain Corbin, "Justice et injustice ordinaire sur les liex de travail d'après les audiences prud'hommales," *Le movement social,* no. 141 (1987): 26-59.

13. Habermas, *The Theory of Communicative Action,* vol. 1, p. xxvi.

14. Thomas McCarthy, "Introduction," to Jürgen Habermas, *The Philosophical Discourse of Modernity,* trans. Frederick Lawrence (Cambridge, Mass., 1987), p. ix.

15. Joan Wallach Scott, *Gender and the Politics of History* (New York, 1988), p. 5.

16. This rather polemical assessment captures, I think, the responses of many writers—John Updike, Ann Tyler, and Malcolm Bradbury come most readily to mind—to the claims and implications of deconstruction. A good scholarly analysis of the "de Man problem" is David Lehman, *Signs of the Times: Deconstruction and the Fall of Paul de Man* (New York, 1990). Bryan Palmer's discussion of Derrida's defense of de Man and his explication of the *Le soir* articles rightly

stresses the incapicity of deconstructionist methodology, divorced from historical context, to arrive at moral judgment in a circumstance where moral judgment is simply unavoidable. Palmer, *Descent into Discourse,* pp. 189-98. For Habermas's examination of Derrida's thought and its affinities with the cabalist tradition, see *Philosophical Discourse of Modernity,* pp. 161-84.

17. François Furet, *Histoire de la France, 1750-1870* (Paris, 1988); John Merriman, informal talk on Schama's *Citizens,* April 1990.

18. Scott, *Gender,* pp. 5-7.

19. Habermas's critique of these threads of thought comprises the heart of his *Philosophical Discourse of Modernity,* lectures 4-10.

20. I insist on the "Leninist" addition. Certainly Furet's updating of Alfred Cobban by calling on Alexis de Tocqueville and Augustin Cochin rejects any Marxist perspective on the Revolution, but, as Sara Maza argues cogently (in "Politics, Culture, and the Origins of the French Revolution," *Journal of Modern History* 61 [1989]: 703-23), this has hardly become the reigning interpretation. On the other hand, the dethroning of Albert Soboul (e.g., in Sonenscher's work) can be viewed not as the collapse of Marxist analysis generally but as the end of the peculiarly positivist and undialectical stamp that Lenin applied to the interpretation of revolutionary change by virtue of his justification of the trajectory and outcome of the Russian Revolution (see Carmen Sirianni, "Productivist Evolutionism and the Dialectics of Labour," in his *Workers' Control and Socialist Revolution: The Soviet Experience in Comparative Perspective* [London, 1982], pp. 245-60). On the viability of Georges Lefebvre's understanding of the peasant revolution (Hilton Root's objections notwithstanding), see P. M. Jones, *The Peasantry in the French Revolution* (Cambridge, 1988).

21. Georg Lukács, *History and Class Consciousness* (London, 1968); Antonio Gramsci, *Selections from the Prison Notebooks,* trans. Quintin Hoare and Geoffrey Nowell Smith (London, 1971).

22. Sirianni, *Workers' Control,* part 1; Charles Bettelheim, *Les luttes de classes en URSS* (Paris, 1974); Neil Harding, *Lenin's Political Thought,* 2 vols. (New York, 1977-81); Alexander Rabinowitch, *The Bolsheviks Come to Power: The Revolution of 1917 in Petrograd* (New York, 1978); Moshe Lewin, *Russian Peasants and Soviet Power: A Study of Collectivization* (New York, 1975); Paul Avrich, *Kronstadt, 1921* (New York, 1988).

23. Sheila Fitzpatrick, ed., *Cultural Revolution in Russia, 1928-1931* (Bloomington, Ill., 1978); William Chase, *Workers, Society, and the Soviet State: Labor and Life in Moscow, 1918-1929* (Urbana, Ill., 1987); Stephen Cohen, *Bukharin and the Bolshevik Revolution* (New York, 1971); Robert C. Tucker, ed., *Stalinism: Essays in Historical Interpretation* (New York, 1977); Leo van Rossum, "Review Essay: Western Studies of Soviet Labour during the Thirties," *International Review of Social History* 35 (1990): 433-53.

24. Perry Anderson, *Considerations on Western Marxism* (London, 1976); Martin Jay, *Marxism and Totality* (Berkeley, Calif., 1984); Andrew Arato, "Introduction," in *The Essential Frankfurt School Reader,* ed. Andrew Arato and Eike Gebhardt (New York, 1978), pp. 3-25.

25. See especially Max Horkheimer, "The End of Reason" and "The Authori-

tarian State" in *Essential Frankfurt,* ed. Arato and Gebhardt, pp. 26-48 and
95-117, respectively; Franz Neumann, *Behemoth: The Structure and Practice of
National Socialism* (New York, 1966); Theodor Adorno, *Negative Dialectics*
(London, 1973); Terry Eagleton, *The Ideology of the Aesthetics* (Oxford, 1990),
pp. 341-65; Herbert Marcuse, *One-Dimensional Man* (Boston, 1964); Michel
Foucault, "What Is Enlightenment?" in *The Foucault Reader,* ed. Paul Rabinow
(New York, 1984), pp. 32-50.

26. This perspective—appropriately annotated—is laid out in greater detail in
the conclusion to Johnson, *Industrial Languedoc.*

27. Ibid., parts 3 and 4; Alex Callinicos and Mike Simons, *The Great Strike:
The Miners' Strike of 1984-5 and Its Lessons* (London, 1985); Tony Dickson and
David Judge, eds., *The Politics of Industrial Closure* (London, 1987); Paul
Schervisch, *The Structural Determinants of Unemployment: Vulnerability and
Power in Market Relations* (New York, 1983); Leonard Fagin and Martin Little,
Forsaken Families (Harmondsworth, England, 1984); Paul Staudohar and Holly
Brown, eds., *Deindustrialization and Plant Closure* (Lexington, Mass., 1987);
Barry Bluestone and Bennett Harrison, *The Deindustrialization of America*
(New York, 1981); Eve Rosenhaft, *Beating the Fascists? The German Commu-
nists and Political Violence, 1929-1933* (Cambridge, 1983); Anthony McElligott,
"Mobilizing the Unemployed: The KPD and the Unemployed German Workers'
Movement in Hamburg-Altoona during the Weimar Republic," in *The German
Unemployed,* ed. Richard Evans and Dick Geary (London, 1979); André Gorz,
Farewell to the Working Class (London, 1982) and *Critique of Economic Reason*
(London, 1989). Habermas's first enunciation of this theme was summed up in
his *Legitimation Crisis,* trans. Thomas McCarthy (Boston, 1975); his failure to
integrate class struggle into this perspective is rightly criticized by Terry Eagleton,
Ideology of the Aesthetics, pp. 402-3, 411.

28. Habermas, *The Philosophical Discourse of Modernity,* pp. 64-66.

29. Ibid.

30. Habermas, *The Theory of Communicative Action,* vol. 2, pp. 338-43.

31. Jon Elster, *Making Sense of Marx* (Cambridge, 1985), pp. 402-27
(quotation, p. 427); see Adam Przeworski, *Capitalism and Social Democracy*
(Cambridge, 1985), on the use of this perspective in social-democratic thought.

32. Happily, much marxist (uncapitalized) scholarship today proceeds from
this assumption. The agenda was laid out clearly in the various studies in Theda
Skocpol and Michael Burawoy, eds., *Marxist Inquiries: Studies of Labor, Class,
and States* (Chicago, 1982).

33. Elster, *Making Sense,* pp. 428-45; David McLellan, ed., *Karl Marx:
Selected Writings* (Oxford, 1977), pp. 277-97; Franz Mehring, *Karl Marx* (Ann
Arbor, Mich., 1962), pp. 200-208; David McLellan, *Karl Marx* (New York,
1973), pp. 246-52; George Lichtheim, *Marxism* (New York, 1982), pp. 122-29.

34. The term *organized,* used by Klause Offe and adopted by Habermas
(*Legitimation Crisis*), has been questioned. See Klaus Offe, ed., *Disorganized
Capitalism* (Cambridge, 1985).

35. Besides Habermas (particularly his interviews with Dews, "Editor's

Introduction"), Gorz (*Critique*) and David Harvey (*The Condition of Postmodernity: An Enquiry into the Origins of Cultural Change* [Oxford, 1989]) especially inform this discussion.

36. Max Horkheimer's "The End of Reason" (1941) perhaps best summed up the despair of his generation (in *Essential Frankfurt*, ed. Arato and Gebhardt, pp. 26-48).

37. Habermas quoted in Jay, *Fin-de-siècle Socialism*, p. 28; Habermas, *The Theory of Communicative Action*, vol. 1, pp. x-xi, 301-19; vol. 2, pp. 10-12.

38. Jürgen Habermas, *The Structural Transformation of the Public Sphere: An Inquiry into a Category of Bourgeois Society*, trans. Thomas Burger (Cambridge, Mass., 1989), pp. xviii, 101, 129-40, 175-80.

39. Ricoeur quoted in Thomas McCarthy, "Introduction" to Habermas, *The Theory of Communicative Action*, vol. 1, p. 9.

40. Habermas, *The Theory of Communicative Action*, vol. 2, pp. 124-26, 135.

41. The development of his concept of the lifeworld is largely based on a dialogue with these three giants of sociological thought. See ibid., chaps. 5, 6.1.

42. Ibid., pp. 77-111, 135-48 (quotation, p. 109).

43. Ibid., p. 118.

44. Ibid., pp. 153-71 (quotation, p. 171).

45. Ibid., pp. 342-73 (quotation, p. 346).

46. Ibid., pp. 374-403 (quotation, p. 395). See also Habermas, *Legitimation Crisis*, part 3.

47. Harvey, *Postmodernity*, p. 56; Eagleton, *Ideology of the Aesthetics*, pp. 384-401.

48. Jay, *Fin-de-siècle Socialism*.

49. Joan Landes, *Women and the Public Sphere in the Age of the French Revolution* (Ithaca, N.Y., 1988), pp. 1-13; William M. Reddy, *Money and Liberty in Europe: A Critique of Historical Understanding* (Cambridge, 1987), pp. 221-23.

50. An excellent analysis of the relevant historiography, which deals with the Revolution as well, is Benjamin Nathans, "Habermas's 'Public Sphere' in the Era of the French Revolution," *French Historical Studies* 16 (1990): 620-44.

51. Possibly the most interesting book on this process and the mechanisms by which "juridification," in Habermas's terminology, ensnared both in the filament nets of the law is Christopher L. Tomlins, *The State and the Unions: Labor Relations, Law, and the Organized Labor Movement in America, 1880-1960* (Cambridge, 1985).

52. Charles Maier, *Recasting Bourgeois Europe: Stabilization in France, Germany, and Italy after World War II* (Princeton, N.J., 1975).

53. Geoffrey Eley, "Labor History, Social History, *Alltagsgeschichte:* Experience, Culture, and the Politics of the Everyday—a New Direction for German Social History?" *Journal of Modern History* 61 (1989): 297-343, provides an excellent overview of this historiography.

RONALD AMINZADE

Class Analysis, Politics, and French Labor History

The absence of a close connection between economic development, class formation, and political change has prompted many social scientists to reject class analysis and proclaim "the autonomy of the political." Among political sociologists, "state-centered" theories of politics have downplayed or ignored the role of class relations and emphasized the autonomy of state managers and the distinctively political determinants of historical outcomes. Theda Skocpol argues for the potential autonomy of political institutions from class forces, claiming that state and party organizations are not shaped simply in response to class struggle, dominant class interests, or socioeconomic changes. In her account, state autonomy, which derives from institutional arrangements as well as linkages to transnational structures, involves "the formulation and pursuit of goals that are not simply reflective of the demands and interests of social groups, classes, or society."[1]

Challenges to the viability of class analysis have also emerged from the ranks of historians of nineteenth-century France, who have rejected the notion of coherent social classes acting politically to defend their interests. Research has documented both the different social class backgrounds of those sharing similar political identities and the divergent political identities of those sharing similar relations to the means of production. Mark Traugott's study of the composition of the groups that participated in the June 1848 insurrection, on both sides of the barricades, found deep class divisions in the political loyalties of Parisian workers.[2] Contrary to the traditional Marxist notion that the lumpenproletariat provided the forces of repression in June of 1848, Traugott found that members of the Mobile Guard, which led the repression of the uprising, and the insurgents had virtually the same social backgrounds. Workers who joined the Mobile Guard developed bonds of solidarity in the context of an organizational setting that forged new collective identities during the relatively brief period between February and June of 1848. The interests that motivated working-class political action were not reducible to social origins or prior class experiences; they were actively constituted during the course of political conflicts. Traugott concludes that "any class-based propensities of actors are conditioned by a set of contingent organizational forces." He emphasizes "the decisive role of political and organizational variables in explaining the course and outcome of collective action."[3]

William Sewell, Jr.'s study of nineteenth-century French politics makes similar claims. After providing evidence that privileged workers whose trades were not degraded by capitalist penetration joined the ranks of radical artisans, Sewell suggests that a wide variety of different experiences, such as migration, unemployment, or lowered incomes, may predispose workers to political radicalism. He attributes the absence of a close connection between occupational conditions and political predispositions to the role of state structures and political discourses in radicalizing workers.[4]

Other nineteenth-century French historians have gone beyond this recognition of the need to integrate class and institutional analysis by questioning the value of class analysis.[5] William Reddy observes that the historical record shows that "political movements draw on broad bands of support, coalesce around principles that transcend the concerns of specific positions in the social structure, and depend on the dedication of selfless innovators." He concludes that we should "set the concept of class aside entirely, with all that it entails." For some scholars, the rejection of class analysis has led to post-structuralist analyses of discourse. François Furet contends that during the course of the French Revolution, language became a decisive determinant of politics, as "speech substitutes itself for power" and "the semiotic circuit is the absolute master of politics."[6]

State-centered theories of politics and historical studies of French politics that acknowledge the relative autonomy of the political have the virtue of highlighting organizational and ideological factors that reductionist Marxist analyses of politics often ignore. In contrast to most Marxist analyses of politics, state-centered approaches recognize the contingent relationship between class structure and political action. They explore the institutional and cultural mechanisms that frame the identities and perceived interests of social groups, help determine the political saliency of particular grievances, and help explain the willingness and ability of people to engage in certain types of political action. Their work makes it clear that although structural positions may define a constellation of class interests that can serve as a potential basis for collective political action, such interests typically compete politically and organizationally with alternative interests rooted in nonclass identities. Their accounts move us away from a structural reductionism in which the centrality of class interests in any particular conflict is given by the mode of production. They remind us of the need to take the identities and perceived interests of actors as problematic and as constituted through political activity. They also sensitize us to the manner in which cultural traditions and inherited political languages shape material interests when they are translated into political objectives. Yet these insights do not necessarily imply a rejection of class analysis. By regarding all social identities, including class identities, as discursively constituted instead of grounded in material interests and production relations and by treating the relationship between material conditions and political forces as purely conjunctural rather than as systematically structured, some scholars have too readily abandoned class analysis.

The Relevance of Class Analysis

A rejection of the notion that interests are structurally given and unproblematic suggests the need for a closer integration of class, institutional, and cultural analysis. Once one recognizes the problematic character of creating interests supportive of unified political action among those sharing similar structural positions, the institutional and ideological dimensions of interest formation and the organizational underpinnings of the diffusion of interpretations and ideologies become a central concern. Recognition of the problematic and historically contingent character of the relationship between class structure and the interests generating collective political action requires attention to the ways in which interests are constituted in a (structured) process of struggle that typically cuts across class lines. Understanding this process requires analysis of the organization of institutional arenas, the strategies and choices of political actors, the cross-class alliances that typically characterize collective political action, the nature of the ideologies underpinning such alliances, and the concrete historical conjunctures within which political actions take place.

These theoretical concerns suggest a clear agenda for historical research on nineteenth-century French working-class formation. Such an agenda includes exploration of how changes in local class relations resulting from the uneven pattern of early capitalist industrialization shaped the strategies of political leaders and the alliances they forged, how changing forms of the state transformed opportunities (and costs) for collective political action, how the institutionalization of political parties altered the nature of contention for state power, and how the ideology and practice of republicanism, which was based on populist and fraternal (i.e., gendered) understandings of politics, shaped collective perceptions of class interests, political alliances, and the character of local politics.

Structural positions within production (i.e., class positions) define a constellation of interests that can serve as a potential basis for collective political action, but such class interests produce politically variable outcomes for at least five reasons. First, such structural positions, understood in terms of social relations of production, often define contradictory class interests.[7] For example, the class interests of many nineteenth-century French republican socialist artisans were contradictory. As small master artisans, their positions within production made them employers intent on resisting the demands of the workers they employed. As producers engaging in manual labor alongside their apprentices and journeymen, however, they had an interest in resisting the innovations of capitalist merchants and manufacturers whose activities threatened the demise of their small workshops. Second, the material interests attached to structurally defined class positions are often complex, with such interests rarely structured in one-dimensional ways. Any given group of workers, for instance, has internally heterogeneous material interests based on their social relationship to the means of production (e.g., short-run and long-term, individualistic and collective). Third, occupancy of class positions, and hence commitment to the interests they define, can vary temporally depending on the extent of mobility between positions. Workers experiencing routine mobility out of the working class to the petite bourgeoisie are less likely to develop strong political commitments to interests defined by occupancy of working-class positions than are workers with little opportunity for such mobility. Fourth, the families in which workers live are often class-heterogeneous, containing not only workers but also household members whose incomes are not derived from wage labor. In the case of nineteenth-century France, the persistence of a household economy founded on multiple sources of income meant that worker households living on industrial wages alone were a minority.[8] Fifth, and in my opinion most important, is the fact that the complex and often contradictory interests defined by class positions are typically contested in a political arena with multiple possible enemies and allies. This means that it is rarely predetermined just how such interests will be defined in political programs and coalitions or how politically salient class-based interests (rather than nonclass interests rooted in racial, ethnic, or gender stratification) will become. Although material interests defined by relations of production may powerfully shape the lines of political cleavage in a society, such interests are typically organized and politically contested in a political arena dominated by organizations that are not class-homogeneous and by mobilizing ideologies that cut across class lines.

The rejection of a class-reductionist understanding of politics does not mean that individuals, as workers, shopkeepers, professionals, or capitalists, do not have material interests that may motivate their political behavior. Workers have an interest in not being exploited by capitalists just as women have an interest in not being dominated by men, but the translation of these interests into political objectives and collective political action is neither spontaneous nor unproblematic. This translation depends on building political organizations and identities that are not simple reflections of objective positions in class structures or of the interests that can be imputed to such positions. Given this perspective on class, one of the key issues for historical research on working-class formation becomes how multiclass political struggles rooted in concrete institutions, like mass political parties, have historically defined and redefined class relations by helping forge collective identities of class against alternative bases of collective identity.

The preceding discussion suggests that the translation of class interests into political objectives occurs in a structured process of conflict and alliances, through organizational and ideological mechanisms linking social structure to political behavior. Translating interests based on one's position as a landowner, shopkeeper, worker, or capitalist into subjective political dispositions and collective political action depends on a process that is not a simple reflection of class structure. Institutions, such as political parties, and ideologies, like republicanism, play a key role in this process. Contrary to what proponents of abandoning class analysis suggest, however, these institutions and ideologies are not independent of material conditions and class forces; nor are they capable of simply creating interests out of discourses, unconstrained by material realities.

My research on nineteenth-century French working-class formation at Toulouse, Rouen, and Saint-Étienne suggests the importance of class relations in shaping the constraints and opportunities facing political actors. Class relations were crucial determinants of local political outcomes in nineteenth-century France not because they determined the political intentions, motivations, or choices of actors but because they helped constitute a structure of choices, or realm of possible strategies and alliances, facing political actors.[9] The class structure of each city helped determine patterns of access to scarce resources (which provided capacities for collective action), imposed important limits on the options available to leaders devising political strategies of contention for power, and helped determine the consequences of those strategies. Local class structures, class struggles, and intraclass divisions constituted central constraints and opportunities facing political actors.

Proper appreciation of the relationship between class and politics requires institutionally grounded class analysis. In mid-nineteenth-century France, the role local class forces played in shaping political developments was mediated through historically specific institutional forms. Prior to 1848, the decentralized character of French politics made it possible for local republican party leaders to choose alternative political strategies suited to local circumstances and thus provided early party leaders with a good deal of autonomy from national dominant class actors and interests. During the July Monarchy (1830–48), local republican parties were able to mobilize electoral support among their city's propertied elite by appealing to dominant-class actors whose interests conflicted with capitalist-class actors who exercised more power at the national level. This was the case at Saint-Étienne in the struggle against the coal monopoly, when local groups of capitalists joined a popular political battle in opposition to national finance capital. It was also the case at Toulouse, where many local grain merchants and landowners, angered by central state tariff policies, joined the opposition, and at Rouen, where state railroad policies enabled republicans to mobilize electoral support among the propertied electorate. The decentralized institutional structure of mid-nineteenth-century French politics enabled local republican parties to capitalize politically on distinctive intraclass divisions in their cities, providing republicans with an opportunity to attract dissident members of the local propertied elite to their cause.

The centrality of class structure in shaping local politics is also evident in the pattern of working-class formation in the cities of Toulouse, Rouen, and Saint-Étienne during the July Monarchy. During this period, each city witnessed the formation of local republican parties that competed with contending forces, especially Icarian communists, to secure the political loyalties of workers and simultaneously attempted to win local elections in which only the most wealthy residents were entitled to vote. Despite a shared commitment to the establishment of a republic, each local party pursued different strategies of contending for power, forged different electoral alliances, and relied to different degrees on a rhetoric of class to mobilize working-class support. An explanation of these differences requires attention to the different patterns of capital accumulation and consequent class structures of each city. At Toulouse, the presence of a relatively strong landed aristocracy fostered a successful electoral alliance with the Legitimist party, which inhibited republicans' ability to compete with Icarians for the political loyalties of workers. This strategy was abandoned after radical republicans and their working-class supporters, mainly artisans in handicraft industries, gained a greater voice in the local party. Such an electoral strategy was never attempted in other cities, like Rouen and Saint-Étienne, where alternative patterns of industrial development created different options and fostered strategies in which the aristocracy remained enemies rather than allies. The choices made by republican party leaders were not the ineluctable result of the structure of class relations, for in each case competing strategies of contention for power generated intense conflicts among republicans.

The above examples suggest that instead of treating the lack of a close correspondence between class position and political action as cause for abandoning class analysis, a recognition of the limitations of an overly economistic perspective on politics can provide the opportunity to rethink class analysis. This rethinking should contribute to the development of a theory of politics that resolves certain anomalies, such as the emergence of revolutionary working-class movements in backwaters of industrial capitalist development, and thereby expands the explanatory power of class analysis.[10] My own contribution to this rethinking has focused on an effort to pinpoint the institutional and ideological foundations of bour-geois hegemony as they emerged historically as a product of the intersec-tion of certain institutional and cultural arrangements (i.e., a localized multiparty system and a contested republican political culture) with a regionally uneven process of early capitalist industrialization.[11] The estab-lishment of bourgeois hegemony in nineteenth-century France was a precarious and conflictual cultural, social, political, and economic process. Although this hegemony always remained contested, growing numbers of people, in their taken-for-granted assumptions and day-to-day activities, came to identify the class interests of the bourgeoisie as the general interests of society. The process entailed political concessions by bour-geois leaders, such as the extension of suffrage to workers and the legalization of trade unions. It also involved contestation over the mean-ing of a liberal-democratic ideology (i.e., French republicanism) that permitted bourgeois leaders simultaneously to transcend their own class identities, mobilize other groups under their leadership, and protect their long-term class interests in maintaining a capitalist system. The transfor-mation of French republicanism from a revolutionary to a ruling ideology and practice, in other words, was a key dimension of the creation of hegemonic class rule.

A second aspect of this rethinking of class analysis involves an attempt to specify more clearly the role of class struggles and intraclass divisions as determinants of local political outcomes. Whereas classical Marxist theory designated class struggle as the central motor of political change, more recent empirical analyses have emphasized the importance of internal divisions within social classes, especially conflicts among "segments" of the dominant class, in determining state policies and political outcomes.[12] The relationship between intraclass conflicts and struggles between classes, however, has not yet been adequately analyzed or incorporated into theory. Careful historical comparisons of this relationship, over time and across cities, should help to ascertain whether there are any systematic patterns in this relationship during the early period of capitalist industrialization, when class interests and identities, and their place in the political arena, were actively contested. The goal should be to carefully document and theorize the transformation of French politics in a manner that avoids the various forms of reductionism that continue to plague Marxist thought.[13] This requires recognizing class relations as a powerful determinant of political outcomes and simultaneously acknowledging the ideological and institutional structuring of class relations and the role of nonclass interests, identities, and political practices.

Proletarianization, Politics, and Working-Class Formation

Many recent accounts of the political consequences of early industrialization in Western Europe have emphasized the consequences of the process of proletarianization. After the accumulation of abundant historical evidence documenting the central role of artisans rather than factory workers in the major political upheavals of the nineteenth century, social and economic historians carefully began to explore changes in the character of artisanal production that may have animated this political behavior. My own earlier work on the formation of the working class of Toulouse during the mid-nineteenth century emphasized the varied ways in which different forms of production were transformed by early capitalist industrialization and the consequences of these changes for French workers, workplaces, and politics.[14] This research emphasized the importance of internal transformations of handicraft production in motivating republican and socialist political activities on the part of artisans and the uneven character of the process of proletarianization over time and across occupations. In this earlier work, I sought to expand the concept of proletarianization to include not simply the separation of workers from the means of production but also the diverse ways in which labor became increasingly subordinated to capital during the course of the nineteenth century.[15] Such a redefinition, however, fails to confront fully problems

arising from the assumption of a direct connection between proletarianization and political allegiances and outcomes. Analyses that assume
such a connection fail to understand the ways in which global class
relations and their institutional expression in the political arena shape
the consequences of capital's shifting strategies of control over labor.
Complex and shifting political class alliances, not simply workers' experiences at the point of production, shaped nineteenth-century French
working-class politics. An understanding of working-class politics, in
other words, requires a more class-relational and less workplace-based
view of politics, which directs attention to the larger political economy,
that is, to the ways in which different patterns of bourgeois class formation were shaped by different city's varied and changing linkages to the
world economy and how this in turn affected the character of cross-class
political alliances and the political allegiances and dispositions of the
working class. Although localities may be the appropriate *units* of analysis for the study of nineteenth-century class formation,[16] the proper
objects of analysis are long-term processes, like industrialization, proletarianization, and class formation, which unfold at a variety of different
spatial levels, including the local.

   The problem with many local studies of proletarianization and politics—
and with theories of working-class formation that highlight labor-market
segmentation or changes in labor processes—is not their unwillingness to
recognize an autonomous political dynamic but their failure to situate
local political developments in the context of the international economy
and to understand the cross-class alliances and relations forged in the
political arena. The focus of research on localities has provided access to
the microdynamics of collective action and to the intentions and day-to-
day interactions of social actors, but it has often meant a tendency to
ignore the larger international scene and the ways in which shifting
global economic relations affect local politics. In nineteenth-century France's
major cities, the nature of the local economy and character of local class
relations, as well as political divisions within local elites, were closely tied
to shifting national and global economic realities. Local political allegiances and alliances were often decisively shaped by the nature of the
connection between a particular urban economy and the national or
world market, with the hotly contested questions of tariffs and railroad-
building providing central issues in cementing cross-class alliances and
fostering intraclass divisions. In short, to understand working-class politics in nineteenth-century French cities, we need to look beyond the shop
floor and the locality and supplement analyses of the proletarianization
of workers and the rise and decline of different local industries with the
study of shifting connections between local, national, and global econo-

mies and the study of the political institutions in which class relations were negotiated.

In mid-nineteenth-century France, the working class was formed not simply as a product of capitalist development but also politically, through the medium of local republican organizations. This is why we need to understand the inner workings of republican "proto-parties"—their organizational structure, competing ideological currents, and internal struggles—to understand the process of working-class formation fully. Just as labor history cannot be written apart from the history of capital, it cannot be divorced from political history. Political institutions, like nascent or "proto" republican parties, constituted the central terrain on which local class relations were actively contested and redefined in mid-nineteenth-century France. The history of French working-class formation is intimately tied to the shifting organizational and ideological features of national and local republicanism during the period from 1830 to 1870, when French democrats created the first mass-based political party in France. Republicans were responsible for initially mobilizing workers into the political arena and establishing the institutional structure and rules of the game under which French parties have functioned since the Constitution of 1875. Republicans mobilized French workers by appealing to issues of class inequality, from suffrage restrictions to regressive taxes to the absence of municipal public services in working-class neighborhoods. In doing so, they helped constitute identities of class for workers and organize politics in terms of class. Labor historians need to explore the institutional context within which local republican parties operated, including the character of local-national party linkages and the internal divisions in social composition and ideology that produced conflict and change in French republicanism during the middle decades of the nineteenth century.

Republican Ideology, Fraternalism, and Working-Class Formation

French republicans shared a common commitment to a republican form of government, a commonality that gained importance in the face of staunch opposition to republican government on the part of the most powerful members of the property-holding class, who preferred some form of a monarchy. Republicans also shared certain common values, including a belief in progress and political rationalism, a hostility to aristocracy and monarchy, and a refusal to accept tradition as a legitimate basis of political authority. Most republicans agreed on a political program that included universal male suffrage, civil liberties, parliamen-

tary government, tax reform, free secular education, and universal obligatory military service. Republicanism was not, however, an internally
consistent and logically rigorous system of thought.[17] Those who identified themselves as republicans differed on a wide variety of key issues
concerning the relationship between the state and the economy.

French republicanism was not a coherent ideology but a contradictory
blend of elements of the discourses of liberalism and socialism. The
articulating principles of republican ideology, summarized in the slogan
of the French Revolution—liberty, equality, and fraternity—were subject
to alternative interpretations throughout the nineteenth century, as republicans elaborated different visions of the republic. For liberal republicans,
the principle of liberty meant freedom from the oppressive and arbitrary
practices of an autocratic state as well as freedom from state interference
in the economy. The principle of equality meant the extension of legal
rights to all men regardless of their wealth or property. The principle of
fraternity referred to the national solidarities that connected all inhabit-
ants of France, regardless of their social class. Socialist republicans also
adopted a language of rights but in a way that attached very different
meanings to the terms *liberty, equality,* and *fraternity.* The principle of
liberty was expanded to include the right to work, that is, state-guaranteed
employment. The principle of equality was extended beyond the boundaries of the political arena to the economy. Whereas liberal republicans
envisioned a republic that would promote class conciliation among all
French citizens, socialist republicans appealed to class antagonisms by
challenging established class inequalities and property relations. The
principle of fraternity was appropriated by republican socialists to foster
the values of collectivism, mutual aid, and class solidarity.

Recent accounts of ideological change have denied or downplayed the
class rootedness of political ideologies, treating them as autonomous
of class forces or suggesting an arbitrary relationship between class
relations and political ideologies.[18] The political ideology of mid-nineteenth-
century republicanism was not autonomous or detached from class relations nor was it simply a class ideology, despite its close connection to the
working-class struggles of the period. The class connotations of republicanism were not given by the nature of the ideology. They were actively
contested in political struggles over incorporating elements of liberal and
socialist discourses and practices into republicanism. The development of
republican ideology was not the result of an internal working out of an
autonomous discourse, of the sort suggested by François Furet in his
study of the French Revolution.[19] It was the complex and creative product of conflicts over alternative visions of the republic, which had distinctive social underpinnings.

Although liberal, radical, and socialist republicanism appealed across class boundaries, different visions of the republic mobilized different class bases of support.[20] Liberal economic themes were congruent with the day-to-day realities of bourgeois life, which fostered values emphasizing risk-taking, wealth-making, and the subordination of wage labor. Republican liberals drew their most prominent spokespersons from the bourgeoisie, especially those merchants and industrialists who were adversely affected by state tariff and railroad policies, and they recruited most of their supporters among property owners and employers, including some smaller urban and rural property holders. Radical republicanism initially drew its support from shopkeepers, small masters, students, clerks, and less-well-to-do professionals, whose social situations fostered the values of thrift, independence, and hard work, more so than risk-taking or wealth-making. During the 1860s radicals expanded their base of urban support to include liberal industrialists dissatisfied with the Imperial Regime's tariff and transportation policies as well as many urban workers and shopkeepers. The experience of wage labor fostered a collectivist awareness of interdependence that was congruent with the associationalist principles of early republican socialism. Republican socialists found most of their support within the working class, especially among artisans, although their leadership came from the ranks of dissident intellectuals and professionals, especially lawyers, doctors, journalists, and educators.

The success of republican ideology depended on its ability to mobilize supporters from various social classes by reconciling what, in the context of the intense class divisions of early industrial capitalism, were antagonistic principles—individual liberty and democracy. This reconciliation was the product of decades of struggle among liberal, socialist, and radical republicans over alternative visions of the republic that amalgamated elements of classical liberalism and early socialism in different ways.[21]

Both liberalism and socialism represented internally diverse and changing discourses rather than rigid positions. Despite sharp differences in their political discourses on the meaning of liberty, equality, and fraternity, in actual political practice, nineteenth-century liberalism and socialism constituted overlapping and mutually interacting practices, each of which was transformed by one another during the course of the nineteenth century. French socialists increasingly came to accept working within the electoral arena and a representative rather than participatory practice of democracy. The harsh repression they repeatedly faced strengthened their commitment to civil liberties and parliamentary restraints on executive power. Republican socialist workers of the late 1860s called for a variety of liberal measures, including civil liberties, the election of mayors rather than their appointment by the central state, and greater municipal freedom. French liberals came to accept not only associational rights but also various types of state intervention to remedy the social ills of the free market, from child labor laws to progressive income taxes. This reconciliation was not natural or inevitable, though. The creation of a republican synthesis that selectively incorporated elements of liberal and socialist traditions in a manner that made democracy safe for capitalism was the outcome of a long, sometimes violent struggle among republicans.

Republican ideology became dominant, or hegemonic, in France only after it incorporated contradictory elements of liberalism and socialism and neutralized their potential antagonism. This ideological synthesis was the achievement of mid-nineteenth-century radical republicans, but it fell to late nineteenth-century republicans to institutionalize the radical republican vision. Although radical republicans rejected socialism, especially its statist versions, and preached class collaboration rather than class conflict, they parted company with liberals by calling for government intervention in the economy to improve the condition of the working class and to guarantee workers the right to organize unions. Radicals acknowledged the intimate connections between economic and political spheres and shared with socialists a willingness to use state power to remedy social problems. Unlike socialists, they were less concerned with reorganizing production than with promoting a more equitable income distribution through tax reforms, government regulation of monopolies, the legalization of unions, and welfare policies. Radicals defended the inviolable rights of property against socialist collectivism but rejected the liberal antipathy toward political authority. Though less committed to economic equality than socialists were, French radicals were committed to social equality. French radicalism, observes Alain Cottereau, "maintained a populist appearance, showing little respect for middle-class styles and proprieties, which gives it a very different coloring than that of English or American radicalism . . . far from sharing in the quest for honorability and for moral recognition by other social classes, the style of the French radicals was very populist and perhaps even 'demogogic' in the eyes of the most 'honorable' social classes."[22]

The success of republicans depended on their ability to reconcile antagonistic class interests by amalgamating elements of classical liberalism, early socialism, and democracy. Struggles among republicans over the character of party platforms and content of the political agenda centered on the contrasting objectives of these three political traditions, which were incorporated in different ways over time and across cities. The outcomes of these key struggles, less visible but perhaps as important as the more dramatic struggles on the barricades and in the streets, were not dictated by the logic of republican discourse or its internal contradictions; they can only be understood by placing a nonreductionist form of class analysis back at the center of the agenda of French history.

Republicans also made an important contribution to the process of working-class formation by fostering a distinctively gendered understanding of both politics and social class. Although republican rhetoric called for political equality, its universalist ethic did not include women, who were excluded from citizenship rights in the republican constitutions of 1791 and 1793 and were denied basic rights of assembly and association under the First French Republic. The Jacobin republican regime of the Convention, fearful of sansculotte popular upheaval, in which women played a key role, suppressed all political activity by women, outlawing female clubs and political associations in October of 1793. Despite some dissenting voices among Girondin republicans like Condorcet, the vast majority of late eighteenth-century republicans shared Rousseau's aversion to public women and embraced a vision of the republic that excluded women from formal political life and asserted their natural domesticity, relegating their civic role to the home where they would perform the duties of republican mothers, raising their children as republican patriots.[23] The French republican vision of democracy excluded ostensible dependents, including women and children, from the suffrage. The general argument used to oppose female suffrage concerned the danger of enfranchising anyone who was likely to follow someone else's orders when voting, which included not only women but also servants, prisoners, monks, and apprentices. Traditional republican notions of civic virtue, which assigned women to the private sphere as republican mothers and as the moral guardians of the home, were also used to justify denying the vote to women, as was the argument that women were too influenced by a reactionary clergy to provide secure electoral support for the republic.[24]

Early French republicanism was built on fraternal organizational forms and a mobilizing ideology that was fraternal in character. Although *fraternity* is one of the three key words in the republican motto, historians have remained remarkably blind to the fraternal features of nineteenth-century French republicanism.[25] Fraternity was not simply a republican expression of community; it was a gendered sociocultural form of solidarity and community that played a central role in the constitution of republican identities. Fraternalism appealed to a particular vision of masculine camaraderie and male authority, allowing republicans to construct solidarities based on fictive kinship, which crossed class lines via shared definitions of manhood and rituals of male bonding.[26] The quasi-familial ties, rituals, and solidarities sustained by republican associations were based on a vision of fraternity that was explicitly restricted to men. Republican secret societies, masonic lodges, electoral associations, social clubs (*chambrées*), and informal cafe gatherings fostered cross-class male bonding, often in an atmosphere of danger. Secret associations, such as the Carbonari societies of the 1830s and the secret societies of 1850–51, and politicized associations of urban sociability, such as masonic lodges, were fraternal forms of organization that helped shape the republican party during its formative years, which were marked by intense political repression. Political repression not only drove republican activities underground into these fraternal associations but also helped valorize masculine virtues of physical bravery and combat by encouraging republicans to embrace revolutionary violence. Prior to 1848, republican rhetoric included a militaristic nationalism that appealed to males who had experienced military service, and, both before and after 1848, it encompassed a patriarchal view of citizenship rights as limited to men. Like the traditional artisans' organizations, the *compagnonnages*,[27] and the predominantly bourgeois masonic lodges, the secret societies and conspiratorial organizations that became prominent during the intense repression of the 1830s and 1850s utilized secret oaths and elaborate rituals to foster male bonding, including oaths of regicide and the ritual stabbing of straw mannequins symbolizing royalty.

Utopian socialists of the late 1830s and 1840s, from Flora Tristan to Saint-Simon, Charles Fourier, and Étienne Cabet, offered an alternative understanding of class and politics. They espoused feminist themes of gender equality and economic independence, envisioned a public role for women, and strove to create organizational forms that, in contrast to those of republicans, were neither fraternal nor electoral.[28] In contrast to republicans, utopian socialists proposed various experiments with different family forms, targeting family as well as workplace organization in their criticisms of the existing social order. The triumph of republican socialism over "utopian socialism" during the 1840s, a turning point that has not been adequately explored by French labor historians, was not simply the victory of an ideology but also the victory of fraternity as a form of political association over a more communal organizational vision, which was more open to female participation.[29] It was also the triumph of a more gender exclusive understanding of working-class politics, which equated productivity, masculinity, and civic rights.

Republican Discourses of Representation and Working-Class Formation

In recent years, feminist historians have transformed our understanding of class formation by focusing attention on the gendered character of the process. Joan Scott's research in particular has reshaped our understanding of French working-class history. Her work carefully documents the gendered character of class identities and political appeals and persuasively argues for an end to "the compartmentalizing tendency of so much of social history that relegates sex and gender to the institution of the family [and] associates class with the workplace and the community. . . ."[30]

By privileging canonical texts, representions, and linguistic codes, by adopting a deinstitutionalized understanding of politics and a poststructuralist epistomology, and by collapsing class and class consciousness, however, Scott marginalizes the socioeconomic and institutional dimensions of the process of class formation. The importance of these dimensions and the rootedness of language in material contexts can be illustrated by an analysis of the transformation of French republican discourse on political representation.

The discourse of republicanism included certain understandings of the meaning of political representation, which was contested and transformed during the 1850s and 1860s. The notion of representation (and leadership) that dominated republican circles throughout the mid-nineteenth century was rooted in the sansculottes' vision of direct democracy, which considered elected officials to be delegates (*mandataires*), not representatives. Whereas elected delegates were obligated to adhere to the binding instructions from their constituents, representatives followed the dictates of their own conscience and convictions. This participatory vision of elected officials as delegates with binding obligations to the voters who elected them contrasted with the liberal notion of elected officials as representatives with some degree of independence from their constituents. The participatory vision also implied the right of citizens to take nonelectoral collective political actions if their elected representatives were not abiding by their mandates. Republicans continued to adhere to the traditional notion of the imperative mandate throughout the mid-nineteenth century. In this understanding of representation, elected officials are bound to carry the expressed wishes and grievances of their constituents.[31]

The sansculottes of the French revolution adopted this imperative mandate view of representation, which was elaborated in the Constitution of 1793 in the statement that the government was the property of the sovereign people and its officials their clerks. Prior to 1870, the notion that elected officials were mandatories was reflected not only in republican hostility toward executive power and in the opposition of most republicans to the direct election of a president but also in the very language of mid-nineteenth-century republican politics, which termed the written platforms of candidates for elected office *mandats*. Republican socialist advocates of direct democracy did not deny the need for representative institutions in a country as large as France, but they regarded the principle of the imperative mandate as a way to ensure popular control of elected officials.[32]

The imperative mandate vision of democracy was summarized in Alexandre Ledru-Rollin's famous statement of 1840: "I am their leader, I must follow them." The republican commitment to participatory democracy was evident in 1848, when radical republicans provided leadership for many of the clubs that proliferated in the aftermath of the February Revolution. Most clubs saw their function as not simply providing a public forum for the discussion of political issues but also exerting direct popular pressure on bourgeois government officials to ensure that the betrayal of 1830 did not reoccur.[33] During the 1860s, radical republican leaders reinterpreted the doctrine of an imperative mandate to give it a distinctive capitalist tone, using the free-market language of binding contracts rather than the sansculotte rhetoric of popular sovereignty. According to radical republican leaders of the 1860s, including Léon Gambetta and Jean Macé, voters were like clients who instructed elected officials to carry out their wishes and these officials, like honest businessmen, were obliged to fulfill their contractual obligations. "Businessman or deputy," wrote Jean Macé, "can an honest man be anything other than a machine for keeping promises?"[34]

The transformation of the meaning of the imperative mandate was linked not only to capitalist development but also to larger institutional changes in French politics, including the growth of political parties and the decline of local neighborhood-based institutions of political participation. The notion of an imperative mandate was initially rooted in a communal and direct democracy vision of politics, which was eclipsed by the emergence of mass political parties. As the electorate expanded and political parties increasingly organized voters, the locus of accountability shifted from ordinary constituents to party leaders, who were responsible for making sure that elected representatives adhered to the principles and platforms of the parties that nominated them for office. In July of 1870, the public prosecutor at Toulouse noted that republican candidates in the upcoming city council election accepted the imperative mandate and "had agreed in advance to vote according to orders given by the republican committee." "This pledge," he observed, "which they are no doubt obliged to make, is remarkable. The result, if they are elected, will be that, although invested with the confidence of around 12,000 electors, they must submit to the absolute domination of an unauthorized and unqualified committee."[35] The emergence of party organizations capable of enforcing discipline on their elected representatives thus transformed the meaning of the imperative mandate, making it possible for government officials to denounce the principle as the basis for oligarchic rule rather than popular democracy.

Why should such shifting meanings of political representation concern French labor historians? Changing republican meanings of representation shaped the process of French working-class formation by privileging certain institutional forms, which in turn privileged the ability of certain social classes to represent their interests. The transformed contractual understanding of the imperative mandate that emerged during the 1860s was premised on parliamentary rather than communal institutions. Given the unequal distribution of resources across the class structure, parliamentary institutions favored the dominant class by placing a premium on such resources as oratory, legal skills, and an ability to organize beyond the local level. The original sansculotte notion of the imperative mandate was rooted in the more participatory, face-to-face relations of such institutions as the clubs, cafes, and neighborhood assemblies. These conferred political advantage to those who possessed different resources, including deference and respect based on long-time residence, age, or patriarchal authority, support from friendship and kinship networks, and centrality to informal communication networks.[36] These were more accessible to wage laborers and small property owners than were the resources required for success in parliamentary politics. In the cafes, clubs, secret societies, and neighborhood assemblies that were a central part of the organizational nexus of local republican politics, workers had greater opportunity to exercise political leadership and to command equality of respect as "citizens" than in a competitive electoral arena that demanded organizational skills and financial resources that were beyond the reach of many workers.

Shifting republican meanings of representation did not alter the gendered understanding of citizenship, which excluded women from public life. Republican notions of accountability to constituents, whether they were contractual or popular democratic understandings, remained based on a fraternalist ideology and politics. Republican meanings of representation, however, did change. The preceding account of this change suggests the social processes that transformed these meanings are not reducible to language. Political meanings were not constituted by autonomous discourses or transformed as a result of contradictions internal to republican ideology. They were developed and transformed in response to changing socioeconomic and political conditions, produced by processes of capitalist development and political party formation.

Conclusion: An Agenda for French Labor History

My agenda for French labor history is guided by the following four principles. First, class analysis is neither dead nor buried, although class-reductionist explanations of politics have been thoroughly discredited. Students of the process of working-class formation must be attentive to material realities as well as discourse. An adequate history of French labor requires the creative combination of class, institutional, and cultural analysis. Second, class formation is a gendered process. This does not simply mean that we need to become more attentive to the role of women in French working-class history. It also means that we must explore the gendered character of ideas and institutions even when women are absent from the scene. Third, class formation in France was as much a political as an economic process. Labor historians therefore need to become more attentive to the role that political institutions, especially political parties, played in shaping working-class identities and interests. Finally, although local studies will probably continue to contribute the most to our understanding of working-class formation, such studies must become more sensitive to the way in which localities are differentially situated in the national and global economy.

Given these guidelines, how should we proceed to write the history of French labor? In my view, we should write narratives based on explicit theorizing and carefully constructed comparisons. Working-class formation was a process in which people actively contested alternative understandings of class and class interests and different strategies for persuing those interests. These conflicts are best captured by theoretically explicit narratives that carefully trace and compare the sequences of events constituting the process. Narratives allow us to capture the unfolding of social action over time in a manner sensitive to the order in which events occur. By making the theories that underpin our narratives more explicit, we avoid the danger of burying our explanatory principles in engaging stories. By comparing sequences, we can determine whether there are typical sequences across cities or regions and can explore the causes and consequences of different sequence patterns. The picture we end up with is unlikely to resemble a random assortment of contingent events or a single path toward liberation guided by the iron logic of capital accumulation. It will more likely portray a structured process that was path-dependent,[37] in which past choices at key forks in the road helped determine the subsequent trajectory by delimiting future options and opening up other possibilities.

Notes

My thanks to Lenard Berlanstein, Barbara Laslett, Mary Jo Maynes, and Erik Olin Wright for comments on an earlier draft.

1. Theda Skocpol, "Sociology's Historical Imagination," in *Vision and Method in Historical Sociology,* ed. Theda Skocpol (Cambridge, 1984), pp. 13-14. Skocpol's work is exemplary in that it manages to avoid many of the problems that have plagued the debate over the relative autonomy of the capitalist state, including an ambiguity regarding what the state is autonomous from and a tendency to treat the state as a unitary structure rather than as a set of diverse institutions that may be subject to varying mechanisms limiting or extending their autonomy. Many state theorists fail to differentiate between different levels of the state—for example, local and national—and do not explore differences across levels in degrees and mechanisms of autonomy. They also tend to treat theoretical claims about the nature and extent of state autonomy as methodological postulates rather than regard the nature and extent of state autonomy as historically as well as institutionally variable. These problems suggest that theoretical claims about state autonomy would benefit from clearer specification of the particular political institutions in question, the particular levels of the state in question, the historical context in which these institutions are situated, the concrete mechanisms fostering or impeding political autonomy, and precisely what these institutions are autonomous from.

2. Mark Traugott, *Armies of the Poor: Determinants of Working-Class Participation in the Paris Insurrection of June 1848* (Princeton, N.J., 1985).

3. Ibid., pp. 184, 186.

4. William H. Sewell, Jr., "Uneven Development, the Autonomy of Politics, and the Dockworkers of Nineteenth-Century Marseille," *American Historical Review* 93 (1988): 604-37.

5. French historians are often quick to dismiss the value of class analysis by pointing to the diversity of motives animating political behavior and the complexity of political struggles. J. F. Bosher describes the political conflicts preceding the French Revolution as a story "of struggles between men with political principles as well as class characteristics, with wills and characters as well as class interests, and with minds for thinking as well as class loyalties. These men are free to win or loose, not bound by historical necessity. Their struggles are infinitely complicated political struggles, not vague underlying class conflicts. . . . " Bosher, "Introduction" to Jean Egret, *The French Prerevolution 1787-1788,* trans. Wesley D. Camp (Chicago, 1977), p. xiv.

6. William M. Reddy, *Money and Liberty in Modern Europe: A Critique of Historical Understanding* (Cambridge, 1987), pp. xi, 71; François Furet, *Penser la Révolution française* (Paris, 1978), pp. 71-72.

7. For a discussion of the concept of contradictory class locations, see Erik Olin Wright, *Classes* (London, 1985) and *Class, Crisis, and the State* (London, 1978).

8. "In addition to one or more industrial wages," notes Alain Cottereau, "there were agricultural incomes (revenue from the sale of owner-produced crops, gathering, agricultural wages, rent revenue); wages as employees or as domestics; revenue from small businesses or gardening; and income from exchanges among relatives and friends outside of commercial circuits." Cottereau, "The Distinctiveness of Working-Class Cultures in France, 1848-1900," in *Working-Class Formation: Nineteenth-Century Patterns in Western Europe and the United States,* ed. Ira Katznelson and Aristide R. Zolberg (Princeton, N.J., 1986), p. 142.

9. My approach borrows heavily from Adam Przeworski, who argues that social relations should be "treated as structures of choices available to actors, not as sources of norms to be internalized and acted. Social relations are the structures within which actors, individual and collective, deliberate upon goals, perceive and evaluate alternatives, and select courses of action." Przeworski, "Proletariat into a Class: The Process of Class Formation," in his *Capitalism and Social Democracy* (Cambridge, 1985), p. 96.

10. This goal is consistent with Imre Lakatos's view of how advances in social science research come about. Lakatos, *The Methodology of Scientific Research Programme* (Cambridge, 1978).

11. For an analysis of the emergence of hegemonic forms of class rule in nineteenth-century France, see Ronald Aminzade, *Class, Politics, and Early Industrial Capitalism: A Study of Mid-Nineteenth-Century Toulouse, France* (Albany, N.Y., 1981), pp. 269-89.

12. See, for example, Maurice Zeitlin, W. Lawrence Neuman, and Richard Ratcliff, "Class Segments: Agrarian Property and Political Leadership in the Capitalist Class of Chile," *American Sociological Review* 41 (1976): 1006-29; and Maurice Zeitlin, ed., *Classes, Class Conflict, and the State: Empirical Studies in Class Analysis* (Cambridge, Mass., 1980). This emphasis on the role of internal divisions among dominant class actors is not limited to Marxist analyses. For a neo-Weberian account of the development of absolutist states in France and England that locates the central dynamic of political change in conflicts among elites, see Richard Lachmann, "Elite Conflict and State Formation in Sixteenth- and Seventeenth-Century England and France," *American Sociological Review* 54 (1989): 141-62.

13. For a discussion of various forms of reductions in Marxist political theory, see Nicos Mouzelis, "Reductionism in Marxist Theory," *Telos* 45 (1980): 173-85. See also his effort to overcome this reductionism by developing political concepts to analyze modes of domination in *Politics in the Semi-Periphery* (New York, 1986).

14. Aminzade, *Class, Politics, and Early Industrial Capitalism.*

15. Ronald Aminzade, "Reinterpreting Capitalist Industrialization: A Study of Nineteenth-Century France," *Social History* 9 (1984): 329-50.

16. As Christopher Johnson observed many years ago and as his own work

amply demonstrates, "There is little question that most new insights into the problems of class formation and the development of class consciousness will derive from intensive local or industry-specific study that utilizes the cumbersome but richly rewarding social data that have come to be the backbone of labor history." Johnson, "Patterns of Proletarianization: Parisian Tailors and Lodève Woolen Workers," in *Consciousness and Class Experience in Nineteenth-Century Europe*, ed. by John Merriman (New York, 1979), p. 82.

17. "No ideology is ever wholly logical or consistent," writes Stuart Hall. "All the great organic ideologies bring together discordant elements and have to struggle to make contradictory ideas fit the scheme. There are always loose ends, breaks in the logic, gaps between theory and practice, and internal contradictions in any current of thought. . . . " Hall, "Variants of Liberalism," in *Politics and Ideology*, ed. James Donald and Stuart Hall (New York, 1986), p. 36.

18. For polemical but insightful critiques of these approaches, see Ellen Meiksins Wood, *The Retreat from Class* (London, 1986); and Bryan D. Palmer, *Descent into Discourse: The Reification of Language and the Writing of Social History* (Philadelphia, 1990).

19. Furet, *Penser la Révolution française.*

20. This discussion borrows insights from Göran Therborn's analysis of ideologies, which emphasizes a "selective affinity" rather than rigid connection between the values fostered by different socioeconomic milieus and political beliefs. Therborn, *The Ideology of Power and the Power of Ideology* (London, 1980), pp. 57-61.

21. My tripartite division of republicans into liberal, radical, and socialist camps does not imply the absence of divisions within each camp. Liberal republicans of the early 1860s, for example, were divided over whether to cooperate with the liberalizing efforts of the Imperial Regime, *la gauche ouverte* headed by Émile Ollivier, or to oppose cooperation with nonrepublicans, *la gauche fermée* led by Jules Grévy and Jules Ferry. Republican socialists were also divided, with some favoring Proudhonian socialism and others, including the followers of Louis Blanqui, adopting a more Jacobin vision. For an alternative classification of the nineteenth-century French left, which utilizes vaguer, more philosophical criteria, emphasizing the romanticism and "Rousseauist" leanings of Alexandre Ledru-Rollin, Louis Blanc, Edgar Quinet, Jules Michelet, and Victor Hugo, the liberalism of Étienne Vacherot and Jules Simon, the positivism and juridicism of Émile Littré, Léon Gambetta, and Jules Ferry, and the revolutionary aspirations of men like Louis Blanqui and Louis Delescluze, see Claude Nicolet, *L'idée républicaine en France, 1789-1924* (Paris, 1982), pp. 152-87. For another approach, which emphasizes means and moral themes as well as goals as the criteria for distinguishing divisions within the mid-nineteenth-century French left, see Stephane Rials, "Néo-Jacobinisme et néo-hérbertisme au milieu du XIXe siècle," in *Révolution et contre-révolution au XIXe siècle* (Paris, 1987), pp. 284-300.

22. Cottereau, "The Distinctiveness of Working-Class Cultures," pp. 150-51.

23. Joan Landes, *Women and the Public Sphere in the Age of the French Revolution* (Ithaca, N.Y., 1988), pp. 66-89.

24. "Not even the fiercest republicans," notes Sian Reynolds, "seriously suggested depriving churchgoers of their vote. It was because women had originally been excluded from the Republic that it was easy to convert an argument about rights into an argument about the putative result of giving women the vote." Reynolds, "Marianne's Citizens?" in *Women, State, and Revolution: Essays on Power and Gender in Europe since 1789,* ed. Sian Reynolds (Amherst, Mass., 1987), p. 113.

25. For a feminist critique of the orthodox historiography of the Republic, see Reynolds, "Marianne's Citizens?" pp. 102-22.

26. This account relies heavily on the pioneering work of Mary Ann Clawson, who identifies four elements that define fraternalism as a unique social form: corporatism, ritual, masculinity, and proprietorship. "A corporatist impulse, a fascination with dramatic ritual, and an attachment to the inter-connected identities of proprietorship and masculinity characterize early modern fraternalism and its nineteenth century counterparts." Clawson, *Constructing Brotherhood: Class, Gender, and Fraternalism* (Princeton, N.J., 1989), pp. 51-52.

27. On the rituals of the *compagnonnage,* see Cynthia Truant, "Compagnonnage: Symbolic Action and the Defense of Workers' Rights in France, 1700-1848" (Ph.D. diss., University of Chicago, 1978). See also Truant, "Solidarity and Symbolism among Journeymen Artisans: The Case of Compagnonnage," *Comparative Studies in Society and History* 21 (1979): 214-26.

28. Flora Tristan envisioned the creation of "worker's palaces," which, writes Joan Landes, were "organizational centers for the achievement of true equality, and forums for the common education of the two sexes—a kind of proletarian public sphere, supported by workers' self-taxation, in which women will occupy a central place." Landes, *Women and the Public Sphere,* p. 182. See also Flora Tristan, *The Workers' Union,* trans. Beverly Livingston (Urbana, Ill., 1983); S. Joan Moon, "Feminism and Socialism: The Utopian Synthesis of Flora Tristan," in *Socialist Women,* ed. Marilyn J. Boxer and Jean H. Quataert (New York, 1978), pp. 19-50; and Leslie Goldstein, "Early Feminist Themes in French Utopian Socialism," *Journal of the History of Ideas* 43 (1982): 91-108.

29. Dorothy Thompson notes a similar process of the exclusion of women from popular politics during the 1840s in England and attributes it, in part, to the growth of electoral politics among skilled workers and the organizational transformation of working-class politics. Skilled workers, she writes, "left behind the mass politics of the earlier part of the century. . . . In doing so, the skilled workers also left behind the unskilled workers and the women, whose way of life did not allow their participation in the more structured political forms. These forms required both regularity of working times and regularity of income for participation to be possible. . . . " Thompson, "Women and Nineteenth-Century Radical Politics: A Lost Dimension," in *The Rights and Wrongs of Women,* ed. Juliet Mitchell and Ann Oakley (New York, 1976), p. 37.

30. Joan Wallach Scott, *Gender and the Politics of History* (New York, 1988), p. 6.

31. This principle did not originate with Rousseau but dated back to the

elections of the Estates General of the Old Regime. Delegates to the Estates General were mandated not to deliberate on issues but to accurately present the wishes of their constituents, as expressed in the documents (*cahiers*) drawn up separately by each order in local and regional deliberative assemblies. Any delegates who attempted to usurp the power of their constituents by exercising initiative and going beyond the explicit mandate elaborated in the *cahiers* were not only punished by removal from office but also subject to judicial and financial penalties. See Claude Soule, *Les États Généraux* (Paris, 1968), pp. 76–78. The form and content of mandates varied across elections and localities, and historians disagree about the latitude given to deputies by their constituents. Whereas Soule portrays the mandate as highly restricted, J. Russell Major argues that most deputies received ample powers whenever royal letters of convocation were not vague. Major, *The Deputies to the Estates General in Renaissance France* (Madison, Wis., 1960), p. 8. Delegates to the Estates General were not chosen in a contested election process, in which candidates offered alternative views of the grievances that should be presented to the king in the Estates *cahier* or appealed to groups with competing interests in the Estate. Delegates were selected before issues and grievances were even compiled in the *cahiers,* so it was not even possible to select delegates on the basis of their positions on given issues. This is not surprising since the function of the delegates was not to represent the views of competing factions within the Estate or *baillange* or to deliberate on issues but to present their constituents' deliberations to the king, following the instructions contained in the *cahier.* Claude Soule, "La notion historique de représentation politique," *Politique* 6 (1962): 19; Ran Halevi, "Modalités, participation, et luttes électorales sous l'Ancien Régime," in *Explication du vote: Un bilan des études électorales en France,* ed. Daniel Gaxie (Paris, 1985), p. 98.

32. Nicolet, *L'idée républicaine en France,* pp. 109–10.

33. On the club movement in Paris, see Peter Amann, *Revolution and Mass Democracy: The Paris Club Movement in 1848* (Princeton, N.J., 1975).

34. Quoted in Katherine Auspitz, *The Radical Bourgeoisie* (Cambridge, 1982), p. 34.

35. Letter of July 19, 1870, Archives Nationales, BB 18 1768.

36. Jane Mansbridge, *Beyond Adversary Democracy* (New York, 1980), pp. 97–114.

37. For a discussion of the concept of path dependency, see Ronald Aminzade, "Historical Sociology and Time," *Sociological Methods and Research* 20 (1992): 462–64.

LAURA LEE DOWNS

Women's Strikes
and the Politics of
Popular Egalitarianism
in France, 1916–18

Historians have long been drawn to the study of labor protest, for strikes suggest the possibility of grasping (however momentarily) at that elusive phantom, the autonomous self-expression of working people. This prospect holds special appeal for labor historians, whose quest for working-class subjectivity is so often constrained by the silence that surrounds their subaltern subjects. As a strike unfolds, the once muffled voices of ordinary women and men ring with a startling, sharp clarity. The historian, hitherto condemned to searching the silence for random bits and clues, is abruptly faced with the task of interpreting the sudden cascade of language and desire unleashed in the collective decision to take shop-floor grievances onto the streets. It is this problem of interpretation, the constructions historians place on the speech and actions of the generally unheard-from, that I discuss here, using the example of France during World War I.

In the spring of 1917, a sudden, massive wave of strikes hit the munitions factories of Paris. Commencing in the aftermath of the Pentecost holiday, the movement spread rapidly from factory to factory and from one industrial suburb to the next. Within days, nearly 43,000 metals and munition workers, most of them women, had left their machines and joined the crowds that marched along the broad boulevards of industrial Paris. Though brief local disputes had broken out in individual munitions factories over the previous year, the May–June movement triggered the most widespread and powerful strikes since August 1914. After three years of fighting, it seemed that low wages and long hours might undo the "sacred union," which, since the onset of war, had bound working class to bourgeoisie in a national crusade against the German threat to the Republic.[1] Within a few short months, political scandal would shatter this domestic truce, but in May–June, its partisans still hoped to preserve the fragile unity. Employers, police, state officials, and even some trade union leaders thus collaborated in the effort to end the street demonstrations and to get the women back to work as quickly as possible.

The May–June strikes clearly mark an important moment in the history of France's "other front." After three years of relative quiet, muffled by the blanket of sacred union and the many sanctions that state and employer wielded in time of war, the working class was starting to recover its independent voice. Yet historians give this movement only a fleeting nod (at best) when recounting labor's fate during the World War I. Certainly, the police and employers who joined in repressing this movement viewed it as a significant event. The widespread work stoppages threatened the military effort by slowing the flow of arms to the front, while the daily demonstrations constituted the first serious rupture of public order since the war began. Moreover, the strikes followed hard on the heels of open revolt among some 40,000 thousand soldiers along the western front.[2] Although news of the mutiny was carefully suppressed (neither the Germans nor France's British ally ever got wind of the event), rumors had traveled back to Paris and circulated among the striking crowds. Police searched vigorously for traitors among the strike movement's ringleaders. They were convinced that the link between mutiny and strike was more than casual, that a nefarious force of German agents had fomented the demonstrations on both fronts.

Max Gallo writes that in time of war, with syndicalist militants dispersed across the landscape and unprecedented powers of discipline concentrated in the hands of state and employers, workers' protests over wages and conditions were themselves the critical force that catalyzed labor's revival.[3] Moreover, under the constraints and prohibitions of war, syndicalism would regenerate only through those apparently nonpolitical protests tied closely to the concrete conditions of work—struggles that initially were fought almost exclusively by women.[4]

Labor history's classic distinction between "narrow" struggles over shop-floor conditions and the more "political" strike, motivated by broader concerns outside the workplace, thus loses force and clarity in the context of the war. Nonetheless, historians have doggedly fixed their eyes beyond May–June, locating labor's "true" renascence in the spring of 1918, when a predominantly male and explicitly pacifist movement swept the war factories. Those who do not bypass May–June altogether simply shrug it off as the act of an apolitical and wage-hungry female crowd, for whom the conduct of the war and other serious political issues were remote affairs.[5] But if French labor first recovered its voice in 1917—and the burgeoning protest that followed in the autumn of that year suggests this was indeed the case[6]—then May–June marks an important passage from invertebrate silence to vocal opposition. Had the voice that first rallied the protest been baritone rather than soprano, perhaps labor history would not have been so quick to banish this movement to its margins. The following case study suggests that historians' dismissive view of women's protest as preeminently unpolitical parallels the opinion of those police and employers who nervously watched and then hastily repressed the movement of May–June 1917.[7]

Life in the War Factories: Conditions of Work and the Resurgence of Protest

The women who downed tools that spring had toiled for two years or more under miserable conditions, which the sharpening pressure of inflation merely exacerbated. With the declaration of war, the government had proclaimed a "state of siege," which remained in force throughout the war. This emergency law curtailed many civil rights—free speech, freedom of the press—and suspended all protective legislation at work—laws concerning maximum hours, prohibitions against night work for women and children, laws requiring that dangerous machinery be fenced to protect the operatives. During the first three years of war, women in the war factories worked thirteen days at a stretch, on rotating shifts of eleven to twelve hours. On the fourteenth day, they rested, in preparation for another grim fortnight.

Within the factories, conditions were often deplorable—cramped, ill-lit workrooms with unfenced machinery, insufficient and filthy lavatories, and inadequate medical facilities for treating the all-too-frequent injuries on the shop floor.[8] Worse, employers ran their equipment continuously and pushed individuals to ever-greater feats of speed at the assembly table or on the machine. By manipulating base rates and production bonuses and deploying the patriotic goad—"A single minute lost, another death at the front," as the newspapers put it—management pressed workers to sustain this rapid pace without flagging.

Labor had scant basis on which to resist the pressure, for the mobilization had scattered syndicalist militants and ruptured the prewar order on the factory floor. In its place stood a divided work force, split fairly evenly into three parts: (1) those entirely new to the industry—consisting of women (25 percent) and foreign workers (10 percent); (2) civilian men (30 percent); and (3) mobilized men (35 percent). The civilians were men ineligible for military duty—older, unfit (a low standard indeed, as time wore on), or noncitizen workers. The mobilized were essentially conscript labor, skilled metalworkers (for the most part) who had been called up in 1914 and then recalled from the front and stationed in the war factories, where they built weapons under the shadow of military discipline.[9] At the slightest murmur of protest, employers could return these men to the depots to be tried in the military courts for indiscipline.

The trade union (*syndicats*) could offer little support to this highly vulnerable work force. Notoriously weak before the war, they had all but collapsed with the mobilization, as members were called up, killed in the trenches, or dispersed across France in defense plants far from their homes and prewar work sites.[10] In addition, the politics of sacred union had divided the union leadership. The reformist majority followed CGT chief Léon Jouhaux into eager collaboration with the government.[11] But Alphonse Merrheim, head of France's main metalworking union, the Fédération des Métaux, had opposed the war from the outset. The Fédération's refusal of war and sacred union allowed it to hear a tale that the more patriotic CGT could credit only with difficulty: munitions workers faced exhausting labor, low wages, and a general reassertion of unchecked managerial authority on the factory floor. Ultimately, this meant that the metalworking union would form one nodal point around which a viable labor movement could reassemble. In the short term, however, a divided union leadership, in conjunction with the collapse in rank-and-file membership, freed employers to restructure work and wages in the metals factories without any significant organized shop-floor resistance.

Employers took ample advantage of these unprecedented circumstances. Armed with exceptional disciplinary powers (especially over mobilized workers) and freed of most legal constraints because of the state of seige, they imposed their new regime with impunity, redividing labor and pushing for higher output while slashing wages. For a variety of reasons, employers often piloted their restructuring projects on women. Recently arrived on the metalworking factory floor, women were unfamiliar with the work and prewar shop traditions.[12] This combined with their uniformly low rate of wages (half to two-thirds of the male rate, on average) to render them especially vulnerable to the speedups and rate-cutting that spread throughout the industry after 1914. To take but one example, when Wilcox-Regnault substituted women for men on grenade work, the firm started the women at half the male rate. There were no changes in the technology or organization of production; women simply came cheaper than men. Not content with their savings, management decided to push for greater output by cutting the already low base rate (8F per day) and offering a production bonus of 1F per hundred grenades. The women responded as the boss had hoped: as the rate fell from 8F to 7F to 5F 50 per day (and as the production bonus fell by half), the women went from 350 grenades per day (on a par with the men they had replaced) to 1,200 and, finally, to 1,700 grenades a day. When management cut the rate to 5F 25 per day, the women struck work. Wilcox fired them all and found replacements immediately, all of whom were started at 5F 25 per day.[13]

Even if the unions had had a more powerful presence at this time, there is little reason to suppose they would have extended wholehearted support to women as they struggled to establish decent wages and conditions for themselves. For one thing, syndicalists deeply resented women for executing task work so rapidly. Women's much-touted speed and dexterity, which so recommended them to their employers,[14] won them the title "toolsmashers" among their skilled male colleagues. "Because of the speed at which they work . . . the fitters claim that a woman's lathe needs five repairs to every one repair for a man's," it was reported. One woman roused particular hostility: "Having proved her great manual dexterity and her will to break solidarity [she] pursued her own earnings without regard to corporative concerns."[15]

In syndicalist eyes, women's "excessive" concern with wages bore witness to a greedy and grasping individualism, which could only work against collective efforts to limit exploitation. In time of war, their productivist zeal was doubly objectionable, and doubly threatening, for every increase in efficiency on the factory floor freed more men for duty in the trenches. "The intensification of women's work leads only to men being sent to butchery,"[16] Merrheim bitterly remarked. The tradition of resisting overwork by limiting output thus took on additional significance and mingled the politics of war with a nascent shop-floor division between women and their more experienced male colleagues.

If syndicalists feared women's aptitude for the swift, precise task work that multiplied in the redivided and reorganized labor process, they nonetheless saw, quite correctly, that metals employers intended to continue hiring women after the war. Faced with this prospect, union leaders began to argue that women, too, should be drawn into the syndicalist fold, if only as a means of defending the men.[17] They suggested that women might be educated out of their "anti-collectivism," that it was the product of women's narrow milieu—home, family, and women's trades—not an eternal feature of female nature.[18] In 1916, the Fédération des Métaux launched the campaign by organizing a new, desegregated union, the Syndicat des Ouvriers et Ouvrières en Métaux de la Seine, which successfully recruited among the increasingly restive "munitionettes." By July of 1917, women, who formed nearly 30 percent of all workers in the Parisian metals and munitions industries, also made up about 30 percent of the region's unionized metalworkers.[19] Yet even this, the most concerted effort to organize women metalworkers, was not without its ambiguities. Although Fédération leader Alphonse Merrheim frequently spoke at union meetings, the Fédération itself held aloof from the union. Not surprisingly, the organized craft elite was not yet prepared to embrace women as full colleagues in this formerly male occupation.

French women thus entered the metalworking industry just when the twin pressures of invasion and the reorganization of work had produced a precipitous decline in conditions and had chased an already weak trade union structure to the edges of the factory floor. Women were not wholly without resources in their struggle to carve out a more hospitable space for themselves, however. During the second year of the war, women developed some of these resources as they began to protest openly against the rate-cutting and overwork endemic in the munitions industry.

Reclaiming the Initiative: Women's Strikes in the War Factories, June 1916 to April 1917

Strikes in the war factory were generally brief, lasting two to four days on average, and were for the most part single-sex affairs. Mixed conflicts, though not unknown, were rare and, aside from the May–June movement, were usually dominated by men. This sexual segregation arose from the conjuncture of two phenomena: (1) the fact that these initial struggles rarely spread from the shop where they first broke out, and (2) shops were generally segregated by sex, because employers preferred to separate women and men by workshop wherever possible. Conflicts would remain spatially contained until May–June 1917, when women introduced the tactic of *débauchage:* leaving work with the express intent of calling out support from other shops, industries, and trades, by violence and intimidation, if necessary.

In time, women's strikes acquired a shape and structure that reflected syndicalism's weak links to these workers. The center of the conflict always lay with the strikers themselves, who met daily in local halls—*bourses du travail,*[20] syndicalist meeting halls, and even Boulogne's

"Mignon-Palace" movie house—to formulate their demands, elect delegates, and vote on other matters relating to the struggle. During the briefest stoppages—those lasting only a few hours—the women remained in the shop, arms folded and machines idle, while a small delegation approached the boss. Though workers sometimes stopped to write out formal petitions, the delegation was usually empowered to speak on behalf of the whole. In the case of longer conflicts, women were more likely to put their demands in writing. Longer strikes, however, carried the risk of dismissal. So long as the women remained inside, arms crossed before their machines, management could not lock them out. Nonetheless, several of these early strikes did last a week or more, and each time the women won at least partial victory.

If the strike was to be a long one, the women would elect a strike committee, which took responsibility for organizing the dispute. The committee wrote up the demands, collected strike funds,[21] approached management or the authorities at the Ministry of Armaments, and made contact with syndicalist leaders at the Fédération des Métaux. The Fédération lent moral, financial, and organizational support during the more prolonged struggles, using the labor press to publicize the disputes, stir public sympathy, and gather strike funds for these women, "most of [whom] have many children, their husbands at the front, imprisoned or shot."[22] In one case, Merrheim even accompanied the women as they pleaded their case to the director. But in no instance was the trade union present at the outset. Women initiated and directed their own actions and invited union participation only in some cases and only after the conflict had begun. This pattern would reemerge with a vengeance in the May–June movement.

Frequently, women's first concern was to gain direct access to higher management. The relations of production in wartime Paris may have been marked by the reassertion of untrammeled managerial power, but most workers, female and male, experienced this authority not from the employer but at the hands of his foremen and shop chiefs. The employer remained a distant figure, unstained by the small, daily torments that some of his junior officers wrought in their minor reigns of terror on the factory floor. Workers of both sexes were often convinced that successful resolution of their grievances lay in capturing the ear of this remote and perhaps sympathetic figure. Surely he would be moved to rectify matters, once he learned how bad things were "down there" in the shops.[23]

The notion that "the king is good" had its counterpart in the idea that foremen and shop chiefs were the main sources of evil on the factory floor. Women workers, whether on strike or not, often reviled these petty tyrants, and not without reason. In January 1917, the foreman at Malicet and Blin prevented women drillers from circulating a petition for higher wages, claiming that if the women needed a raise, he would give it to them himself. The shop chief then took the petition and promised to pass it along to the director. Eight days later, the woman who started the petition was fired on the pretext that her work was unsatisfactory. Her entire shift (321 women) stopped work and stormed into the director's office, where they learned he had never even seen their petition.[24]

The eleven-day strike at the Dion factory—the first significant conflict to rupture the labor peace that had hitherto reigned in the war factories—is in many ways a classic example of the women's strike before the May–June movement. In June 1916, the chief in the all-female gun shop announced that the work was to be "reorganized": henceforth, each woman would operate three machines, where formerly she had handled two. In addition, management proposed to slash the rate, so that even with a higher work load, workers feared they could not maintain their current earnings. When the 110 women stopped work and sought to lodge their protest with the director, the foreman blocked their efforts with words of contempt: "The Dion factory never yields to a strike as a matter of principle . . . it has never yielded to men and it is even less likely to yield to women."[25]

Even if the women had made direct contact with their employer, however, it is unlikely that he would have given their case a sympathetic hearing, for the Marquis de Dion ruled his works in the best tradition of France's "divine right employers";[26] any demand rising from the factory floor was tantamount to mutiny. Ultimately, the intransigent marquis would yield only to government arbitration, and the Ministry of Armaments dispatched one of its labor controllers to settle the dispute.[27] At that point, the strike committee ceased trying to capture the boss's ear and turned to the controller.

In its letters to the controller, the strike committee outlined a fairly typical set of demands: wage guarantees, protection of strikers against victimization, and more respect for women on the part of foremen. The committee also added two demands that testify to the harshness of life in the war factory: (1) women be given as much time off as possible during their husbands' leaves from the front, and (2) if a woman fell sick on her shift, day or night, she not be fired or simply dumped at the factory gates to make her own way home. The record is mute on the resolution of these last two issues, but it does show that the ministry's arbitration brought at least partial victory to the women at Dion. Although the work load was increased, workers were guaranteed their former level of earnings, and management agreed to rehire those it had fired for having participated in the strike.[28]

Women thus found an unexpected ally (of sorts) in the Ministry of

Armaments and in its chief, Albert Thomas. Thomas, a right-wing social-ist and partisan of the sacred union, had been appointed in May 1915 to coordinate arms production and oversee conditions in the war factories. Adopting what one scholar has termed a Jacobin ethos of centralist (and nationalist) war socialism,[29] Thomas favored improving wages and condi-tions in the war factories, so long as the improvements came through state intervention, not from labor's own initiatives. A resolute adherent to the politics of sacred union, he could brook no independent action from workers so sensitively placed vis-à-vis the national defense. Should muni-tions workers of either sex take matters into their own hands, the minis-ter was prepared to unleash the state's considerable repressive force against them.[30]

Nonetheless, Thomas did lend his patronage to women's demands for improvements in wages and conditions. His most important intervention came on January 16, 1917, when he published a detailed wage list, the "Thomas scale," which raised the minimum rates for workers of both sexes while narrowing the gap between women's and men's wages.[31] Thomas imposed his wage list by fiat, hoping the new minimum rates would bring an end to the growing agitation among (mostly women) metalworkers. In the very short run, he was successful, and the tempo of strikes relaxed in the weeks that followed.[32] But this success owed as much to coercion as it did to concession, for in the same decree that established the new wage scale, Thomas had effectively outlawed the strike, enjoining workers and employers to accept government arbitration in the event of a dispute. Although reformists (such as Jouhaux) wel-comed the added strength that arbitration might lend to labor's cause, men like Merrheim fulminated against the new strictures placed on a labor movement that was just beginning to show signs it still lived. Any lull in strikes probably owed as much to compulsory arbitration, that "redoubtable weapon against the working class,"[33] as it did to the improve-ment in wages. In any event, the relative calm did not last beyond April.

Throughout the spring of 1917, many of the largest employers in the region (Renault, Salmson, Vedovelli) stubbornly refused to implement the widely published Thomas scale. Wartime inflation had already cut real wages by an average of 23 percent. Taking 1914 as a baseline (100), prices stood at 139 in January 1917.[34] As the cost of living climbed ever more steeply that spring, reaching 183 in June, workers of both sexes grew restive and then indignant at employers' failure to grant the new minimum wage. Given the increasing severity of conditions that spring, it is perhaps surprising that the strikers held out as long as they did, waiting until the end of May before taking their multiple grievances to the streets. The following case study traces one part of this broad movement, beginning at the Salmson aircraft factory on the avenue des Moulineaux in Boulogne-Billancourt (an industrial suburb west of Paris), where 4,100 workers, 1,100 of them women, toiled each day, building weapons for the national defense.

The Struggle at Boulogne-Billancourt, May–June 1917

On Tuesday morning, May 29, 1917, thirty-eight women aviation workers at Salmson returned to work after the Pentecost weekend. Although Salmson had expected them back on Monday, the women had prolonged their holiday by the time-honored working-class practice of observing "Saint Monday," that is, extending the weekend by simply failing to show up Monday morning. Taking off for "Saint Monday" was a traditional and highly popular means of evading time discipline and seemed especially reasonable in this situation, for the other big munition employers in that dense industrial suburb had given their workers Pentecost Monday off. But their late return was just the excuse Salmson had been waiting for. No sooner had the prodigal thirty-eight punched the clock than five found themselves on the street again, walking papers in hand. The shop chief had apparently long since identified them as "troublemakers."

Irate at having been singled out and victimized in this fashion, the five women departed, only to return later that afternoon, leading a band of two hundred women, including strikers from the Iris Lamp Factory, women temporarily laid off from Citroën, and laundresses from the Boulogne district.[35] In the words of one police observer, the five had been "transformed into ringleaders." The group gathered beneath the factory windows and sought to bring out the 1,000-plus women who remained at their machines. When this effort failed, they moved on to the nearby Hanriot airplane works and successfully called out the 150 women working there. The cortege then proceeded to the local *bourse du travail,* where the Hanriot women signed a petition demanding a substantial wage increase, half-day Saturdays, and Sundays off altogether (the so-called English week, or *semaine anglaise*).[36] Upon returning to the factory, however, the Hanriot women disavowed their action, claiming that the strikers from Salmson had forced them to sign.

The following morning, the five returned to Salmson, this time at the head of a cortege numbering some one thousand women (strikers and unemployed) from different industries in the Paris region.[37] One of the five, Pauline Dantan, carried the red flag. Another waved a banner declaring "We want our soldiers." On the other side, it bore the legend "We want the English week," blending the politics of the war with those of the workplace. The leaders returned to their positions beneath the factory windows. This time their imprecations met with success, and about half of Salmson's women streamed out to join the throng.

Now 1,500 strong, the women turned their force back on the factory, pushing in the gates and surrounding the shops. Having staged a mass walkout, they decided to ensure that all work at Salmson ground to a complete halt. While the main part of the crowd guarded the machines, a delegation approached the bosses to demand that the five leaders be rehired immediately.[38] Management responded by firing the entire work force, male and female. Undaunted, the women regrouped and marched on several other local defense plants—Hanriot, Farman, Astra, and Kellner—where they garnered some additional force before proceeding to the biggest target, Renault's vast "factory agglomeration," where more than 10,000 workers (4,000 of them women) toiled each day.

Renault's empire was, in some sense, the war factory writ large. The means of repression and organization of production that other employers had adopted in piecemeal or sporadic fashion—huge gates that locked tightly behind the workers each morning; a doorkeeper who kept track of latecomers and enforced the fines for lateness; a liberal sprinkling of *mouchards* (police informants) among the workers;[39] vast mass production; and assembly halls, where thousands stood or sat alongside one other, enjoined to silence as they worked swiftly at a fragmented task whose pace was unrelenting—were all honed to perfection at Renault. For instance, not only was Renault's staff crawling with police informers, but the streets around the factory were patrolled by the local gendarmerie, assisted by sixty foot soldiers whom management had brought in expressly to maintain order in the works.[40]

The turbulent, overwhelmingly female crowd gathered outside the factory gates. Rumors flew as the strikers called out to their compatriots, urging them to flee the shops and join them in the streets: "At Argenteuil, the men and women stopped work yesterday, except for the Gnome plant [airplane engines]. But today, [the strikers] have brought the women out of that factory by violence . . . the soldiers at the front have begun to mutiny and are coming to Paris to support their wives' demands; in St. Étienne, two hundred women [have] been killed by colonial soldiers, the French soldiers having refused to shoot."[41] And, of course, Pauline Dantan continued to carry the red flag, symbol of syndicalist revolt since May Day 1890, when it had found a permanent place in the working-class iconography of protest.

Police, employers, the state, even organized (male) labor were all committed to the notion that this urgent rising was, like all instances of women's militancy, an unpolitical phenomenon. It sprang from that unstable encounter between the pragmatic and the demonic that constituted women's character, arising at the conjunction of their practical, appropriately feminine concern with wages and their notoriously "hotheaded," undisciplined natures. These men refused to consider the possibility that the strike wave might be grounded in a discernible and meaningful set of moral-political affiliations and attachments, a refusal that had significant consequences when it came to suppressing the movement, as I will discuss later. Police and employers thus duly recorded the language and events of May–June 1917, while giving scant recognition to its clearly political aspect. Nonetheless, this aspect stands revealed in gesture (waving the red flag) and in the language that women used to exhort their fellow workers to lay down their tools: "The soldiers will come back sooner, the war will end of its own accord on the day we cease building weapons and munitions of war."[42]

The women at Renault responded with alacrity: 2,000 of them poured onto the streets of Boulogne-Billancourt. These streets, ordinarily patrolled by Renault's private police force, became worker territory, although not without a struggle. At the nearby Place Nationale, the largely female crowd came up against a human barrier—municipal police, fortified by Renault's own agents and soldiers. Hoping to swarm back into the works and occupy them, the women surged against this barrier.[43] They smashed in the factory windows with their fists and then receded momentarily to await the lunch break of those women who had not yet come out. At one o'clock, the remaining 2,000 had to pass through this agitated crowd on its way to the local canteens and cafes. Few returned for the afternoon shift.[44]

By now, the cortege had turned away from the factories and was headed toward Reuilly, where the soldiers whose job was to maintain order in the factories and streets of Paris dwelt. Women marched on the barracks crying, "Down with the war! The draft dodgers to the front and our husbands will come back!" As they marched, they continued to raise the inevitable cheer, "Vive nos poilus!" The demonstrations at Reuilly reflected a particular kind of protest over the conduct of the war, a protest that distinguished the heroic *poilus*—those husbands and relatives lost to the trenches—from the cowardly *embusqués* (draft dodgers)—men who had taken a dishonorable refuge in the factories. Some of the hated draft dodgers were men with no experience of metalworking (or, indeed, of factory labor at all). Posing as skilled metalworkers to escape the front, they had taken advantage of the confusion and grim desperation surrounding the first recalls of mobilized labor. Not all mobilized men were such bold draft dodgers, though; most were skilled metalworkers, including the very foremen and shop chiefs on whom semiskilled and unskilled women workers depended for the repair and regulation of their machines.[45]

As the shell of sacred union cracked apart, tensions between women workers and their foremen, already high by the second year of war, began to emerge in the open. Police and trade unions alike report more than one instance where the mutual antagonism erupted into an outright exchange of blows. Sometimes, the story is one of women using their fists to defend themselves against the foreman's repeated brutality.[46] Other times, the women themselves took the offensive. Police spies recount the misadventures of "La Boxeuse," who first earned her title at Panhard. The firm eventually dismissed her, presumably for her violent disposition, but in the sellers' market that was wartime Paris, she soon turned up at another war factory, where she repeated her antics, this time in the company of two similarly inclined women. The three colluded in relentlessly harassing the foreman, but it was "La Boxeuse" who finally gave in to the urge to knock him flat.[47]

In attacking the cowardice of the "draft-dodging" craftsmen, women drew a parallel between the politics of war and the politics of the factory floor, constructing a political vision that implicitly linked their own subordinate shop-floor position to the vulnerable condition of their brothers and husbands who, under a spurious sacred union, were sacrificed on the battlefield ahead of the syndicalist fat cats. Police thus overheard one group of women sneer that "trade union leaders are disgusting people who earn fat wages while our husbands have gone off to be killed for a quarter franc per day."[48] Convinced that their factory had become a haven for draft dodgers, nearly a third of the work force (2,500 women and 150 men) at Delaunay-Belleville put down their tools and joined their compatriots in the streets.[49]

In both cases, women challenged the manifest inequality of sacrifice at the front and in the factory, which by 1917 seemed to increase daily under the straining facade of the sacred union. This challenge formed part of a larger politics of "equality in suffering," a popular egalitarianism that demanded the burdens of war be distributed more evenly across the population.[50] By 1916, women all across the city had begun to espouse this vision in protests over food shortages and the mobilization of younger military classes. A handwritten placard, posted in a working-class neighborhood on the northeastern edge of Paris on January 14, 1916, captured their vision:

> Equality—Equality—Equality
> For those who are suffering[51]

Women workers thus came to understand and express their experience of inequality on the factory floor less through a syndicalist vocabulary of labor-capital polarity than through the wartime language of equality in sacrifice. As the shape and progression of women's strikes reveals, shop-floor divisions intertwined with the politics of war at every level and every turn and would continue to do so until after the armistice. One cannot, therefore, speak with assurance of women's "narrow" concern with wages and conditions and men's "broader" grasp of war and politics, as though a clear line distinguished the two. Yet historians continue to do so, reflecting in their own work the very categories and convictions by which police, employers, and male trade unionists characterized as "unpolitical" the sudden menace of women metalworkers surging through the streets, waving the red flag, and demanding that cowardly draft dodgers be sent to replace their own soldier relatives ("*our* soldiers") at the front.

Women workers' egalitarian call to arms has thus passed unseen and unmarked. As a political vision, it recalls the Jacobin idea of a common "tax in blood," levied by the Republic in danger.[52] Yet the women's conception of equal sacrifice to the nation has fallen from view, lost in scholastic distinctions between the narrow archaism of a mere wage movement (all that the undeveloped female consciousness is capable of conceiving) and the more evolved "political strike" toward which mature (i.e., organized, native French, skilled male) elements in the working population strained after 1914. It is a dubious division, one that undoubtedly rests on the same series of gendered polarities—male-female, rational-irrational, political-sexual—by which police and employers strove to defuse the strike's clearly threatening aspect.[53] As the unwitting heirs to this analytic tradition, labor historians have also placed women metalworkers and their strike outside the realm of politics, in this case, beyond the bounds of a narrative concerned solely with a single political trajectory: the development of an explicitly pacifist and male-directed protest against the war.[54]

The women's assault on the barracks at Reuilly gave tangible form to official fears that behind the growing strike wave lurked the ever-present danger of defeatism. The many thousands on strike had already shattered both the image and the experience of public order under the sacred union, openly challenging the growing inequities that were sheltered under its patriotic aegis. Now the angry mob of women threatened to spread the pacifist "contagion" to the men in uniform. Official concern turned to genuine alarm when, in keeping with the city's long insurrectionary tradition, the soldiers at Reuilly began to fraternize with the women.[55] Together, workers and soldiers marched along the broad avenues, singing popular songs and bits of the Internationale in the bright spring air. One journal reported that a large group of young women workers crowded into a cafe on the rue de Paris at the eastern end of the city, filling all the tables, even those on the terrace, and consuming mountains of food, "slabs of charcuterie, fistfuls of cherries . . . [and] many glasses of white wine. At the end of the meal, the order was given and the women all rose and departed," leaving an unpaid bill behind them.[56]

The munition strikes of May–June were not the first protest to shake Paris during that weary third springtime of war. Throughout the previous months, increasingly widespread bread rioting bore witness to Parisian women's growing resentment over the spiraling cost of living. Then, in the second week of May, the *midinettes* (dressmakers) from Paris's most fashionable shops struck work and took to the posh boulevards around the Opera. Again, the triggering incident was redundancy. On May 11, two women from the Maison Jenny had been told they would no longer be needed for the Saturday afternoon shift. Enraged, they put down their needles and urged their compatriots to join them in demanding the English week (without any reduction in pay) and a 1F per day cost of living bonus.[57] Lifting the tricolor flag aloft, the long corteges (ultimately embracing some 10,000 women) sang as they marched:

> On s'en fout
> On aura la semaine anglaise
> On s'en fout
> On aura nos vingt sous[58]

The mid-May strikes of women-doing-women's-work struck a responsive, sympathetic chord in the hearts of men across the political spectrum. The rightist journal *L'Eclair* termed the corteges "very rue de la Paix," while socialist militants at *Humanité* were overcome by the women's "charm" and appealingly feminine strike tactics: "On the grand boulevards a long cortege advances. It's the Parisian dressmakers, blouses fragrant with lilacs and lily-of-the-valley. They run, they jump, they sing, they laugh, and yet it is neither the feast of St. Catherine nor the mid-Lent holiday."[59]

Women metalworkers would rouse no such sympathy from the press. Where the *midinettes* had pinned on lilies of the valley and waved the national colors, the "munitionettes" waved the red flag of working-class revolt and generally presented a less gentle and feminine spectacle. "If the young women must claim the English week, at least they could do so in a more discreet fashion, without parades, or calling in the streets," declared one journal.[60] Where the *midinettes* pranced and smiled, the *munionettes* presented a more menacing aspect, smashing windows, fighting with scabs in the factory yards, yelling threats, and even attacking the police as they strove to restore order.[61] Worst of all, these rough, burly creatures showed scant loyalty to the nation, halting their vital war work with selfish calls for more money, their husbands, and an end to the war. Unlike the *midinettes,* whose movement ended with a peaceful return to work, the *munionettes* would face arrest, interrogation, imprisonment, and widespread victimization of those identified as ringleaders.

Clearly, the May–June strikes were a multivalent movement, erupting as thousands of women were protesting over wages, food prices, and working conditions. The gay assault on local cafes and restaurants might have reflected munitions workers' anger at the pinch of high prices. Or the self-made free lunch, accompanied by singing and dancing, might have expressed a less sharply focused sense of carnival. Having temporarily seized control of the streets around their factories, women and men were, perhaps, enjoying their brief exercise of power in a society that offered little recognition to women or to its working class. As Simone Weil was to observe nineteen years later, during the sit-down strikes at Renault, the very act of seizing control had transformed the factory from a site of exploitation to a space in which women and men moved throughout the shops with dignity and ease: "Independent of all demands, this strike is itself a joy; pure and unadulterated.... What a joy to walk freely through these shops where one had been rivetted to one's machine, to gather in groups, to converse, to eat together. What a joy to hear music, singing and laughter, instead of the relentless clamor of machines, stark symbol of the harsh necessity before which one bends.... What a joy to pass before the foremen with one's head held high ... to see them compelled to be our familiars, to fold their hands, to renounce completely all giving of orders."[62] In 1917, the point was to flee the works altogether, to occupy (and thus reclaim) the streets *around* the factory, transforming those spaces from a locus of police/employer surveillance to a terrain on which workers could meet and move, converse and act, without fear of reprisal. Women's brief occupation at Salmson, as well as their effort to repeat the trick at Renault, was a means to that end, a tactic for reinforcing the numbers who held the streets.[63]

May–June 1917 thus combined a kind of festive quality with a widespread and mounting sense that things could no longer go on as they had in the war factories. For over two years, women had toiled eleven to twelve hours daily at jobs that were taxing and relentless in pace.[64] Conditions remained atrocious—at least one historian suggests they actually worsened sharply over the course of the war[65]—and women's wages, though well above the normal rates paid for "women's" work, lagged far behind the soaring cost of living (not to mention behind the wages of their male colleagues.)

But the sudden agitation that swept the defense plants of Paris that spring was not solely, or even predominantly, a protest over wages and hours. The war had endowed the already powerful employers with tremendous authority over labor. Moreover, the politics of the sacred union guaranteed that these men could exercise their enhanced powers unobstructed by any effective trade union organization. The incident that sparked the protest in Boulogne-Billancourt—the unjust dismissal of the five "troublemakers," arbitrarily singled out and victimized for an infraction (taking off holy Monday) that others had also committed—suggests that women's experience of unchecked managerial authority played an important role in triggering the strike.[66] Furthermore, whatever faith women had had in the employer as a higher court of appeal against the iniquities of foremen seems to have dissipated over the course of the May–June movement. The strikers thus took their cause not to the director but to the streets of the city itself.

If the women were all too aware of their many grievances, management and police officials alike seem to have been utterly obtuse, first stunned, then baffled by the sudden, sharp upheaval: "It is incomprehensible, when one considers what high wages we pay [them]."[67] These men agreed that women were "hotheaded" and "undisciplined," prone to such "effervescence." The question was why—how had these apolitical (if hotheaded) creatures ever been moved to such action in the first place? Police and employers both looked to the fearsome "outside agitator"—the only possible explanation available to them, given their account of women as unpolitical animals: "From the moment the women from Salmson first made contact with the *Bourse du Travail,* the movement seems to have changed in appearance. Elements who were foreign to metalworking, and to the factory world of Boulogne and Billancourt intervened with the clear intention of spreading and aggravating the conflict."[68] Elements "foreign to metalworking" rapidly became elements foreign to France, and a powerful conviction that the real danger lay in "Kraut insurgents" led employers to demand that police exercise "a discreet but active surveillance, as active as possible" *around* their factories to hold at bay a defeatist contagion, whose "foreign origins it is not difficult to discern."[69]

Restoring the Labor Peace: Repression and Concession in the War Factories

The Paris-wide strike wave, which peaked around the first of June, involved 42,336 munitions workers (nearly 75 percent of whom were women) in more than sixty separate strike actions.[70] Although these actions did not constitute a full-blown general strike—42,000 workers represented only one-sixth of the total number employed in metalworking at the time—they were by far the most extensive and threatening protests unleashed by the working class since the war had begun. Like previous strikes among women munitions workers, the May–June movement was sudden and sharp, with the metalworkers' union entering in only after the fact, hoping to direct and support the women's action and also to enroll them as dues-paying members. But the trade unions played only a minor role in May–June 1917. From the outset, women took the initiative, opening the protest, developing their own organization and forms of struggle, and formulating their demands with little or no intervention from the formal structures of the labor movement.

By the middle of the month, most of the strikers had returned to work. Poorly paid and lacking access to union strike funds, few women could afford to pass a full week without wages. As they slowly drifted back to the factories, the women took advantage of the fear their action had implanted in managerial hearts to demand increases in wages and leisure time.[71] At Renault, they circulated a petition demanding a raise of 10 centimes per hour plus a 1F 25 cost of living indemnity. They promised further direct action if their demands were not met. Unimpressed, management failed to respond, and on June 3, only half the nightshift turned up for work. Renault then conceded the raise, effective July 1, and suspended all night work for women.

The pattern was similar across the city. Over the period from May 29 to June 4, women deserted the factories in droves, joining heartily in street demonstrations and lively confrontations with the police. They then gradually returned to work, armed with specific demands that often took the form of written petitions. The petitions usually called for some kind of improvement in wages, along with Sundays off and half-day Saturdays. On the matter of wages, the strikes were a roaring success, and employers all over the city conceded the long overdue improvements. Where employers could not come to terms with the women, the Ministry of Armaments stepped in and arbitrated, usually granting the minimum levels that the Thomas scale had set the previous January. In the favorable conjuncture of the war, with tight labor markets and a sympathetic minister of armaments, women's self-organized direct actions proved highly effective, winning far more at the level of wages and conditions than the still-cautious trade unions were prepared to demand. However, most employers refused to grant the English week, and none would meet women's initial demand that the victimized "ringleaders" and "troublemakers" be rehired.

By mid-June, order had been restored through a combination of concession and repression, as police and employers collaborated in identifying and purging ringleaders of both sexes. Over the course of the movement, they arrested some 390 individuals (277 of them women), many of whom were subsequently prosecuted for having "obstructed the freedom of work." On the morning of May 31, following the assaults on Renault and Reuilly, the five ringleaders from Salmson were swept into the dragnet. After a day's interrogation, police let the women go.

From the reports, it is quite clear that police evaluated women and men according to very different standards. Male militants were investigated according to a political litmus test. Did they have any open ties to revolutionary or syndicalist groups? Had they been seen hanging about at such meetings, or were they simply lazy bums who would rather be paid by German agents to stir up trouble than do an honest days work building bombs? Women were evaluated by a set of "moral" criteria that were actually related to sexual conduct, behavior that was carefully spied on and recorded. Were they married? Did they have children? Were they known to have many lovers? Were they cheating on soldier husbands? If so, this was evidence of a character wholly given to debauchery, incapable of sustaining any kind of loyalty to home (*foyer*) or nation. Further, a woman's giving herself over to open "debauchery" outside the factory gates was seen as translating into laziness and a lack of seriousness on the job: "Marie Testud . . . is a worker who is neither serious nor hardworking. Since her husband's disappearance [missing in action] she has openly abandoned herself to debauchery and many workers and soldiers visit her. She is a hotheaded character . . . [but] . . . she has no known connections in revolutionary circles."[72]

In a neat piece of Aristotelian reasoning, police reports observed that since all husbands were absent, the rational part of the proletarian household was missing—the wifely "heart and soul" of the working-class *foyer* had lost her head.[73] As a result, the dark side of her "true," unchained nature was prone to erupt—"aggressive and insolent, hotheaded and fierce": "Marie Louise Pouchet [is] aggressive and, insolent, and proved one of the fiercest during the strike of the Boulogne factories. She has no known connections in syndicalist or revolutionary circles; we know only that she receives many men at her home, apparently workers, whom she takes as lovers."[74]

Sometimes police simply could not find an adequate explanation for individual action within the parameters of the strict political-male/moral-female polarity. For instance, Pauline Dantan was a good worker, to judge by her earnings. Moreover, "her private conduct is good . . . [and] she is far less hotheaded than the others."[75] But it was Dantan who had borne the red flag, leading that long and angry cortege through the streets of Boulogne-Billancourt. Another of the original ringleaders, Louise Piat, also enjoyed a good reputation; no amount of police snooping could uncover a single illicit affair. Her combative behavior therefore bewildered police investigators but did not lead them to question their basic assumption: among women, labor militancy (or any aggressively asserted political stance) sprang from an unchecked sexuality. Had they been interested in alternative accounts of women's activism, they might have listened to what Louise Piat herself had to say: "She complained bitterly that her two daughters, employed at the Iris Lamp Factory, had been laid off for the time being." In a time of acute hardship, Piat had become a sole breadwinner and could hardly absorb the cost of being fired herself. But Piat's interrogators, having duly noted her complaint, concluded that there was "no reason for her to have been mixed up in the movement of the past few days."[76]

This pattern repeated itself as police investigated the women they had rounded up outside Salmson's gates that morning. In their determined preoccupation with the women's household and living circumstances, they managed to uncover the one quality these five women had in common: all had been sole breadwinners at the time that Salmson had fired them.[77] This singular fact did not register, however, as police doggedly dug for the kinds of "moral" information that in their eyes constituted an intelligible explanation for the leaders' aggressive action.

The neat link between political activism and manhood placed women outside the magic circle of rational political action and thus compelled police to construct nonpolitical explanations for women's manifestly political acts. In the case of Pauline Dantan and Louise Piat, the police ultimately had to leave unanswered the question of why these women had protested so vehemently, so they could uphold the boundary separating women from politics, lest it dissolve altogether in the face of a more complex reality. This dualistic conception, besieged as it was on the female-moral (sexual) side, could also break down on the male-political side—and so it did, in the case of a small band of nine deaf-mutes whom the police also investigated that day. Eight of the nine were male, yet the police applied the moral/sexual criteria usually reserved for women. The inspection of their personal life was deemed relevant because several of the men in this group led a "particular life [according to] special morals," that is, they had been identified as homosexual lovers. For police and employers, concerned about rooting out the sources of this potent strike movement, the political was recast as personal if you were a gay man or a "hotheaded" (and therefore promiscuous) woman.[78]

The May–June movement was to represent the apogee of women's autonomous activism in the war factories. Women formed a strong and active contingent in the strikes that swept the aviation industry in September, during which they put forth their own demand for equal pay,

grounded in their temporary status as head of the family: "as our husbands are all at the front, we have a right to the same wages as the
men."[79] But the initiative was passing gradually from women to men, as
men began to throw off the cloak of silence imposed by the sacred union
(and the mobilization). By the spring of 1918, when a more unambiguously
antiwar movement swept the war factories, women made up only 30
percent of the audience at syndicalist meetings, compared with 40 percent the previous year.[80]

As the form and structure of the May–June movement suggests, however,
unionization rates offer a distorted vision of women's militancy, for women
looked to the unions only after they had initiated a protest, and then only
sporadically. More important, women remained a prominent and vocal
presence in the crowds that took to the streets during the vast insurrectionary strike against the war in May 1918. When the men at Thomson-
Houston were ready to abandon the struggle after only a few days, it was
their shop steward, Mme Martin, who urged them to stay out with the
sharp reproach, "Enough of this war! Peace now and we'll strike until the
end!" She then suggested that what was really needed was an assault on
the works to force out the treacherous "scabs," who were content to
remain "idle" (i.e., on the job) while their more courageous colleagues
risked harassment and arrest in the streets.[81] The strikers adopted this
plan with alacrity.[82]

As in 1917, police and employers watched the women activists carefully.
They recorded their words and actions in hopes of controlling them, but
their anxieties grew as women became more emboldened: "The women
workers gather in groups on the streets, and feel free to call loudly for
peace."[83] They still, however, shaped their observations within the contradictory framework of women as hotheaded yet apolitical wage-hounds,
moved to strike solely by the prospect of earning more money. They
consequently continued to ignore the politics of "equality in suffering,"[84]
the vision that linked women's shop-floor experience to their husbands'
sacrifice on the battlefield and demanded the burdens of war be spread
evenly across the population.

This vision still animated women strikers; indeed, its outlines had
grown sharper and the tone more acid as the war took its toll. When
Panhard fired a Mme. Garnier for her militant role in the strike, she
responded by listing her own sacrifices to the war effort. She had two
children and a wounded husband languishing in a German prisoner of
war camp; Panhard therefore did not have "the right . . . to put (her) out
on the street." Across the city at the Gnome et Rhone aircraft plant, a
Mme. Martelet remonstrated with equal vehemence: "As they've taken
my husband in order to defend the bosses' profits, it is just that they

should furnish me with the means to live and raise my children."[85] Despite these sharp challenges to a system that had failed to distribute the costs of war equally, police investigators persisted in offering the (by now) standard interpretation of women's activism: although women were often "the first to want to strike" (hotheaded), they seemed "content to return to their munitions work, where their wages remain high, permitting them to lead a relatively pleasant existence."[86]

The May–June movement of 1917 had provoked very different reactions among police and employers, state officials, and organized (male) labor. For the police and employers, the strikes disrupted the patriotic order of the sacred union and threatened the flow of arms to the front. Their main priority was to contain the women's "effervescence" and to get everyone back to work before the dangerous aura of rebellion, freedom, and irresponsibility spread to the male work force: "Whatever else they may be, these women's strikes are creating among the men themselves—mobilized or not—a spirit which the Government should look into."[87] The bureaucrats at the Ministry of Armaments were also concerned about ending the demonstrations and resuming production, but these were men of the left, broadly speaking (most were radicals and right-wing socialists). Though determined to end the upheaval and restore order in the streets and the factories, they had some sympathy for the material difficulties that workers faced. They consequently received the news of the strike with an air of understanding; after all, prices had soared since 1914, and many industrialists had failed to apply the ministry's recommended minimum wages. The state thus supported the women's wage demands, stepping in to arbitrate on their behalf where necessary.

CGT men were of (at least) two minds about the women's action. It was, after all, the first serious rupture in their increasingly punishing agreement to lay down the weapons of labor militancy and join in the patriotic social peace. For the reformist partisans of the sacred union, however, any break with the devils' deal of sacred union threatened to nullify that measure of respectability labor leaders had bought for themselves by their willingness to roll over and die for the Republic. For this reason, Léon Jouhaux repudiated the women's action: "As long as it was a matter of strikes among women garment workers, the CGT was able to distance itself from the movement. But now, with the efflorescence of women's strikes within the defense industries, the CGT must discipline all movements, so that we will not be held responsible for any disorder."[88] On the other hand, Alphonse Merrheim's more militant Fédération des Métaux threw its weight behind the movement; indeed, those who concurred in Merrheim's strong antiwar stance muttered that the women had not gone far enough in opposing the war. Police and employer reports, however, suggest that the majority of male workers saw the strike as a welcome departure from the self-imposed muzzle of sacred union and supported the strikes with whatever means available, direct and indirect.[89]

Yet the opinions of these diverse groups of men, who had such varied, even opposing stakes in the outcome of this struggle, were bound together by a common conviction that the women's strike movement issued from some place other than the political. Despite their very different reactions to the strike, none of them interpreted it as a political event. As a result, one finds an odd convergence in the language of police, employer, and organized labor on the subject of women's "unpolitical" nature.[90] On May 24, 1917, union spokesman L. Lefèvre urged his fellows to create a more welcoming atmosphere at syndicalist meetings by focusing on "the questions which interest them [women] . . . reducing the workday, raising wages and winning the English week . . . we must not mingle political issues in our speeches . . . when they are present."[91] A few weeks later, industrialist André Citroën remarked that "one of the most striking differences between male and female workers is the latter's dislike of all mutualist and trade unionist efforts."[92] And, in the face of overwhelming evidence to the contrary, police and employers grimly adhered to the theory that the women had not acted on their own initiative but had been "advised to go on strike by certain leaders." For police, employer, and male worker alike, women's "corporate" identity as women—an identity resting in part on the notion that women and politics were disjoint entities—overwhelmed any other identity, such as worker, that women might also carry. The police thus spoke of "women, temporarily transformed into wartime workers,"[93] and they viewed this human mass as malleable (indeed, volatile) material in the hands of unscrupulous men, whether anarchist, syndicalist, or paid agent of the Kaiser's war machine.

Notes

The research for this essay was completed thanks to a travel grant from the Society of Fellows at Columbia University. The Society of Fellows heard an early version of this paper, as did the Center for the Study of Social Transformations at the University of Michigan. I am grateful for the questions and comments I received at each session. Finally, I would like to thank Mary Dearborn, Pieter Judson, Karen Merrill, and Sabine MacCormack for their astute and helpful criticisms of this essay in its earlier incarnations.

1. This famous *union sacrée,* in which men from all shades on the political spectrum buried their differences in the effort to free France from the enemy,

emerged spontaneously at the funeral of Jean Jaurès, the beloved, undoctrinaire socialist from Carmaux (the Midi) who had been assassinated on the eve of the war (August 1) by Raoul Vilain, a rabidly nationalist, right-wing loon. At his funeral, veteran Communard Edouard Vaillant fell weeping into the arms of his long-standing political foe, the conservative Catholic politician Count Albert de Mun. At that moment, men of the left, center-right, and center forged a government of national defense and "sacred union." The union was destined to hold until the summer of 1917, when the pressure of strikes on the home front, mutinies along the Chemin des Dames, and rumors of corruption and spying conspired to bring Minister of Interior Louis Malvy (and, by association, his leftist colleagues) under suspicion. (Malvy was accused of not having prosecuted with sufficient vigor known leftists and pacifists, listed on France's famous Carnet B.) By the end of September, the cabinet of sacred union had been replaced with a hard-line nationalist government, which under Georges Clemenceau's leadership was determined to hang on until the American arrival by quelling rebellion at home and in the trenches.

2. Guy Pedroncini, *Les mutineries de 1917* (Paris, 1967). Throughout April and May, collective acts of disobedience shook the very armies that General Robert Nivelle had hurled over the top in a series of suicidal attacks against the German forces along the Chemin des Dames. Pedroncini counts 151 cases, of which 110 were collective demonstrations, and notes that over half the divisions in the entire French army were affected. Soldiers refused to proceed to the front, stacked their weapons, commandeered trains, and streamed toward Paris. The mutiny continued for several weeks and was ultimately ended through a combination of brutal repression (shootings and internment) and concessions. General Nivelle, who had sent so many thousands to a senseless death, was replaced by General Philippe Pétain, master of the defense and hero of Verdun. Pétain stopped throwing French at the German machine guns and instead settled the army down to wait for the Americans. He also improved rations and conditions, in particular, with more equally distributed rests and leaves.

3. "Action and syndicalist demands allowed [the activist] to break the power of conditioning and inertia . . . to rediscover that he was not isolated. . . . " Max Gallo, "Quelques aspects de la mentalité et du comportement ouvrier dans les usines de guerre," *Le mouvement social,* no. 58 (July–Sept. 1966): 30.

4. Ibid., p. 9. Women formed nearly 70 percent of all strikers between June 1916 and July 1917.

5. Among those who more or less ignore May–June are Gallo, "Quelques aspects," and R. Wohl, *French Communism in the Making, 1914-1924* (Stanford, Calif., 1966). James MacMillan and Jean-Louis Robert do not ignore the movement, but both contribute to the apolitical reading of these strikes. See J. L. Robert, "Les luttes ouvrières en France pendant la première guerre mondiale," *Cahiers de l'Institut Maurice Thorez* (1977): 23; and J. MacMillan, *Housewife or Harlot? The Place of Women in French Society, 1870-1940* (New York, 1981). MacMillan's infelicitously titled book uses the strike to illustrate the regrettable fact that once again women failed to achieve the kind of political maturity manifested in

permanent, mass adherence to the trade unions. At no point does MacMillan question the relevance of trade union organization in a circumstance where employers, ruling by "divine right," refused to receive shop stewards, would not accept the legitimacy of workers' demands, and even failed to apply the minimum wages prescribed in the Thomas scale (see the later discussion of Thomas). Alfred Rosmer, a leftist eyewitness to the wartime labor movement, gives the women's strikes a serious and detailed consideration that underscores their crucial role in reviving labor protest. See A. Rosmer, *Le mouvement ouvrier pendant la guerre,* 2 vols. (Paris, 1939).

6. A brief general strike (men and women) swept the aviation industry in September, and the 3,000 women at the Vincennes cartridge works staged a short, massive demonstration in November.

7. There is an abundant and ever-burgeoning literature on historians' implicit adoption of the gendered categories by which their subjects divided and understood their world. Joan Scott's important essay "Women in *The Making of the English Working Class,"* in her *Gender and the Politics of History* (New York, 1988), comes to mind, as does Mary Poovey's prismatic study of gender ideology in mid-Victorian Britain, *Uneven Developments* (Chicago, 1988). See also Jacquelyn Dowd Hall, "Disorderly Women: Gender and Labor Militancy in the Appalachian South," in *Unequal Sisters,* ed. E. DuBois and V. Ruiz (New York, 1990), pp. 298–321; Denise Riley, *Am I That Name?* (Minneapolis, 1988); Barbara Taylor, *Eve and the New Jerusalem* (New York, 1981); Jane Flax, "Postmodernism and Gender Relations in Feminist Theory," *Signs* 12 (1987): 621–43; Sandra Harding, "Feminism, Science, and the Anti-Enlightenment Critiques," in *Feminism/ Postmodernism,* ed. L. Nicholson (New York, 1990); and Sandra Harding, "The Instability of the Analytic Categories of Feminist Theory," *Signs* 11 (1986): 645–64.

8. Lack of protection, long hours, and the relentless pace of work combined to produce a high rate of rather spectacular accidents, particularly in factories where people worked with explosives. In the Paris region alone, explosions and fires in powder, fuse, and grenade works killed over one hundred munitions workers and wounded hundreds of others, some of whom merely had the bad luck of living nearby. Figures for deaths and mutilation are highly uncertain, since the press was heavily censored and appears to have consistently underreported the carnage. For instance, in 1916, the Billaud grenade factory exploded into flames. The press reported some 30-odd deaths, but workers from a nearby factory counted 125 corpses being carried from the smoldering sheds, "not to mention the women and children, horribly wounded and transported to the hospital, where they must surely have succumbed. . . . " Report from a meeting of the Syndicat des Ouvriers et Ouvrières en Métaux de la Seine, held at the Bourse du Travail on December 11, 1916, p. 4, Archives Nationales (hereafter AN) F7 13366.

9. All figures are for July 1917. See L. Downs, "Women in Industry, 1914–1939: The Employers' Perspective" (Ph.D. thesis, Columbia University, 1987), p. 549. Belgians were classed as noncitizen civilians rather than as foreigners, perhaps

because so many had worked in French industry before the war. See Gary Cross, *Immigrant Workers in Industrial France: The Making of a New Laboring Class* (Philadelphia, 1983). The civilian category included men from industries and occupations other than metalworking, while mobilized men were experienced metalworkers for the most part (a few militarily unfit characters also turned up in this category, as well as the infamous *embusqués,* draft dodgers who, though lacking any factory experience whatsoever, leapt at the chance to escape the trenches and were able to do so because of the initial confusion surrounding France's scramble to build weapons.) Although these men were recalled to work at their prewar occupations, they were rarely returned to the factories in which they had labored before the war. August 1914 thus constituted a sharp break in the continuity of personnel on the factory floor. The proportion of mobilized men, which peaked in 1915 at just under 50 percent of the work force, fell over the next two years as military inspectors toured the factories in search of soldiers. By July 1917, only 35 percent of Parisian munitions workers were mobilized men; by the armistice, just under 30 were mobilized. See Rosmer, *Mouvement ouvrier,* for an account of the execrable conditions under which these conscripts labored.

10. See Duncan Gallie, *Social Inequality and Class Radicalism in France and Britain* (Cambridge, 1983), chap. 12.

11. Confédération Générale du Travail (CGT) was the national umbrella organization for the syndicalist movement; all trades and locals were federated to this large, loose confederation. The collaboration with the government remained informal; unlike Britain, trade unions had no official voice in setting policy in the war factories. See Downs, "Women in Industry," chaps. 2, 3.

12. Few were strangers to paid employment, since the war industries drew women from traditionally "feminine" industries—trades like needleworking, textiles, and domestic service, which had contracted with the mobilization. Only a handful, however, had ever worked with metals before; a scant 5 percent of the prewar metalworking labor force was female.

13. In 1916, Paris still swarmed with unemployed women, thrown out of work by the mobilization and subsequent shift from the inessential luxury trades in which they were clustered before the war. See Downs, "Women in Industry," chap. 2. The information on Wilcox-Regnault is taken from a police spy report of a meeting of the Union des Ouvriers Mécaniciens de la Seine, held at the Bourse du Travail in Paris on November 27, 1916, pp. 6–7, AN F7 13366. Some 250 people attended, including a group of women.

14. One labor inspector reported the employers' glee at women's productivity: "It seems that women do not share most men's concern with limiting their efforts to that which will gain them the necessary salary; women produce to the extent their strength permits, in order to earn as much as possible." Neither the inspector nor the employers whose delight he recorded seems to have reflected on the fact that, with a base rate of half to two-thirds that paid to men, women were constrained to work as rapidly as possible to take home the necessary (subsistence) rate that men could earn at a more leisurely pace. Fonds Albert

Thomas (Minister of Armaments), Note 2, on the recruitment of female labor, p. 2, AN 94AP 348.

15. Pierre Hamp, *L'information ouvrière et sociale,* April 7, 1918, p. 1.

16. A. Merrheim, speaking at the Bourse du Travail in Nantes, June 4, 1916, AN F7 13361. If women often brought the ardor of the neophyte to their new occupations, it is also true that they, too, feared rate-cutting and overwork. Thebaud, Dubesset, and Vincent mention a strike, in mid-October 1916, by twenty-six women lathe workers, demanding that management fire two others who were outproducing the rest. Not surprisingly, management was not terribly receptive to the idea. F. Thebaud, C. Vincent, and M. Dubesset, "Quand les femmes entrent dans les usines" (Unpublished mémoire de maîtrise, Paris, 1974), p. 309.

17. "Given that to a certain extent women will be called upon to replace men in the factories after the war, it is their duty to join their respective trade unions . . . if they wish to realize their just demands." Jules Bled, secretary of the Union des Syndicats de la Seine, a wartime labor coalition, speaking to a gathering of some 200 workers (mostly women) at the Maison Commune, Levallois-Perret, August 14, 1916, AN F7 13366. Max Gallo offers the following brusque but accurate summation of the syndicalist position: "The unionized woman worker would defend herself better, work less and earn more, so that she would not be as serious a competitor for the male worker." Gallo, "Quelques aspects," p. 17.

18. See, for instance, the labor pamphlet *Le travail de la femme pendant la guerre,* published by the Comité Intersyndicale d'Action contre l'Exploitation de la Femme (Paris, 1917). The Comité was formed in July 1915 and included representatives from the clothing, printing, and metals industries.

19. Thebaud, Vincent, and Dubesset, "Quand les femmes," p. 285. The Syndicat was formed in April 1916 from the amalgamation of several Fédération locals. By mid-summer, following a series of successful strikes in the war factories, some 800 women had enrolled in the new trade union. May–June 1917 delivered an additional 5,000 women (and 450 men) to the young union. By July 1917, the organization boasted 10,090 members, 70 percent of whom were women. This was a considerable advance over the scant 200 (out of 15,000 members) organized in the Fédération in 1913. All 200 worked in the state artillery at Vincennes and were organized separately from the men. See R. Picard, *Le mouvement syndicale durant la guerre* (Paris, 1927).

20. The *bourse du travail,* a distinctively French institution, was a local labor exchange controlled by the trade unions, which also functioned as a meeting hall for organizations of every trade in the town, neighborhood, or region. The *bourse* often housed reading rooms and libraries, combining elements of worker self-education with a practical purpose (job postings). Most important, the *bourses,* like the trade union's meeting halls, were autonomous, worker-controlled spaces where strikers could meet and formulate demands. See F. Pelloutier, *Histoire des bourses du travail: Origines, institution, avenir* (Paris, 1971); and Jacques Julliard, *Fernand Pelloutier et les origines du syndicalisme d'action directe* (Paris, 1971).

21. Such funds were rare; women generally struck work without any savings or support. Records emphasize women's concern for democratic procedure, in particular, the insistence on using secret ballots when voting on whether to strike. Records also show that women strikers, like their male counterparts, preferred to act in unanimity.

22. The passage continues: "Worker solidarity must incline in their favor. . . . " From an article soliciting contributions for the women strikers at Dion, in *Humanité,* July 4, 1916.

23. The notion that remote bosses formed a court of higher justice was by no means confined to women workers. In August 1917, workers at Nieuport, Caudron, and Voisin decided to protest the removal of two wounded war veterans, who had been returned to the front for having led a wage protest. The 550 men and 150 women decided to take up a collection for these men and then send a petition, not only to the director but also to his mother. Report from August 22, 1917, AN F7 13367.

24. After a nine-day strike, the women won the 0F 75 minimum wage for which the drillers had initially petitioned. *L'Union des Métaux,* Dec. 1916–Feb. 1917, p. 6.

25. Cited in Thebaud, Vincent, and Dubesset, "Quand les femmes," p. 333.

26. The phrase is Senator Paul Faure's, used to criticize Eugene Schneider's domination of factory and town in Le Creusot. Cited in Donald Reid, "Industrial Paternalism: Discourse and Practice in Nineteenth-Century French Mining and Metallurgy," *Comparative Studies in Society and History* 27 (1985): 581.

27. The labor controllers were military officials attached to the Ministry of Armaments who monitored working conditions and labor deployment in the war factories. The man in question here was a captain in the army and regional controller for the Seine Department.

28. Thebaud, Vincent, and Dubesset, "Quand les femmes," p. 333.

29. Gallo, "Quelques aspects."

30. Thomas sharply criticized women for their frequent resort to the strike weapon, and on January 17, 1917, successfully shamed women at the Schneider works (Harfleur) into abandoning their struggle altogether: "Suddenly and without warning you stopped work yesterday. Have you considered the gravity of your error? Have you thought of the enemy, who never ceases his labors, of your brothers, you husbands who impatiently await the means of defense which you provide them? . . . the government does not wish to brutally employ its legal sanctions; it appeals to your patriotism, to your love for the soldiers at the front, to your reason. . . . Be here on the job tomorrow, each and every one of you." *La bataille* (the official organ of the CGT), January 25, 1917.

31. See Downs, "Women in Industry," chap. 2. In 1916, women had a base pay of between 0F 35 and 0F 50 per hour, which translated into an average piecework earnings rate of 0F 57 per hour. Men earned between 0F 50 and 1F 20, depending on the skill required for the job. The Thomas scale did not seek to eliminate the male-female wage gap, but in lifting the rates of the least well-paid, it had the effect of narrowing that gap from 31 percent to 18 percent. Unskilled

women were to receive a flat time rate of 0F 65, while the base rate for semiskilled women was 0F 75 to 0F 90. The ceiling for women was 1F 10 per hour, paid to polishers, who were the most highly skilled women in the war factories. Unskilled men were offered a time rate of 0F 80, while semiskilled men's base was 1F to 1F 30 per hour. See Rosmer, *Mouvement ouvrier,* vol. 1, for wage levels before the Thomas scale; and *Tarifs et règlementation des salaires applicables pour les fabrications de guerre et de la région parisienne,* January 16, 1917, pp. 19–20. See Madeleine Guilbert, *Revue française du travail* (Paris, Nov. 1946), p. 663, for information on the male-female wage gap over time.

32. The tempo of strikes relaxed but did not abate altogether; for instance, on March 3, 1917, 2,000 women at the Vincennes cartridge plant struck work in search of higher wages.

33. From the Fédération des Métaux's blanket condemnation of the decree, voted on February 21, 1917. Cited in Thebaud, Vincent, and Dubesset, "Quand les femmes," p. 294. That women continued to strike under such conditions indicates the increasing severity of life during that third year of war.

34. In addition, the array of goods available was sharply reduced by wartime rationing. Flour, bread, potatoes, and other staples were especially scarce, and women who worked long shifts in the war factories were doubly hit because they had no time to stand in the long lines. Rising food costs were especially serious at a time when, on average, workers spent 60–70 percent of their income on food alone. Michelle Perrot, "On the Formation of the French Working Class," in *Working-Class Formation: Nineteenth-Century Patterns in Western Europe and the United States,* ed. Ira Katznelson and Aristide Zolberg (Princeton, N.J., 1986), p. 104.

35. Iris was located in Issy-les-Moulineaux, one of the depressing little industrial towns on the city's southwestern perimeter. A traditionally heavy employer of women, Iris was not under a munitions contract and therefore was unable to guarantee steady employment throughout the war (they had no assured supply of raw materials). Citroën was under contract but, like many other defense factories, had to lay off part of its work force temporarily because of recurrent shortages of steel and coal. The presence of laundresses is an interesting harbinger of the shape this conflict would assume, that is, a protest that not only transcended the four walls of any single factory but also brought out workers (mostly women) from all trades in a kind of festive upsurge that Michelle Perrot characterizes as a typical form of protest in France. See Michelle Perrot, *Les ouvriers en grève: France, 1871–1890,* 2 vols. (Paris, 1974).

36. Report on the May–June Movement in Boulogne-Billancourt, June 1, 1917, AN F7 13366. At a time when the unrealized Thomas scale set women's hourly minimum wage (on piecework) at 0F 85, the strikers demanded 1F per hour. The call for the English week had been a long-standing demand among French workers of both sexes. The relentless pressure of war production, in conjunction with the mounting problems women faced in acquiring food (because of shortages, rationing, and long bread lines) and finding time for domestic chores, led workers to redouble their effort to reduce the work week.

37. According to Gilbert Hatry, the crowd that gathered that morning included women from Thomson-Houston (electrical equipment) and Hanriot; apparently the latter had changed their minds yet once again. Hatry, *Renault: Usine de guerre* (Paris, 1972), p. 120.

38. This was the last time during the war (the last time I found, at any rate) that women approached the higher-ups in hopes of redressing injustices and ill-treatment suffered at the hands of foremen and shop chiefs.

39. According to one estimate, as many as one out of every 1,600 munitions workers in the Paris region was a paid police spy. See Thebaud, Vincent, and Dubesset, "Quand les femmes."

40. The use of soldiers to keep order at home and workers at the job grew more common after the women's strikes of May 1917. Indeed, when Georges Clemenceau took over the premiership in September, he held two battalions in reserve solely to keep order among the workers of Paris. See P. Bernard, *Le fin d'un monde* (Paris, 1975).

41. Argenteuil is another industrial suburb, due north of Boulogne, and was also dominated by metals, aviation, and other war industries. All the rumors are taken from police dossiers collected in AN F7 13366; reports on the May–June strikes dated June 1, June 3, and June 4 (quotation from the June 4 report, p. 4). The rumors of mutiny at the front are a bizarre blend of truth and wishful thinking (see note 2, above). The soldiers' motives were many, but the desire to support the women's strike demands was probably not at the top of the list. Given the authorities' careful suppression of all news of the mutinies, it is interesting that the women knew of the movement (even though they imputed their own motivations to it and circulated particular and unsubstantiated embellishments, for example, that it was the Annamite troops who had refused to march. It is also interesting that colonial troops figure so prominently in these stories.) Another curious point was Philippe Bernard's report that a variant of the rumor that women were being shot by colonial troops circulated among the soldiers during the May and June mutinies. In the soldiers' tale, the women being massacred were on the outskirts of Paris rather than Saint-Étienne, and the colonials in question were said to be Indo-Chinese. Bernard, *Le fin d'un monde.*

42. Police report, June 4, 1917, p. 4, AN F7 13366.

43. According to Michelle Perrot, women were far more likely to support a strike by occupying the works than were men, who seem not to have gotten the idea until 1936. See Perrot, *Ouvriers en grève.*

44. The crowd actively blocked women's reentry into Renault, but it did allow the mobilized men to return to work undisturbed.

45. Because women were paid by the piece, their wages fell off sharply each time their machines were stopped for retooling or repair.

46. At Salmson, for instance, one foreman "brutalized" a woman he had long tormented, while the other foremen and shop chiefs stood by. Only when the woman responded, blow for blow, did the other foremen intervene. See *Le populaire,* May 3, 1918.

47. When management tried to dismiss this lively trio, the other workers

resisted, staging a brief solidarity strike on their behalf. The firm refused to rehire "La Boxeuse" but did take back her two more decorous companions. AN F7 13366.

48. The soldier's daily allowance was 25 centimes. This is the only instance I found of women believing the 1917 strike wave to be syndicalist in origin. Most correctly took it as their own movement.

49. In 1917, there were 2,800 women employed at Delaunay-Belleville (around 30 percent of the entire work force). Conditions were sufficiently poor that the firm was referred to in local newspapers as "a women's penitentiary." Jean-Louis Brunet, *St-Denis, la ville rouge* (Paris, 1980), p. 176. Brunet also notes that strikers at Delaunay-Belleville took an especially hard line on the question of who should be sent to the front, crying, "The bosses to the front, our soldiers will return." Ibid., p. 177.

50. See John Horne, "L'impôt du sang: Republican rhetoric and industrial warfare in France, 1914-18," *Social History* 14 (1989): 201-23.

51. The poster continues: "over the seventeen months of this horrible war, not all women have suffered. She whose husband is stationed in the factory has happiness and money; she whose breadwinner has spent those seventeen months in the army has known nothing but misery and privation. . . . Wives, mothers, sisters, fiancées, he who has spent seventeen months in the factory should replace him who has languished in the trenches. For Equality and Justice. Demand from your Deputies relief for the mobilized men. Equality for all." According to police, the placard was written "in a woman's hand" and posted on the door of number 6 Place Martin Nadaud (in the twentieth arrondissement). Archives of the Prefecture of Police, Ba 1545; cited in Thebaud, Vincent, and Dubesset, "Quand les femmes," p. 254.

52. John Horne has traced this notion in socialist and left-republican rhetoric after 1914. See Horne, "L'impôt du sang." Not surprisingly, the women's conception of egalitarian sacrifice to the nation differed from men's, rooted as it was in (1) the divergent political experience of this disenfranchised subset of the citizenry, and (2) the different meanings that sacrifice held for factory workers pure and simple versus those directly confronted with a stint in the trenches.

53. Perhaps they hoped that pronouncing it "unpolitical" might contain the movement's force, extent, and significance. As we shall see, however, these men deployed a further set of oppositions—appropriately feminine workers (dressmakers) versus dangerously masculinized metalworkers, individualistic, selfish women workers versus properly social, collectivist male workers—which dwelt in uneasy cohabitation with the first series, threatening to disrupt the vision of unpolitical yet activist women constructed through the first set of oppositions.

54. It would be interesting to trace how and why historians have ended by appropriating the categories by which male participants understood the women's action. Unfortunately, such an ambitious archeology lies well beyond the scope of this essay.

55. In 1789, 1830, 1848, and 1871, revolutionary risings got going in earnest when guards sent to control crowds of women joined with them in protest instead.

56. The article continues: "The police watched, as powerless as the rest, and let the strikers move on so that they might quench their thirst in similar fashion a bit further down the road. Cafe owners, consider yourselves warned!" *La Seine Départmentale,* June 10, 1917.

57. The movement gathered force more gradually than in metalworking; by May 14, only 200 women were out. A few days later, however, the strike had spread to some thirty fashion houses. With 10,000 women out, the entire industry was paralyzed. Workers from other "women's" trades (hats, corsets, shirts, and furs) joined in, and Minister of Interior Louis Malvy (a leftist) finally stepped in to arbitrate. On May 22, the bosses met the women's conditions (including a "no victimization" clause), and work resumed on May 23.

58. Y. Delatour, "Le travail des femmes, 1914-1918," *Francia* 2 (1974): 489.

59. *L'Eclair,* May 20, 1917; *Humanité,* May 14, 1917.

60. *Journal des débats,* June 2, 1917. This was a journal of the center/right-center.

61. At Citroën, where 680 women and 70 men joined the strike, women turned "ferociously" on the gendarmerie, seeking to tear off their uniforms. Eyewitness report of "M. R.," cited in Thebaud, Vincent, and Dubesset, "Quand les femmes," p. 331.

62. Simone Weil, "La vie et la grève des ouvrières métallos," in *La condition ouvrière* (Paris, 1951), pp. 230-31. Weil had worked at Renault (and other Parisian metal factories) for some eighteen months before the sit-down strikes erupted. Her factory journal records the torment of a woman who was especially ungifted at rapid physical labor and for whom the complete denial of initiative to unskilled (women) workers was, perhaps, the hardest aspect of a harsh factory regime: "Every gesture is simply the execution of an order. . . . One is merely a thing attached to the will of another. . . . How one would love to leave one's soul in the carton by the door, and reclaim it upon leaving!" Ibid., pp. 227-28.

63. Michelle Perrot put it beautifully in her essay on French working-class formation: "The factory colonized the neighborhood, or rather created it altogether. The French working-class suburb was not a void, but a place of fairly dense sociability. . . . As an instrument for exercising pressure, the strike was then also, to a greater extent than in our own time of industrial and union concentration, a means of expression in which the working class and the people within which it encased, met again in the street they have reclaimed." Perrot, "On the Formation of the French Working Class," pp. 102, 106.

64. A year earlier, one *gendarme,* reporting on "morale" in the war factories, observed sagely (and with some satisfaction) that "the workers put in an average of 11 hours per day. Under these conditions, they don't even dream of attending syndicalist meetings." "Dans les usines de guerre," May 25, 1916, AN F7 13366.

65. Gallie, *Social Inequality,* chap. 12.

66. As William Reddy has written of the May Day demonstrations among textile workers in the Nord, "The 1890 strike . . . turned into a dramatic denial of deference . . . [it] was not a bargaining maneuver, it was a gesture in an ongoing struggle over the legitimacy of certain ideas about authority and submission."

Reddy, *The Rise of Market Culture: The Textile Trade and French Society, 1750-1900* (Cambridge, 1984), pp. 308-9.

67. High management official at Renault, "Grèves à Boulogne," *Le petit journal,* May 31, 1917.

68. Report on the May–June strikes in Metalworking, dated June 4, 1917, p. 3, AN F7 13366.

69. A. Dutreux, Administrateur-Delegue, S.E.V. (Société Anonyme Pour l'Equipment Electrique des Véhicules), letter to the Police Commissaire, Issy-les Moulineaux, dated May 31, 1917, found in the GIM Archive, AN 39 AS 914.

70. Delatour, "Travail des femmes," p. 488.

71. Leisure time means time off from work, though it is doubtful that a woman's Sunday off was truly leisured, since most of them seem to have used the time to do housework and laundry.

72. Report from June 4, 1917, p. 12, AN F7 13366.

73. See Aristotle's *Politics,* Book I, for an early statement of the pervasive argument that social hierarchy and levels of rationality dovetail in both the household and the polity, providing the means of establishing relationships of ruling and being ruled. In the household, these relationships—between husband and wife, master and slave—are depicted as natural and fixed. In the Middle Ages, the Catholic church drew Aristotelian conceptions of social order into a larger portrait of the seamless, ordered chain linking heaven and earth, highest and lowest in an organic, sensible hierarchy. These Catholic notions of social-moral order turn up repeatedly in the ideologically secular Third Republic.

74. Report from June 4, 1917, p. 11, AN F7 13366.

75. Ibid., p. 12.

76. Ibid., p. 14. High earnings meant the woman was a swift and steady worker, because women were paid on a piecework basis or, more commonly, a basic (time) rate with a substantial piece-based production bonus on top.

77. Police also investigated three other ringleaders that day, women from other factories who had joined the original five at the head of the corteges in Boulogne-Billancourt. All eight were struggling to support themselves and their relatives and children on a rapidly diminishing real wage. Most of the women were in their thirties or early forties, widowed, or married to soldiers who were variously listed as missing in action, prisoners of war, and so forth. Only two were in their twenties; one was married to a man who was missing, the other lived with her mother and was the only single woman in the group. The demographics of these militants—older workers supporting dependents—are quite unlike those of the typically young (sometimes adolescent), unattached male militants who led the strikes that shook England and Germany in those last two years of war.

78. Report from June 4, 1917, p. 8, AN F7 13366. The identification of obstreperous women as promiscuous recalls some of the statements by the police who patrolled the *maisons de tolérance* (state-controlled bordellos). See Jill Harsin, *Policing Prostitution in Nineteenth-Century Paris* (Princeton, N.J., 1985). See also Jacquelyn Daud Hall, "Private Eyes, Public Women: Images of Class and

Sex in the Urban South, Atlanta, Georgia, 1913-1915, in *Work Engendered,* ed. Ava Baron (Ithaca, N.Y., 1991), pp. 243-72.

79. Report from September 22, 1917, AN F7 13366. During the war, most peasant and working-class wives took on the role of "head of the family," de facto and de jure. As the "Intersyndical Committee against Women's Exploitation" argued, "Carrying the same burdens which the man previously carried, she must have a wage equal to his." Comité Intersyndicale d'Action contre l'Exploitation de la Femme, *Travail de la femme,* p. 8.

80. By this time, mobilized men were coming out in droves. The army was ruthlessly combing out the mobilized workers, desperately seeking more machine-gun fodder to meet the final great German offensive that spring. Mobilized men no longer had much to lose by striking, since they were likely to end up at the front no matter what they did.

81. Perrot notes that in the early twentieth century, "the strike was such a positive act, from the vantage point of working-class morality, that those who stayed out of it were called, by a significant twist of language, 'idle.' " Perrot, "On the Formation," p. 106.

82. Report of a strike meeting of 350 workers from Thomson-Houston, May 16, 1918, AN F7 13367. Mme. Martin was one of nine women shop stewards on whom I found records in this period (1917-18). Before, during, and after the war, Thomson-Houston was an especially heavy employer of women, which perhaps explains why it had female shop stewards.

83. Ibid.

84. See the earlier discussion of the politics of equality in suffering.

85. Mme. Garnier based her right to work on a notional contract; the wartime state and defense profiteers clearly owed the Garniers for their visible contributions and sacrifices to the war effort. From police reports on militants at Panhard and Gnome et Rhone, May 13, 1918, AN F7 13367.

86. Report from the strike at Delaunay-Belleville, (Saint-Denis), May 26, 1918, p. 2, AN F7 13367. The police spy went on to report that after returning to work, one woman confided to her friend: "Today I made ninety pieces. I must make up the time lost last week." The spy further commented that such sentiments were common among the 2,800 women who had struck Delaunay-Belleville: "They work as hard as they possibly can, in hopes that their fortnightly earnings won't have fallen off too much as a result of the eight days' work stoppage." (Women made up nearly a third of the Delaunay-Belleville work force, which totaled 9,600 in 1918.)

87. Report on the strike movement, June 1, 1917, p. 1, AN F7 13366.

88. Léon Jouhaux, speech before the Comité Confédéral, June 2, 1917, AN F7 13617.

89. Many joined the women in the streets; nearly 12,000 of the 42,000 on strike were men, after all. Others (presumably mobilized men) stayed in the factories but crossed their arms and refused to work. Still others shouted encouragement to the women or suggested shops that were ripe for *débauchage.* See reports on the May-June strikes, 1917, AN F7 13366.

90. It would be interesting to know whether women concurred in this interpretation of their movement. It would not be terribly surprising if they did, yet there is no evidence in the police and employer reports to support even the shakiest conjectures regarding their self-perceptions.

91. L. Lefèvre, speech before the Comité Générale de l'Union, May 24, 1917, AN F7 13667. Lefèvre was a member of the metalworkers' Federation Executive Committee.

92. Thebaud, Vincent, and Dubesset, "Quand les femmes," p. 285.

93. Report from June 1, 1917, p. 1, AN F7 13366.

LEORA AUSLANDER

Perceptions of Beauty and the Problem of Consciousness: Parisian Furniture Makers

Venturing onto the uncertain terrain of "the new labor history," this essay tackles some of the field's oldest questions: What did workers want? How did they come to those desires? Where, when, and how did they say what they desired? And, what do the form and content of the expression of those desires imply about class consciousness? A pair of assumptions has undergirded much earlier work on these problems: ideally workers came to a (unified) recognition of their interests through a process of class formation grounded in a shared relation to the means of production; and organized labor (sometimes joined by left political parties) was the most authentic expression of workers' consciousness. This essay questions those assumptions, suggesting instead that workers spoke in many, often incompatible but nonetheless equally "authentic" voices. An analysis of what nineteenth-century French furniture makers said about their hopes and expectations of their work, where they said it, and why they chose those contexts will demonstrate the possibilities of this approach. Even as this essay challenges some of the assumptions of labor history, its origins are canonical within the discipline, for they lie in my own experience on the shop floor.

When I was working as a cabinetmaker in and around Boston in the early 1980s, I assumed that my coworkers would be contesting our hours, wages, and working conditions through union organizing.[1] Although they would have appreciated improved material circumstances, they were far more distraught about the aesthetic failure of their labor. They found the objects we made ugly, devoid of creativity, artistry, and imagination, and useless, contributing nothing they valued to the world. Their response to this form of the alienation of their labor was not to organize but to stay in the factory after hours, using the machines and stealing wood to make things they considered beautiful and useful. Two colleagues built guitars—one acoustic and the other electric—a third crafted a maple sled with carved bubinga (an African wood) runners, and a fourth redid the interior of his '72 Ford in mahogany veneer.[2] These artisans were in full possession of their craft, but they were not being paid for its expert deployment on the job. Furthermore, although deeply troubled by this loss, they did not perceive union organizing as a solution.

Like many other fledgling artisans of intellectual origins, I ended up studying the lives of cabinetmakers and union organizers rather than working as one myself. As I pursued my reading in histories of industrialization, labor, and the working class in the nineteenth century, I became confused. In my experience, woodworkers in late twentieth-century Boston were most outraged by the lack of beauty or utility of the objects they made at work, so why did little hint of any such preoccupation appear in the histories of European workers?[3] Were late nineteenth-century French artisans really only concerned with hours, wages, control of the production process, and working conditions, as the literature implies, or had labor historians, trapped by their own vision of what workers "should" have wanted, neglected to look at the full range of artisanal desires?[4]

Labor historians have been partially blinded. They, too readily perhaps, have accepted that by the nineteenth century, workers were selling their labor rather than the product of their labor, and they have therefore eliminated those alienated commodities from the story. Furniture makers directly expressed their desire to make beautiful objects at work in the context of the world's fairs of the 1860s and 1870s. Workers were, however, silent on the same matter in the context of organized labor. Each of these contexts had its historical logic; deciphering that logic leads to a deeper understanding of the social meaning of labor and of workers' experience. To explain why furniture makers said what they did from the 1860s to 1890, we therefore need to know something of the story of their lives at labor in that period.

Making Beauty: Skill, Knowledge, and Craft Sense

Labor history, because of the primacy granted to a particular definition of worker consciousness and militancy, has analyzed skill and creativity within the context of collective action, attempting to discover whether
workers had the greatest tendency to organize when they were skilled,
unskilled, or in the process of being deskilled.[5] Or it has revealed how
unions used skill as an artificial boundary-making device to exclude
women, temporary laborers, foreigners, and others, from highly waged
labor.[6] There is, however, another set of questions to be asked about skill.
What must artisans have possessed, in their hands and minds, to make
objects they found beautiful? Had they really been thoroughly deprived
of their craft by the second half of the nineteenth century? If artisans still
knew how to make objects they found beautiful and useful but were not
being allowed to do so on the job, why were their employers depriving
them of this possibility?

Like their twentieth-century descendants, nineteenth-century artisans
found that the full practice of the trade required inventiveness; it was not
enough to make exact copies of beautiful objects. The bitterness of Henri
Fourdinois, a furniture manufacturer, concerning consumers' unwillingness
to buy furniture of novel design reveals the intensity of this issue for
artisans: "If one of us . . . wants to offer himself the luxury of demonstrating that he too is capable of making a beautiful piece of his own design,
without worrying about known styles, like in the time of the Renaissance
or under Louis XIV or Louis XVI, he will pay a high price for this excess
of pride."[7]

To be able to innovate, furniture makers needed skill, knowledge, and
craft sense. Possessing basic skill—the ability to plane a board so the two
faces were true, to saw in a straight line, or to cut the male and female
parts of joints so that they would perfectly meet—brought the capacity to
copy an object in wood.[8] The second level of skill entailed abstract
visualization. Having learned how to project three-dimensional objects
from a two-dimensional drawing, the artisan could construct pieces of
great complexity.

More complicated and enabling than the ability to read a drawing was
the ability to make one. Drawing pushed the abstracting capacity from
the relatively passive act of "reading a blueprint" and translating that act
of absorption into a chair to the more active accomplishment of "drawing
a blueprint" and then making the chair. The first and simplest level of
drawing was technical drawing, or the "*trait*," by means of which the
artisan formalized an object or a sketch into a blueprint. Technical
drawing, however, entailed only imitation and copying, not innovation. A

knowledge of technical drawing was sufficient if the task was to make a blueprint from an existing object or sketch, but if the aim was the creation of a new form, then a different kind of drawing capacity was needed. The second level of drawing involved the rendering of figures as well as flora and fauna. This drawing was done freehand from nature or the model and trained the eye to more sophisticated perception and the hand to greater sureness than did technical drawing, which was done with the aid of compass and ruler. The next step was "free" drawing. Free drawing was the depiction on paper of images born in one's imagination. Free drawing therefore occupied a transitional space between skill and knowledge.

Knowledge allowed the artisan to conceptualize a new piece of furniture. While skill consisted of learning a number of strategies for arriving at a defined goal, knowledge gave the artisan the possibility of defining that goal. Acquiring knowledge meant learning the histories of art, architecture, and furniture and through that study obtaining an agility of mind and the means of grasping the full range of possibilities and functions for visual forms. Besides a semiotic repertoire, an understanding of the dynamic of aesthetic change, and a stock of forms and images, furniture makers needed geometry to invent new furniture aesthetics. Artisans had to understand how two-dimensional shapes and three-dimensional volumes were constructed and could be joined. Geometry was necessary as the basis of a simple kind of structural mechanics. To make chairs that would withstand the weight of a well-fed customer, bookcases that would not list, and spiral staircases that would not collapse, it was helpful to know that a triangle is a much stronger form than a rectangle and that one could easily turn one weak rectangle into two much stronger triangles. A knowledge of geometry (and arithmetic) thus provided the technical and theoretical knowledge necessary to create the imagined designs, as well as ideas of what was, in fact, possible.

The last element of the trilogy of skill, knowledge, and craft sense is perhaps the hardest to define. It was of the same epistemological order as common sense; it consisted of informal, practical knowledge vital to the practice of a trade, which was passed from one person in a community to another and from one generation to the next. Possessing craft sense meant being able to judge what a log would look like on the inside, where its faults would be, and what it was destined to make; sensing when glue was the appropriate consistency to match the weather and the woodgrain; and knowing how a flaw in the wood would react to the bite of a plane's knife. Craft sense was not a mystical phenomenon; it was taught but not in the same way that skill and knowledge were taught, because it contained a large component of experience, time, and habit. Notions of both tastefulness and innovation were contained within craft sense. At the same time that old tricks were passed down, artisans encouraged each other to invent new forms and new techniques.

The majority of artisans from as early as the eighteenth century had possessed only fragments of what they would have needed to create objects they found beautiful. Furthermore, making beauty required not only mastery of one's craft but also a degree of control over the production process. Only a small minority of woodworkers had ever been in a position to practice their trade in this way.[9] Until the mid-nineteenth century, however, those who had knowledge, skill, and craft sense had learned it from other artisans in the trade, supplemented perhaps by an occasional evening course.[10] By the end of the nineteenth century, the transmission of knowledge, skill, and craft sense was supposed to be controlled by the state and private philanthropists and effected through schools, museums, and libraries. But skill, knowledge, and craft sense were not to be transmitted as a tripartite whole by the schools, museums, and libraries. Those who drew and those who chiseled were no longer to be the same person. Efforts were made not only to separate skill, knowledge, and craft sense but also to fragment each of them. Some workers, for example, were to learn technical drawing; others, destined for a higher social status, were to learn free drawing. These efforts were not entirely successful; "underground" transmission of the integral trade continued, but its subterranean status transformed its place in artisans' lives.

The Culture of Production, Masculinity, and Beauty

I have called the system by which artisans transmitted skill, knowledge, and craft sense during the Old Regime and the first forty years of the nineteenth century the culture of production. Artisans entered and maintained this culture as they were trained in their craft, and they in turn taught others. Training took place in two stages: apprenticeship and journeymanship. The artisan then either became the master of his own shop or continued life as a waged worker.

To get started in a trade, a child would be sent out in early adolescence to live, work, and learn in the house and workshop of a master.[11] The parents would sign a contract with the master specifying the terms of the apprenticeship, including whether or not the apprenticeship was to be free. It was presumed that the master would teach apprentices the basics of the trade so they could emerge five, six, or seven years later as competent journeymen. The length of the apprenticeship, however, was set as much by the perceived labor needs of the trades as by the length of time it took to master the craft. It was also an accepted, if tacit, feature of the system that apprentices took on a certain amount of errand running, cleaning, and preparatory rough work—tasks not central to their education but necessary to the running of the shop. The role of the master and spouse as substitute parents was, in contrast, an explicit element in the arrangement.[12] They were responsible for the moral as well as trade education of the apprentice. Apprenticeship thus served multiple functions: it provided the industry with cheap labor for some of the dullest, heaviest, and least skilled tasks; it was a period of hazing, of teaching boys to be men;[13] and it was the time to begin acquiring the skill, knowledge, and craft sense necessary for the trade.

This structure seems to have deteriorated steadily in the nineteenth century.[14] By the last quarter of the century, apprentices appear to have been systematically exploited by being specialized too soon. In the eighteenth century and the early part of the nineteenth, apprentices may have been beaten, abused, taught to drink too young, and otherwise given a rather brutal introduction into working life, but they were also generally taught the trade. In the second half of the nineteenth century, complaints concerning the sketchiness of training abounded. The criticisms expressed by the cabinetmaker delegates to the 1867 World's Fair were not unusual: "The apprentice cabinetmaker should not do veneer work, sand, or varnish until after he has learned to plane, rip [saw planks lengthwise] and assemble, or he will become a bad worker, something which happens altogether too often these days. . . . "[15]

Complaints of this nature—not that artisans were not being taught any skills but that they were learning them in the wrong order and thus being deprived of a proper understanding of the craft—were far more frequent than accusations of physical brutality or complete negligence. The experience of Laurent Azzano, who entered the trade sometime around the end of the century as an apprentice in the shop where his father was employed, appears to have been typical of an apprentice privileged by his position as a legitimate heir to the trade.[16] Azzano seems to have put in a great deal of time heating glue—an unskilled, unpleasant, and very necessary task—as well as fulfilling other similar obligations.[17] He was eventually given the opportunity of more skilled work, but with only minimal instruction. Apprentices were systematically being treated, and behaving, as unskilled or semiskilled laborers rather than as heirs to a craft. In fact, by the late 1860s, the official apprenticeship period had become three years, and many artisans were leaving well before that.[18] The young were not the only ones with something to lose as a result of this transformation. Masters were deprived of the possibility of ensuring their reproduction in their craft. "The workshop is the true school . . . the employer . . . wants to train his students according to his taste, to his way of seeing, so that they can continue his tradition."[19] Shop owners, however, felt they could not afford to invest the time training a worker who had little commitment to their shop and perhaps little to the trade as a whole. In addition, new production pressures encouraged the early specialization of workers in the interest of increased efficiency.

Nearly everyone from the 1860s onward, whether artisan or employer, agreed the institution of apprenticeship was moribund. Some thought it should be revived, others suggested its replacement by trade schools, all agreed that something had to be done. The failure of the institution may, paradoxically, be seen in the following apprenticeship contract written up by the Conseil des Prud'hommes (an organization created to arbitrate in labor disputes) in Bordeaux: "art. 2. Monsieur _____ should correctly house and feed the young apprentice, should treat him gently, and behave towards him like a good *pater familias.* He should use him only in the work and services which are directly involved in the exercise of his trade, excepting, following custom, tasks such as sweeping the workshop and some errands to customers or suppliers. But these, exclusively, and without excess."[20] At first glance, this would appear to imply that all was well in apprenticeship, for apprenticeship had been a relation governed by written contract in its heyday. This contract was on different terms, however. In the Old Regime, only apprentices whose parents had paid heavily for the privilege of the apprenticeship were liberated from household and mundane duties; those who came without fee became members of the household in all senses, including an obligation to do chores, that is, to contribute to the social reproduction of the household. This 1902 model contract did not mention payment and yet liberated the apprentice from household duties. It appears to represent, therefore, an effort to create a new institution masquerading as an old. The pseudoparental and substitute familial relation characteristic of apprenticeship had always involved a contractual exchange of services—either the apprentice provided whatever labor the household needed, or he provided money. To ask a master to feed, house, and train a young boy out of the kindness of his heart in exchange for only a few errands and a bit of sweeping indicates how far the apprenticeship system had moved from its original purposes.

I would like to suggest that apprenticeship had worked when the societal model of familial relations included reciprocal responsibilities of the parents and children; the children had an obligation to assist in the material survival of the family, and the parents were to prepare their children for adulthood. By the 1860s, this understanding of the family had been challenged for thirty years by a competing image of the domestic, sentimental family. According to this ideology, the family was to be bound together largely by ties of love.[21] Apprenticeship, because it assumed that children would work to support the family with which they lived, and sentimental families, because they were based on the assumption that children would not, were incompatible visions of society. Even though working-class families did not have the luxury to dispense with their children's labor, denaturalizing (and to a large extent delegitimating) that labor made the apprenticeship system anachronistic by this period.[22] Furthermore, the split between the spheres of production and reproduction was accompanied by other new divisions of labor and responsibility. Training, or education, and production were increasingly divided, with the state playing a new role in the former. If the National Assembly could legislate mandatory schooling, it could also take responsibility for workers' ability to practice their trades. Demands on apprentices considered unremarkable in the first half of the century had become defined as abusive by the second. Likewise, the next step of training—the *compagnonnage,* or journeymen's organizations—had equal difficulties surviving in the new world of industrial capitalism.

Compagnonnage was the unofficial and illegal organization of male workers who had finished their apprenticeships and were embarking on their *tour de France* as journeymen.[23] The tour lasted from three to seven years and was intended to give young workers the opportunity to finish their training and to learn a variety of techniques in their trade. Elaborate initiation rituals, the requirement that one be single, and the intensive work and mobility ensured that the journeymen would come to have an identity based on work and on an allegiance to a trade and the *compagnonnage.*

Breaking ties with real kin and building a social network of brothers were central elements in the creation of a culture of production—an intensely masculine culture focused on the transmission of knowledge, skill, and craft sense. Both the passage from *compagnonnage* to master and the resolution of conflict among rival groups (or sects) within the *compagnonnages* involved contests over the aesthetic and technical mastery of the trade. The best journeymen and the most powerful and manly group of journeymen were those who could make the most beautiful object by whatever means necessary. The *compagnonnages* were not nearly as concerned about the labor process as they were about the appearance and soundness of the finished object.

This trade structure worked effectively only as long as the *compagnonnage* mirrored the structure of the larger society; its integrity and cultural logic were fatally fractured by the end of the corporate system of the Old

Regime. When apprenticeship and *compagnonnage* became atavistic in the second half of the nineteenth century, it was both a cause and an effect of the changing configuration of influences in the culture of production in the furniture trades.[24]

A corollary of the culture of production in the domain of distribution was the ideal of direct sale of custom-made goods from producer to consumer.[25] The artisans who made the goods were understood to have the expertise and authority to sell them.[26] While many more mediated forms of distribution also existed, they were outside the norms.[27] In custom sales, consumers committed themselves to buy on the basis of an abstraction—a model or a drawing—of the objects they were to acquire. This gave the producer considerable control over the process and authority over, as well as responsibility for, the aesthetic success of the purchase. Accurately "reading" models or drawings took skill the consumers rarely possessed. Customers had access to little other information—advertising was in its infancy, the display of goods was primitive, and few decorative arts magazines existed. Furniture was bought largely on the advice of friends and relatives and especially on the basis of the reputation of the artisan. To earn a reputation as a gifted furniture maker, one needed taste as well as technical expertise, and that taste was judged by one's (male) colleagues. Artisans learned definitions of taste from other artisans, and they competed with other men through contests over who could make the most intricate, skillful, and beautiful objects. When the culture of production had been the means of transmitting taste to the artisans of the furnishings trades and direct sale had been the dominant mode of distribution, taste and a concern with beauty and style had been androgynous, perhaps even manly, attributes.

The culture of production was itself the product of an era characterized by a system of classification of people unlike that which would follow the Enlightenment, the French Revolution, the development of industrial capitalism, and political economy. The definition of productive labor changed; in the Old Regime, consumers were not distinct from producers if they were from the same social class. Despite the real ubiquity of people who made their living selling things that other people had made, the role of distributor was not yet fully assimilated into the social taxonomy. Likewise, in this system women and men were not defined as either producers or consumers. Both were both.

This changed during the mid-nineteenth century, for political economy described and created relations of not only production but also consumption. Just as the culture of production—in which workers sold the product of their labor rather than their labor and had property in their craft to pass on to their apprentices—was incompatible with political economy, so too was a society in which all people made and bought goods. Political economists, while fully aware that most women worked for wages, often wrote as if men were the only producers and women the only consumers of value. Men were to sell their labor for the highest sum they could receive for it; the content or product of that labor was not to be of concern. It fell to women, in their role as consumers, to buy the alienated commodities men made at work. The erosion of the culture of production was simultaneous with and reinforced by the gradual shift in distribution from custom to ready-made sales. The capacity to assess beauty was now to be sharpened in bourgeois women (who had innate, latent good taste because of their gender and class) and taught to working-class women (whose class position produced an absence where tastefulness ought to have been). The invention of beauty was to lie in the domain of a specialized group of middle-class men. In the 1860s, however, all of this was still in flux. The culture of production no longer worked, but it had not yet been replaced by any other system of training artisans.

This new void in the authority over taste contributed to radically expanding and redefining a group of workers in the decorative arts who previously had only been involved in the most expensive furniture: the taste professionals. These taste professionals worked not with their hands or even necessarily with a pencil and sketch-pad but with a pen and writing paper. They included architects interested in interior decor; the owners of the largest and most prestigious furniture companies—men who had typically built furniture in their youth but who had become businessmen;[28] the most successful interior decorators and designers; members of the Union Central des Arts Décoratifs and other such organizations; writers concerned with taste and beauty, including the writers of etiquette books; and legislators preoccupied with aesthetics and working-class dwellings. The taste professionals helped organize the private and public trade schools of the late nineteenth century, as well as the museums, libraries, and world's fairs.[29] They wrote articles for the *Revue des arts décoratifs* and other magazines and books on how to furnish one's home tastefully.[30] In general they earned their living through their role as taste professionals, not through the sale of particular objects. There were also many amateurs. The taste professionals often disagreed with each other and engaged in fierce debate, although they did systematically, if individually, assert their legitimacy in the face of distributors' new claims to aesthetic authority. They were not an entirely new group in the late nineteenth century; there had been individuals working in these professions and expert amateurs since the eighteenth century, but the taste professionals, as an identifiable assemblage of subgroups, increased greatly in importance in the 1870s.

Most of the taste professionals were men, although a significant minority were women. But gender is not as simple as biology, and beginning with the appearance of dandies in the third decade of the nineteenth century, men who passed their lives worrying and writing about matters of beauty were not perceived as entirely men anymore.[31] Taste was generally understood as falling within the feminine domain, and male taste professionals may have come to constitute part of the "third sex."[32] Yet good taste was one of France's major claims to international prestige and a place in the new industrial world. The dissonance and anxiety created by France's reliance on expertise defined as feminine for distinction and solvency is evident in the many efforts by taste professionals and others, including political economists, to find a way to remasculanize taste at least partially. In an 1868 text, Armand Audiganne, a social investigator associated with the Académie des Sciences Morales et Politiques (one of the institutional homes of political economy), commented on this issue. He attempted to assert France's coexistent masculine prowess *and* tastefulness by tracing the origins of French aesthetic superiority to the tournaments of the Middle Ages, where manly men jousted for women's approval. This rhetorical move is rather baffling, until one arrives at the phrase claiming that the world's fairs were contemporary jousts. In the fairs, men were competing to produce beauty, not because they cared about the beautiful but because women did. Men competed through beauty for women. Even if men produced beauty, it was women who ultimately judged and consumed it.[33] The torturous recourse to medieval jousting indicates the anachronism of the image, however. By the 1860s, the traditional masculinity of the woodworking trades could not be comfortably reconciled with the recently feminized connotations of aesthetic judgment. Furniture makers without taste were nothing, yet furniture makers with taste were no longer fully men. This had not always been the case; there had been a time when manly men could think about beauty. In the second half of the nineteenth century, the world's fairs kept that moment briefly alive, while trade unions left it behind.

Trade Unions

The apparent late nineteenth-century successors to the role of *compagnonnage* in transmitting and defending the culture of production in the wood trades were mutual aid societies, trade unions, and strikes. Despite superficial similarities, the new associations and actions intervened in artisans' lives at a very different level than had the *compagnonnage*. A thorough reading of the expressed concerns of furniture workers participating in unions, mutual aid societies, and strikes reveals a discourse dominated by demands for improvements in the material conditions of everyday work life: shorter hours, higher wages, and safer working conditions.[34] Little was said about the skill, knowledge, or craft sense that had defined workers as artisans capable of creative labor and innovation.[35] From their tentative beginnings in the 1830s and 1840s to their consolidation during the depression of the 1880s, unions, mutual aid societies, and strikes did not argue for artisans' continued control of the transmission of knowledge, skill, and craft sense. The question is not what organized labor had to say on these matters but why did it say nothing at all? What happened to the culture of production in the course of union organization?

The process of unionization in the Parisian furniture trades was typical, according to the historiography of the French working class in the nineteenth century, of a relatively militant male-dominated artisanal trade. There was an initial period of collective action and informal organization (parallel to the *compagnonnage*) from the beginning of the century to the Revolution of 1848. The mutual aid societies were entirely devoted to providing pensions and benefits in case of illness or unemployment, thus taking over two of the old functions of the *compagnonnage*—material aid and a trade community—but leaving behind the effort to transmit knowledge, skill, and craft sense.[36] Efforts to control production took the form of producer cooperatives.[37] The decades from the 1860s to the 1880s and intensifying in the 1890s saw union organization in many of the trades that made up the furniture industry and numerous strikes over issues of wages, hours, and control.[38] All of the organizations—mutual aid societies, unions and cooperatives—were plagued by ideological conflict and financial instability. The issues consistently raised throughout the nineteenth century were related to economics and, to a more limited degree, control over the labor process. They fought over wages, the employment of foreign workers and women, competition from prisoners and sweated labor, responsibility for worker welfare, and unification across trades.[39]

At first glance, this silence concerning knowledge, taste, and beauty would seem to indicate that the culture of production in which innovation and creativity played central roles was dead by mid-century. Looked at more closely, however, the explanation of the unions' silence appears to have had little to do with whether the members of the unions were concerned with making objects they found beautiful but a great deal to do with what battles furniture makers were able to fight in the context of mutual aid societies, unions, and strikes.

Labor historians have put vast energy and effort into examining the discourses of organized labor. While they have by no means reached consensus concerning what workers were really demanding or why they were asking for those things, they have rarely seriously questioned the appropriateness of looking primarily to the discourses of organized labor to discover the real (or at least dominant) interests and concerns of workers.[40]

Mutual aid societies, trade unions, and strikes functioned as speech communities; they created a relatively unified discourse that transcended the differences between crafts and constructed alliances in the increasingly fragmented and adversarial left of the late nineteenth century.[41] These speech communities could be either long-standing and reified into institutions, as in the case of mutual aid societies and unions, or transient, as in the case of strikes. In each case, coherence within the group, as well as the agreement needed for action, was created by limiting the range of topics for discussion. Legitimate topics for conversation within organized labor were defined to create at least temporary consensus. Many matters of interest to even a majority of members of the organization may have disappeared into silence, to be discussed elsewhere or lost forever.[42] For example, furniture unions, like others, often explicitly deemed politics to be beyond discussion.[43] Beauty and knowledge were never formally banned from debate, but I suspect the topics seemed so inappropriate there was no need to suppress them. Although the notion of speech community may help explain the limited range of demands framed within the context of organized labor, it does not fully explain the logic behind the choice of acceptable issues.[44]

Discourses used within speech communities must accomplish at least two things: (1) at a minimum, they must be intelligible, and hopefully persuasive, to their interlocutors; and (2) they must help consolidate and preserve the group. Labor historians have convincingly argued that the primary audience for much labor action was the state, and feminist scholars have persuasively argued that much of organized labor (except in trades where women formed a clear majority of the work force) was fundamentally masculine in identity.[45] Both of these attributes of the discourse of organized labor shaped what could and could not be said.

Because the dominant interlocutor was the state, it made sense to speak not only the language of political economy but also a familiar (however inverted) language of class. The work of social investigators (like Louis Villermé) in the 1830s argued that the laboring—and dangerous—classes had special needs. This work marked the founding of a conservative concept of class that was clearly separate from the socialist heritage. Just as the *compagnonnage* mimicked and inverted relations with the masters, the unions and socialists accepted and inverted the terms of conservative class definition. The possibility for claims based on both the commodification of labor and membership in a class formed by relation to the means of production limited the available language. Once artisans accepted that they were entering these negotiations as vendors of their labor—as the dominant language of capitalism, political economy, dictated—they were limited to material demands. In a crude sense, what they had to sell was their bodies and the ability of those bodies to do the tasks demanded of them. They could claim better terms for the sale, but they could not offer another object. Had they struck over the right to define the knowledge needed to practice the trade, to control the transmission of that knowledge, and to make objects they found beautiful, it is unlikely that they would have won anything at all or that they would even have been understood. There was no clear way to put a price on knowledge, skill, craft sense, or innovation.

The material orientation of the claims of organized labor was further reinforced by the logic of class as the basis for worker solidarity. An emphasis on material grievances would have helped foster unity among the trades, diverse in their skills and knowledge but common in their experiences of wage cuts, long hours, and increasingly limited control over the labor process. An emphasis on knowledge and taste had already proved to be divisive—to the point of pitched battle—in the *compagnon-nages.* Journeymen of different trades fought over who was truly skilled and knowledgeable and therefore the legitimate heirs of the ancient tradition of *compagnonnage.*[46]

Finally, discussions of the beauty or even the usefulness of objects workers made within a discursive space defined as masculine were becoming increasingly problematic as the century reached its end. With the multiplication of the taste professionals from the 1870s onward, the category of beauty and aesthetic pleasure may have become increasingly suspect in the aggressively masculine context of organized labor. The taste professionals were both male and female, they occupied a space not clearly masculine or feminine, they were neither producers nor consumers, and they worked on the interior but did so from the outside and were often paid for it. The solidarity of unions was fundamentally a masculine solidarity, defending labor in terms sometimes reminiscent of Gracchus Babeuf. It was an alliance of manly men who wielded tools and could bear arms.[47] The union world was also a homosocial one in the context of the perceived blurring of gender boundaries. Male artisans were preoccupied with protecting themselves against the female artisans, who were "encroaching" on their territory.[48] Questions of beauty and knowledge had played a different role in the equally, but differently, masculine culture of production, when rivalries between men were often played out through competition over who could produce the most beautiful object. The culture of production contained very fixed gender positions; women did certain things within the shop and did not do others, and as consumers, they were dependent on the authority, knowledge, and good taste of the producer. In that culture, there was no need to create a definition of masculinity in terms of absolute opposition to femininity. In contrast, organized labor responded to the threat posed by women workers underselling them by fiercely defending a version of masculinity taken from the political economists. Organized male workers sabotaged themselves by participating in this gender system. Organized labor's acceptance of the logic of political economy in which men produced and women consumed further undermined unions' capacity to defend workers' right to make beautiful objects; beauty and utility were to be judged by the consumers, assisted not by producers but by distributors and taste professionals. An interest and expertise in matters of aesthetics came to be defined as both feminine and effeminate, for in fact it was the taste professionals, at least as much as the consumers, who became authoritative in matters of taste. The taste professionals played a new crucial role of mediating between the now alienated producers and consumers.

The logic of political economy, the exigencies of creating a sentiment of cohesion among workers from different trades with varying histories and often a powerful sense of rivalry, and working-class men's sense of what it meant to be a man in the context of the union hall all framed the discourse of organized labor. Unions helped create the working class as much as they represented it.[49] There was no one true discourse common to all artisans but rather individuals who were choosing at one moment to participate in the discourse of organized labor and at other moments to look elsewhere.[50] Given this perspective, labor historians' tendency to privilege union discourse above other expressions of working-class desires in an effort to find the one "true" voice speaking for the class of artisans is highly problematic. Historians have been preoccupied with understanding when and how workers decided to organize unions, to strike, or to revolt and for what goals. What emerges from their efforts, however, is a falsely unified image of a working class concerned above all with hours, wages, working conditions, and narrowly defined revolutionary politics. Although these issues were crucial, they were not the only issues of intense concern to late nineteenth-century Parisian cabinetmakers.

Furniture makers were also interested in maintaining the aesthetic traditions and creative possibilities of the trade. Knowledge and aesthetics did not exist beyond, above, or outside power relations but were deeply embedded within them. Late nineteenth-century artisans preoccupied with knowledge and aesthetics had several options. They could turn to other institutions besides those of organized labor, such as the world's fairs, trade schools, museums, and libraries. They could also adopt extra-institutional strategies: some put creativity into their work by intentionally distorting historical styles; some practiced informal resistance within the workshop; and some continued to transmit knowledge, skill, craft sense, and taste through informal networks based in the workshop (and bar).[51] Those networks, because of their informality, were relatively immune to the changes of the late nineteenth century. Just as neither the anonymous forces of industrial capitalism nor the efforts of the taste professionals could succeed in completely robbing artisans of their culture of production, so the seeming hegemony of the logic of political economy did not silence artisans altogether; it only constrained what they said in the union hall.

World's Fairs

World's fairs were ubiquitous in the industrial world during the second half of the nineteenth century, occurring as often as twice a decade.[52] The fairs of the 1850s and 1860s were a hybrid combining the last vestiges of the Old Regime's culture of production and the new, bourgeois consumer regime of the late nineteenth century. They provided artisans with a site in which they could say what could not be said in the context of organized labor, and they helped transmit knowledge, skill, and craft sense. By the end of the century, decades of economic crises had rendered demand a matter of increased concern, and it was the consumer, rather than the producer and certainly rather than the worker, who became the honored guest at the fairs. But for a moment, in the 1860s, artisans used the fairs to speak their minds and express their concern for the objects of their labor. From their speech, we can see that Audiganne's 1868 characterization of the fairs as jousts, where the real prize was the female consumers' love, was premature. Male artisans could still voice their concern with beauty for its own sake and their own satisfaction in the 1860s. The process of feminizing taste and beauty, the increasing stratification of the furnishings trades, and the new centrality of consumption would drive these voices underground by the 1880s.

The universal exhibitions were not only suspended between the exigencies and interests of production and consumption but also located at an ambiguous juncture between organizations of bourgeois and artisanal initiative. There can be no doubt that the fairs were bourgeois in origin, the result of an alliance between the state, moral reformers, and taste professionals. They were part of the state's effort to respond to the "crisis in taste" provoked by the fading of the culture of production.[53] This crisis was worrisome both economically and politically; the luxury trades produced goods important in the export market, and unemployed artisans were understood to have revolutionary potential. The fairs of the 1850s and 1860s were conceptualized, in part, with the goal of promoting French "art industries" and French products in general and maintaining class peace. Parisian artisans wrote reports on the 1862 Exhibition in London, and artisans were invited by Napoleon III to participate as "worker delegates" in the Exhibition of 1867.[54] These formal invitations from those at the center of power have tended to make historians suspicious of the authenticity of workers' expressions at these fairs,[55] but the worker delegates were not hesitant to express their complaints about the organization of the exhibitions themselves. They also used the fairs, as well as the reports published after the fairs, as an alternate forum to organized labor. It suited the interests of the organizers for the artisan participants to be ostentatiously uncensored.

The general commissioner of the 1867 World's Fair, the sociologist Frédéric Le Play, arranged the most extensive worker participation of any fair in history.[56] He established the Commission for the Encouragement of Workers' Studies, composed of sixty members—manufacturers, economists, bankers, and engineers. The commission formed committees in each *département* (local administrative unit) to see to the election by universal suffrage of worker delegates, assisted by local mutual aid societies.[57] Their responsibilities as delegates were to go to the exhibitions, to study the state of French production and the nature of the competition, and to assess the problems and merits of French production techniques, products, and prices in light of competing exhibits.[58]

In contrast to union and strike meeting reports, while artisans speaking in the context of the expositions also addressed issues of wages and collective organization, they went on at greatest length concerning artistic training, aesthetic control, the quality of the pieces produced, and recognition for their creative labor: "We will not conclude without thanking the entire *corps d'état* [trade] for the knowledge and the care which it has brought to the execution of all of the cited master-pieces. A large part of the successes earned by the exhibitors are ours by right and the active part which we have taken is not less obvious for the fact that it is not officially recognized and consecrated."[59]

These upholsterers thought they brought to their work not only *connaissances* (more concrete, multiple, contextual, and always plural form of knowledge) but also *savoir* (more abstract, unitary, atemporal, and usually singular knowledge) and *soins,* or care.[60] In making that distinction, they were refusing to accept the fragmentation of their craft and the loss of creative possibilities at work.[61] The jigsaw operators emphasized the importance of abstract knowledge in a different way:

> In order for the results to be varied, beautiful, [and] artistic . . . one needs to be not only a jigsaw operator [*découpeur*], one also has to be a draughts-man [*dessinateur*], and thoroughly imbued with the needs of architecture and ornamentation, having completed beforehand a special study of all those things. And . . . regardless of all the talent that he might possess, an artist draughtsman for ornament, decoration and architecture [*artiste dessinateur pour l'ornementation, décoration et architecture*], could never produce anything new and remarkable in découpage, if he does not know the resources of this last branch [architecture] of the industry.[62]

The emphasis here on the finished product is striking. They wanted greater knowledge so they could produce more successful, innovative products. They also specifically insisted on the importance of architecture, the most abstract of the listed forms of knowledge, to the successful practice of the trade.

The artisans in all of the furniture trades were not lacking ideas on how to resolve the "taste crisis." The jigsaw operators suggested the founding of a school specializing in decoupage because those in existence were limited, teaching only what was already being done, not what was possible.[63] The chair turners and furniture designers further specified that they thought the public schools should teach drawing.[64] Many worker delegates asserted that there was a need for both a revived and improved apprenticeship system and training in school.[65] Other artisans thought the aesthetic crisis could be resolved through the creation of specialized libraries[66] or museums,[67] paid study time,[68] or the elimination of consumer influence.[69]

The question of access to new and old masterpieces from which one could get ideas was inflammatory. Cabinetmakers strongly regretted the abolition of the practice of leaving finished objects in the shop for a few days before sending them out to the customers. This period of "shop-viewing" had allowed neighborhood artisans to inspect and learn from newly completed custom-made work.[70] The fairs were supposed to provide the same service, but as the makers of "antique" furniture complained, the cost of exhibiting a piece was prohibitively high.[71] This expense was not a result of display charges but a side effect of the role of the world's fairs as sites of international competition. Artisans, or rather entrepreneurs controlling workshops, devoted enormous resources to exhibition pieces in the hopes of winning prizes of considerable commercial value. Unlike the pieces earlier displayed in the workshops, which had been partially paid for before any work was invested, exhibition pieces were made on speculation and were often never sold. Few artisans could afford the luxury of making a masterpiece of this order. The displays now served the interests of the consumers and manufacturers rather than the educational needs of the artisans. The fairs gave consumers access to the newest and the best in the art industries, and they provided a site for free advertising for the manufacturers. This was a betrayal, or at least a transformation, of the role of the world's fairs in perpetuating a version of the culture of production.

That culture of production was also defended through the vigorous protests made, on aesthetic grounds, against piece-rates. The makers of "antique" furniture complained that piece-rates meant not only that artisans were not earning enough to eat but also that the quality of the work deteriorated: "The worker obliged to obtain a certain wage to feed his family, pay his rent, to supply all of those needs which are so expensive today, works without taste, putting aside all of his pride as an intelligent, skilled, worker, he sets his sights on only one thing—to produce, because one has to eat."[72] The makers of "antique" furniture went on to say that when workers were paid by the day, they did creative work, "because, whatever one says, the worker is proud of earned praise. . . . "[73]

This varied list of suggestions to improve artisans' knowledge of the disciplines constitutive of a fine aesthetic sensibility could be even more detailed. The crucial point here is the amount of attention artisans in the context of the fairs, in contrast to that of organized labor, were paying to this problem in particular. Furthermore, they were making these demands not in terms of defending wages or the traditional labor process but rather in the interest of producing beautiful objects. This is even more striking because these delegates were selected with the assistance of the mutual aid societies and may therefore have been participants in organized labor.

Besides having access to the knowledge as well as the skill they needed, artisans were very concerned about authorship. Delegates expressed great irritation over employers' refusal to give credit to the workers involved in producing a piece. In turn, the cabinetmakers refused to give the names of either the employers or the workers and recounted the following anecdote to justify their decision:

> After having admired one of the masterpieces of French cabinetwork, and especially after having announced our role as worker delegates, we asked the representative of the exhibitor:
> —Would your employer allow us to name the workers who executed this wonderful work?
> —First of all, Sirs, it was the employer who conceived and drew this piece of furniture, with the help of a designer, it's true; but he only detailed the ornaments on the employer's plan.

—OK, but the sculptures, whose details are so elegant and so well finished, who did those?

—Oh, as far as the sculpture is concerned, you can name the artists, but then you will have to name all of them and there are more than sixty. No one of them can claim to have sculpted this piece of furniture, all of whose parts were executed under the direction and surveillance of our employer. If you name a sculptor, as all of the work is very well done, you will have to name all of them.[74]

The cabinetmakers clearly did not accept the argument that employers could legitimately take credit for the pieces emerging from their workshops. In face of the representative's obstructionism, the cabinetmakers were willing to accept the anonymity of the cabinetmakers and other workers, but when it became clear that no worker (and they use the word *worker,* not *artisan*) was to be named, they rebelled. These workers did not accept that they were selling their labor; they had indeed sold their labor, but they wanted recognition for their talent and knowledge.

Worker delegates focused on two other issues of central importance to artisans concerned with the objects they made: specialization within the trades and the role of middlemen. The *découpeurs marqueteurs* wanted greater specialization by trade within the exhibitions so that they would be able to work independently from the cabinetmakers.[75] But since the *marqueteurs* only did marquetry on the surface work of a piece, and whole pieces of furniture had to be displayed rather than just elements of a piece, the *marqueteurs* were forced to cooperate with the cabinetmakers. Although some artisans involved in the union movement and left politics often voiced the importance of eliminating all barriers among people united by their relation to the means of production, in another context, many expressed deep reluctance to abdicate the historical definitions of the particular trades in the interest of working-class solidarity.

Echoes of the protests against the end of shop displays and remnants of Old Regime corporatism can be seen in the protest against distributors. The worker delegates made the argument that middlemen drove wages down because they took a cut in the finished object. The workers could not accept that the distributors added necessary value and performed a useful service for which they should be paid.[76] They also understood that the new occupations of distributor, advertiser, and salesclerk transformed their relation with the consumer and undermined their aesthetic authority— or at least competed with them for it.

These reports from the workers' delegates of 1867 are thus crucial in making the argument that the voices of artisans in unions were not their only voices and that artisans were indeed concerned with issues of taste, education, and knowledge. They used the forum provided them to express their desires to maintain their culture of production, albeit with help from the state. These discourses within the fairs were not, of course, any less dependent on their context than were those produced in the context of unions. The workers were essentially hired as experts to assess the state of their craft and make suggestions concerning what would make those crafts more competitive on the world market. Their emphasis, then, on the products of their labor and their desire to innovate and create beauty was just what was expected of them. But just as union discourse did not adhere absolutely to a line that would have been maximally effective vis-à-vis the state, so the worker delegates sometimes wrote things to which this other manifestation of the state was deaf. The agency of the workers was, in both cases, created contextually.

Even if this may explain why, in this locus, artisans were able to talk about beauty and may even have felt obliged to talk about it, what happened to their gender qualms? If it was threatening to the collective masculinity of the artisans in unions to talk about aesthetics, why was it not as worker delegates? It was not demasculanizing for artisans to talk about beauty—they had been doing so for a long time in the context of the culture of production—it was only impossible in the gendered construction of organized labor. The world's fairs of the 1850s and 1860s, which were a bridge between the old culture of production and a new world, retained qualities of each.

As the century neared its end, it became more and more difficult to persuade workers to participate in mixed-class events. Artisans became increasingly committed to separatist organizations.[77] Even within the context of the exhibitions, the unions eventually came to dominate. After 1867, the worker delegates were chosen by unions and not by a "universal" vote in the locality, assisted by the mutual aid societies. There were fewer written worker reports; the last ones were from Vienna in 1873 and Philadelphia in 1876. The world's fairs could no longer fit into the space between the artisanal culture of production and the taste professionals' vision of artistic renovation. That positioning had depended on the possibility of cross-class alliances and the didactic function of the fairs. Both of those possibilities had in turn depended on a society dominated by relations of production and by a worldview in which production played a central role. By the end of the century, consumers were beginning to replace producers on center stage, and institutions of distribution were starting to rival institutions of production as the central locus of preoccupation.[78]

Although organized labor was deeply constrained by its intimate dialogue with institutions governed by the logic of political economy, the language of the world's fairs of the 1860s and 1870s was a Creole, made from the collision between the language of the "culture of production" born in the Old Regime and the language of the mid-nineteenth-century version of political economy. The world's fairs of the 1880s then left the producers of goods aside altogether—and left them speechless—as the fairs moved into the service of a mature bourgeois consumption regime.

Conclusion

By the 1920s, the old artisanal tradition of Parisian furniture production had been definitively broken and existed only in vestigial form. The descendants in trade of the cabinetmakers of the Old Regime and the first seventy years of the new had become marginally skilled workers, petit bourgeois managers, designers, low-level engineers, sales clerks, and decorators, leaving only a few in artisanal production. This story has often been told as the inevitable outcome of the anonymous development of industrial capitalism or as the result of bourgeois conspiracy. Although structural determinants and class fears were important, the story is more complicated.

Legislators and other bourgeois concerned with the fate of the luxury trades in the late nineteenth century were trapped by their understanding of those trades. First of all, the lack of innovation was perceived as the fundamental problem of the French furniture industry in the late nineteenth century (which was not necessarily the case). Second, the knowledge necessary for tasteful innovation was understood to be dangerous in the hands of the working class, especially the furniture makers well known for their revolutionary tendencies.[79] While concrete skill was safe, abstract knowledge led to revolution; both, however, were needed to make tasteful furniture. Third, they were getting no help from the labor unions, which were worried about other, more material matters.

Organized labor became the loudest voice of the artisans, but its voice could not even whisper desires for beauty. The aesthetic experts became bourgeois women and bourgeois and petit bourgeois men perceived to be of dubious masculinity, who knew little of the production process; but the making of furniture was carried out by "he-men," who had deprived themselves and been deprived of overtly caring about beauty.

Artisans in the second half of the nineteenth century also faced a series of dilemmas. Their old means of transmitting knowledge, skill, and craft sense was no longer viable. They themselves could no longer persuade their young colleagues to complete apprenticeships, and few could afford to take them on. The state was increasingly intervening in education and the workplace. Moreover, they were part of a society that distinguished among men who labored to produce exchange value, women who consumed aesthetic value, and the men—neither fully men nor members of the artisanal class—who produced and assessed aesthetic forms. Artisans who wanted to defend their possibilities of acquiring and deploying their knowledge, skill, and craft sense to make beautiful objects at work risked both their gender and their class, and that was a terrible price to pay. The artisans sustained a defense for a moment in the already anachronistic institutions of the production-centered world's fairs, but the more thoroughly "modern" and therefore ultimately hegemonic trade unions left the field.

This abdication of the field of beauty was but partial. Even in late twentieth-century North America, far more distant from a strong craft tradition than was early twentieth-century France, workers continue to care about beauty subterraneously and subversively and to make beautiful objects. Both gender and class identities may be harder to fix, and it may be harder to deprive people of knowledge than one would have thought. As things became inexpressible or even forgotten in one context, they were remembered and discussed in another. When making beauty became something unmanly, working men no longer did it for wages, but they started creating aesthetically satisfying objects for pleasure.

Notes

I would like to thank Joan Scott for her comments on this essay. The Social Science Research Council, and Tocqueville, Chateaubriand, and Fulbright fellowships funded this research.

1. I worked at F. W. Dixon in Woburn, a company that employed sixty workers and included a cabinet shop, an architectural model shop, an experimental machine shop, a display shop, a pattern-making shop; Brouwer Woodworks in Boston, which consisted of a custom woodworking shop in Cambridge that specialized in spiral staircases and a small production shop in Boston, where we made good quality hardwood furniture of Japanese inspiration; and the Emily Street Cooperative, a workshop where there were fifteen or so independent woodworkers, who collectively owned the big machines and bought wood together.

2. Although this is a well-known phenomenon, it has been analyzed most eloquently by Michel de Certeau in his *The Practice of Everyday Life*, trans. Steven F. Randall (Berkeley, Calif., 1984).

3. I am referring here to the classics of the old "new" labor history of France published in the 1970s and early 1980s. Some of the central monographs are Ronald Aminzade, *Class, Politics, and Early Industrial Capitalism: A Study of Mid-Nineteenth-Century Toulouse, France* (Albany, N.Y., 1981); Robert Bezucha, *The Lyon Uprising of 1834: Social and Political Conflict in the Early July Monarchy* (Cambridge, Mass., 1974); Michael Hanagan, *The Logic of Solidarity:*

Artisans and Industrial Workers in Three French Towns, 1871-1914 (Urbana, Ill., 1980); Yves Lequin, *Les ouvriers de la région lyonnaise (1848-1914),* 2 vols. (Lyon, 1977); Bernard Moss, *The Origins of the French Labor Movement, 1830-1914: The Socialism of Skilled Workers* (Berkeley, Calif., 1976); Michelle Perrot, *Les ouvriers en grève, France 1871-1890* (Paris, 1974); Joan Wallach Scott, *The Glassworkers of Carmaux* (Cambridge, Mass., 1974); William H. Sewell, Jr., *Structure and Mobility: The Men and Women of Marseille, 1820-1970* (Cambridge, 1985); Edward Shorter and Charles Tilly, *Strikes in France, 1830-1968* (London, 1974); and Rolande Trempé, *Les mineurs de Carmaux, 1848-1914* 2 vols. (Paris, 1971). William Sewell's methodological approach in *Work and Revolution in France: The Language of Labor from the Old Regime to 1848* (Cambridge, 1980) is far more textually based than the above and helped to bring a shift in the orientation of American writing of French labor history. Despite the "linguistic turn" of this book, the object and the goal of the study is the same as the others cited. An important counterexample is Lee Shai Weissbach's "Artisanal Responses to Artistic Decline: The Cabinetmakers of Paris in the Era of Industrialization," *Journal of Social History* 16 (1982): 67-81.

4. There are by now many critiques of the labor literature oriented toward uncovering "true consciousness" or denouncing false. For an eloquent plea for another approach, see Michelle Perrot, "On the Formation of the French Working Class," in *Working-Class Formation: Nineteenth-Century Patterns in Western Europe and the United States,* ed. Ira Katznelson and Aristide Zolberg (Princeton, N.J. 1986), esp. p. 71.

5. The classic argument is that workers' organization was a result of proletarianization; workers were most militant not when they were in the process of losing their skill and control over their labor but when they had lost it. One of the most elegant statements of this position is Trempé, *Les mineurs de Carmaux.* Lequin, *Les ouvriers de la région lyonnaise,* vol. 2, chap. 1, on the other hand, takes the currently more popular position that workers struck to resist the process of proletarianization. Bernard Moss, in *The Origins of the French Labor Movement,* situates militancy in yet another location with respect to skill, arguing that it was the most skilled workers who were the most militant.

6. This has been most clearly written about for the British case. See, for example, John Rule, "The Property of Skill in the Period of Manufacture," in *The Historical Meanings of Work,* ed. Patrick Joyce (Cambridge, 1987), pp. 99-118; on the gendering of the concept of skill, see, in the same volume, Maxine Berg, "Women's Work, Mechanisation, and the Early Phases of Industrialisation in England," pp. 64-98. See also the classic analysis by Cynthia Cockburn, *Brothers: Male Dominance and Technological Change* (London, 1983), esp. pp. 113-37.

7. Henri Fourdinois, "De l'état actuel de l'industrie du mobilier," *Revue des arts décoratifs* 5 (1884-85): 537-44.

8. This discussion is derived from reading the approximately 150 technical manuals dating from 1760 to 1920 currently available at the Bibliothèque Forney, the Bibliothèque des Arts Décoratifs, and the Bibliothèque Nationale, as well as from my own practice of the trade.

9. The historiographic attacks on the romanticization of the "golden age" of labor when workers were free are innumerable. The classic text for France is Emile Levasseur, *Histoire des classes ouvrières avant 1789,* 2 vols. (Paris, 1901). The focus of Michael Sonenscher's *The Hatters of Eighteenth-Century France* (Berkeley, Calif., 1987) and *Work and Wages: Natural Law, Politics, and the Eighteenth-Century French Trades* (Cambridge, 1989) is somewhat different but reinforces the argument.

10. Free evening courses for artisans were available from the late eighteenth century at the École Spéciale de dessin and at the École Polytechnique. For the offerings, see Archives Nationales (hereafter AN) F21 1422: École Spéciale de dessin (rue de l'École de médecine), 1832; and F17 12530: École Polytechnique.

11. For eighteenth-century apprenticeship within the guild, see *Statuts, privilèges, ordonnances et réglemens de la communauté des maîtres menuisiers et ébénistes de la ville, fauxbourgs et banlieues de Paris* (Paris, 1751); see also Pierre Verlet, *L'art du meuble à Paris au XVIIIe siècle* (Paris, 1958), p. 22.

12. For a discussion of the paternal role of the master, the contractual nature of the relationship, and the obligations of the apprentice, see Hippolyte Blanc, *Les corporations de métiers: Leur histoire—leur esprit—leur avenir* (Paris, 1898), pp. 133-37.

13. For a discussion of the importance of apprenticeship in teaching masculinity, see Ava Baron, "Questions of Gender: Deskilling and Demasculinization in the U.S. Printing Industry, 1830-1915," *Gender and History* 1 (1989): 178-99; and Keith McClelland, "Masculinity and the 'Representative Artisan' in Britain, 1850-1880," *Gender and History* 1 (1989): 164-77.

14. Ministère du Travail, Office du Travail, *L'apprentissage industriel: Rapport sur l'apprentissage dans les industries d'ameublement* (Paris, 1905). For a nuanced analysis of the status of apprenticeship in the Parisian furniture trades, see Lee Shai Weissbach, "Entrepreneurial Traditionalism in Nineteenth-Century France: A Study of the *Patronage Industriel des enfants de l'ébénisterie,*" *Business History Review* 57 (1983): 548-65. Yves Lequin claims that apprenticeships continued in factories in the late nineteenth century, but he does appear to agree that the general situation was deteriorating. Lequin, "Apprenticeship in Nineteenth-Century France: A Continuing Tradition or a Break with the Past?" in *Work in France: Representations, Meaning, Organization, and Practice,* ed. Steven Kaplan and Cynthia Koepp (Ithaca, N.Y., 1986), pp. 456-74. Lenard Berlanstein is equally bleak in his estimation of the success of the apprenticeship system by the nineteenth century. Berlanstein, "Growing Up as Workers in Nineteenth-Century Paris: Case of the Orphans of the Prince Imperial," *French Historical Studies* 11 (1980): 551-76.

15. Alphonse Baude and A. Loizel, "Ébénistes," in *Exposition universelle de 1867 à Paris. Rapports des délégations ouvrières contentant l'origine et l'histoire des diverses professions, l'appréciation des objets exposés, la comparaison des arts et des industries en France et à l'étranger. L'exposé des voeux et besoins de la classe laborieuse, et l'ensemble des considérations sociales intéressant les ouvriers,* ed. M. F. Devinck, 3 vols. (Paris, 1868), vol. 1, p. 6. The pagination in this text

starts over with each new article. Authors are also often given only by last name; when that is the case, I will do the same.

16. Laurent Azzano, *Mes joyeuses années au faubourg: Souvenirs du faubourg Saint-Antoine* (Paris, 1985), pp. 19, 21, 23.

17. Ibid., p. 27.

18. See AN F22 255: Apprentissage, 1861-1923; AN F12 7621: Enquête d'apprentissage; AN F12 6358-6363: Office du Travail, Enquête sur l'apprentissage industriel, 1901; Office du Travail, Apprentissage industrielle; and Office du Travail, Rapport sur l'apprentissage.

19. AN F12 7621: Enquête d'apprentissage, Syndicat des sculpteurs-décorateurs, Paris.

20. AN F12 7621: Enquête d'apprentissage, 1902, doc. 228—Model apprenticeship contract.

21. For support for this argument, see Lee Shai Weissbach, *Child Labor Reform in Nineteenth-Century France: Assuring the Future Harvest* (Baton Rouge, La., 1989), esp. pp. xiii, 2, 86, 141-42; and Colin Heywood, *Childhood in Nineteenth-Century France: Work, Health, and Education among the Classes Populaires* (Cambridge, 1988), chap. 7.

22. For the more standard and more economistic analysis of the collapse of apprenticeship, see Pierre Quef, *Histoire de l'apprentissage* (Paris, 1964), pp. 125-61.

23. The debate on the meaning and logic of the *compagnonnages* is energetic. While William Sewell argues that the *compagnonnage* existed in a symbiotic relation with the corporations of the Old Regime and produced a mirrored world of their ritual (Sewell, *Work and Revolution in France*), Michael Sonenscher disagrees fiercely. See his "Mythical Work: Workshop Production and the Compagnonnages of Eighteenth-Century France," in *The Historical Meanings of Work*, ed. Joyce, pp. 31-63. Sonenscher argues that if the *compagnonnages* mirrored any Old Regime organization, it was the trade-specific confraternities, not the corporations, but that such arguments are in any case inadequate because they cannot account for the durability of the *compagnonnage* in the first forty years of the nineteenth century. Cynthia Truant, on the other hand, emphasizes the ritual function of the *compagnonnage* and argues for the importance of those rituals in breaking the artisans away from their birth families and fully incorporating them into the trades. Cynthia Truant, "Compagnonnage: Symbolic Action and the Defense of Workers' Rights in France, 1700-1848" (Ph.D. diss. University of Chicago, 1978). Mary Ann Clawson makes a similar argument, emphasizing the masculine quality of these organizations, "Early Modern Fraternalism and the Patriarchal Family," *Feminist Studies* 6 (1980): 368-91. I am not fully persuaded by any of the arguments alone, and while this is not the place to develop a fully elaborated critique of this literature, my discussion here is an attempt to pirate from all of them fruitfully and respectfully.

24. It has been claimed that the *compagnonnage* did not play an important role in training cabinetmakers but was limited to carpenters and finish carpenters—to the woodworkers more properly in the construction business. See, for example,

Pierre du Maroussem, *La question ouvrière: Les ébénistes du faubourg Saint-Antoine* (Paris, 1892), p. 68. While it is true that the *compagnonnage* was first and foremost an organization of workers in the building trades, this was not exclusively the case. In addition, many cabinetmakers were recruited from within the ranks of the finish carpenters. For this argument, see the reliable Ministère du Travail, Office du Travail, *Associations professionnelles ouvrières* (Paris, 1894–1904), vol. 2, pp. 674–75; and Remi Gossez, *Les ouvriers de Paris* (Paris, 1967), p. 143.

25. For the regulations of the furniture guilds concerning distribution, see AN AD XI 22: "Menuisiers, ébénistes, tourneurs, layetiers (1670–1780)."

26. Verlet, *L'art du meuble à Paris au XVIIIe siècle*, p. 72.

27. This norm was true despite the existence of several guilds that sold and did not make furniture: the guild of *tapissiers, miroirtiers,* and *marchands de meubles* (upholsterers, mirror-makers, and furniture dealers) and the guild of the *marchands merciers, grossiers,* and *jouailliers* (dealers in fabrics and notions, wholesalers, and jewelers). See AN AD XI 27: Tapissiers, miroirtiers, marchands de meubles (1611–1756). Included here are the relevant court rulings concerning the guild. It was the ruling of April 18, 1598, that gave the *marchands tapissiers* (upholstered furniture dealers) the right to sell furniture if they bought it from a *maître menuisier* (master furniture maker within a guild) and stamped it with their mark. For an old but useful account of the guild of merchants, see Pierre Vidal and Léon Duru, *Histoire de la corporation des marchands merciers, grossiers, jouailliers* (Paris, 1911); see also AN AD XI 22, which contains the documentation on this guild.

28. A classic example is Henri Fourdinois, who created and ran a leading Parisian furniture shop, la maison Fourdinois. In the 1880s, when the shop was well established, he started publishing thoughts on taste and furniture, including "Quelques reflexions sur le mobilier à propos de l'union centrale," *Revue des arts décoratifs* 3 (1882–83): 161–72; "De l'état actuel de l'industrie mobiliaire," *Revue des arts décoratifs* 5 (1884–85): 537–44; and the monograph *Etude économique et sociale sur l'ameublement* (Paris, 1894). He donated the drawings and photographs of his company to the Bibliothèque Forney, the library created to serve Parisian furniture makers. They now form an essential component of the iconographic collection there. He also lectured on taste and participated on commissions devoted to assessing education in the furniture trades.

29. The Union Centrale des Arts Décoratifs, devoted to improving the situation in the decorative arts, was founded in 1864. Two years later a library was founded under its auspices, and four years later a private school devoted to these trades, the Collège des Beaux Arts Appliqués à l'Industrie (Middle School for Fine Arts Applied to Industry) was established. A public school, the École Professionnelle d'Ameublement (Furnishings Trade School), or the École Boulle (named after a famous seventeenth-century French cabinetmaker, André-Charles Boulle), was founded exactly twenty years later, and a public library for the decorative arts, the Bibliothèque Forney, was created in 1886.

30. Decorating magazines and books proliferated dramatically in the last

third of the nineteenth century. While this expansion included both trade journals and books and periodicals intended to guide consumers, it is the consumer
guides whose multiplication was especially striking. Besides the *Revue des arts
décoratifs* (1880), one may cite, *Art pour tous* (1861); *L'art* (1875); *Art et
décoration* (1897); and *L'art décoratif* (1898), among many other magazines and
books proffering decorating advice.

31. I am endebted to George Chauncey and Carla Hesse for bringing this
point to my attention. On dandies and the question of the masculinity of men
interested in aesthetics, see Marylene Delbourg-Delphis, *Masculin singulier: Le
dandysme et son histoire* (Paris, 1985); and Michel Lemaire, *Le dandysme de
Baudelaire à Mallarmé* (Paris, 1978).

32. On the "feminine" nature of taste, see, among many other texts, Antony
Valbregue, "Les arts de la femme," *Revue des arts décoratifs* 18 (1898); and
Armand Audiganne, *La lutte industrielle des peuples* (Paris, 1868), pp. 184-89.
Two famous taste professionals of the late nineteenth century whose sexuality
certainly caused some speculation were the brothers Goncourt.

33. Audiganne, *La lutte industrielle des peuples,* pp. 184-89.

34. There is a large archival basis for the argument in this section. The
Archives de la Préfecture de Police (APP) in Paris has extensive records of worker
organization, as do the series F12 and F17 in the National Archives (AN). The
archival series and printed texts I have used to constitute this "discourse" are AN
F12 2370-2374: Organisation ouvrière, salaires, 1849-69; AN F17 14406:
Associations professionnelles, renseignements et statistiques sur l'organisation
professionnelle, 1888-1918; AN F17 13636: Fédération nationale de l'ameublement, 1909-26; AN F17 13845 and 13846: Grèves Ameublement, ouvriers des
fabriques de meubles, 1911-34; APP Ba 148: Chambres syndicales des ouvriers
ébénistes, 1872-86; APP Ba 168: Grève des ébénistes, menuisiers, ouvriers en
meubles sculptés, 1871 à 1889; APP Ba 181: Grèves des ouvriers tourneurs sur
bois, 1881-82; APP Ba 182: Grèves des ouvriers tapissiers, 1882-83; APP Ba
1,372: Grève des ouvriers ébénistes de 1891 à 1909; APP Ba 1433: Menuisiers à
façon de 1876 à 1879; APP Ba 147: Société de solidarité et de prévoyance et
Chambre syndicale des tourneurs en chaises, 1871-95; Chambre syndicale des
ouvriers en meuble sculpté, 1872-79; Union corporative et syndicale du meuble
sculpté, 1879-85; APP Ba 1422: Ébénistes en meuble sculpté, 1886-1904;
Ébénistes en tables de nuit, 1893-97; Ébénistes, 1884-85; Employés du commerce
—meuble, 1895.

The most salient primary printed sources are Association des Ouvriers Ébénistes
[Paris], *Statuts* (Paris, n.d.); Coster, *Organisation du travail. Ébénisterie française.
Projet d'annonciation générale dans toute la France entre fabricants ouvriers et
commissionnaires* (Paris, 1851); Anon., *Chambre syndicale des ouvriers ébénistes
de la Seine* (Paris, 1881); Jean-Paul Mazaroz, *Les deux phases d'organisation de
la corporation du meuble sculpté de Paris, suivi de la dénonciation des corporations politiciennes contre les patrons et ouvriers du travail national* (Paris, 1881);
Jean-Paul Mazaroz, *Causes et conséquences de la grève du faubourg Saint-
Antoine d'octobre à novembre 1882* (Paris, 1882); *Société de secours mutuels*

des ébénistes de Paris (Paris, 1881, 1883-84, 1887, 1888, 1889, 1896); Chambre syndicale de l'ameublement, *Bulletin* (Paris, 1882-1935); V. E. Veuclin, *Quelques notes inédites sur la corporation des mouleurs de bois de Paris* (Bernay, 1888); and Chambres syndicales de la ville de Paris et du département de la Seine, *Historique des métiers composant le groupe et de leurs syndicats* (Paris, 1900).

35. For a somewhat different approach to this problem, see Weissbach, "Artisanal Response to Artistic Decline."

36. Ministère du Travail, Office du Travail, *Associations professionelles ouvrières,* vol. 2, pp. 186-87.

37. Gossez, *Les ouvriers de Paris,* pp. 141-43.

38. Ministère du Travail, Office du Travail, *Associations professionnelles ouvrières,* vol. 2, pp. 691-700.

39. See, for example, the major furniture makers' strike in the fall of 1881, where the central issue was a wage cut of 10 centimes per hour. APP Ba 168: January 8, 1882. As in other trades, the standard strike-breaking strategy was to hire foreign workers, especially German and Italian workers. See, for example, APP Ba 168: November 26, 1881.

40. Good examples of this approach include Perrot, *Les ouvriers en grève;* Hanagan, *Logic of Solidarity;* and Shorter and Tilly, *Strikes in France.*

41. For a theoretical discussion of this concept, see, among many others, Joshua A. Fishman, *Sociolinguistics: A Brief Introduction* (Rowley, Mass., 1970); Dell Hymes, *Foundations in Sociolinguistics: An Ethnographic Approach* (Philadelphia, 1974); and John Gumperz, *Discourse Strategies* (Cambridge, 1982).

42. For a discussion of this kind of mechanism in the abstract, see Erving Goffman, *Forms of Talk* (Philadelphia, 1981), pp. 68-69.

43. APP Ba 1422: Union meeting of February 27, 1890, where it was stated that there was to be no discussion of politics. See also APP Ba 1422, April 15, 1889, which contains the new statutes of the trade union. This was a new group that split from the local for political reasons. Perhaps still healing from that schism, they prohibited all political discussion.

44. It should be noted that while I am talking about strikes, mutual aid societies, and unions in one breath, there are distinctions salient in other contexts that I am intentionally ignoring here. For example, Michelle Perrot sharply distinguishes unions from strikes. She argues that strikes developed in response to economic liberalism and that their development was independent from that of unions. In fact, the heyday of strikes—from 1864 to 1890—was brought to an end by the domination of heavily organized unions. Perrot, *Les ouvriers en grève.* An important analysis of the relation between mutual aid societies and other forms of labor action may be found in Michael David Sibalis, "The Mutual Aid Societies of Paris, 1789-1848," *French History* 3 (1989): 1-30.

45. The argument for the state as interlocutor is common to all of the labor histories cited above. The masculinity of organized labor, which at times veered toward misogyny in its tendency to articulate its conceptualization of women workers as evil competition, has also been well documented. See, for example, the classic text, Marie-Hélène Zylberberg-Hocquard, *Femmes et féminisme dans*

le mouvement ouvrier français (Paris, 1981). For two important analyses of the British case, see Sonya O. Rose, "Gender Antagonism and Class Conflict: Exclusionary Strategies of Male Trade Unionists in Nineteenth-Century Britain," *Social History* 13 (1988): 191-208; and Barbara Taylor, " 'The Men Are as Bad as their Masters . . . ': Socialism, Feminism, and Sexual Antagonism in the London Tailoring Trade," *Feminist Studies* 5 (1979): 248-66. For an analysis of the gendering of labor within political economy to which organized labor was responding, see Joan Wallach Scott, " 'L'ouvrière! Mot impie, sordide:' Women Workers in the Discourse of French Political Economy, 1840-1860," in *The Historical Meanings of Work*, ed. Joyce, pp. 119-42. For French workers' discourse on women, see Joan Wallach Scott, "Work Identities for Men and Women," in her *Gender and the Politics of History* (New York, 1988); and Michelle Perrot, "L'éloge de la ménagère dans le discours des ouvriers français au XIXe siècle," *Romantisme* 13 (1976): 105-21.

46. For a very different approach to the transition from defense of a craft to defense of a class, see Margot Stein, "The Meaning of Skill: The Case of the French Engine-Drivers, 1837-1917," *Politics and Society* 8 (1979): 399-427.

47. For an insightful discussion of this phenomenon in the United States, see Elizabeth Faue, " 'The Dynamo of Change': Gender and Solidarity in the American Labor Movement of the 1930s," *Gender and History* 1 (1989): 138-58.

48. This argument is supported, in a different geographic and temporal context, by Merry E. Wiesner, "Guilds, Male Bonding and Women's Work in Early Modern Germany," *Gender and History* 1 (1989): 125-37. Wiesner argues that journeymen's organizations came to exclude women most emphatically at the moment when men's and women's social roles were overlapping more.

49. For this notion of class being created by the process of representation, see Pierre Bourdieu, "What Makes a Social Class? On the Theoretical and Practical Existence of Groups," *Berkeley Journal of Sociology* 32 (1987): 1-17.

50. For a cogent analysis of the multiplicity of speech communities (and identities) that members of the working class may inhabit and possess, see Stuart Hall, "The Problem of Ideology—Marxism without Guarantees," in *Marx 100 Years On*, ed. Betty Matthews (London, 1983), pp. 57-85, esp. p. 77. Even Hall, however, assumes here too much fixity of identity. He does not articulate the possibility that one individual could interact in the world in different roles at different moments—sometimes as a worker, sometimes as a father, sometimes as a consumer—and that each of these roles or identities might be perceived as multivocal and multilocational. A worker does not always speak in the same voice or in the same way or say the same thing, even about his or her life at labor. This approach has been most thoroughly elaborated by feminist theorists, although in an ahistorical way, tending to assume that this process of fragmentation or multiplication is always more or less the same, even if the identities might shift. See Denise Riley, *Am I That Name? Feminism and the Category of 'Women' in History* (Minneapolis, 1987), chap. 1.

For one of the few studies that convincingly treats this fragmentation of identity historically, that is, as resulting from a particular moment in the development of capitalism (and in the process understands it as producing alienation), see Henri Lefebvre, *Critique de la vie quotidienne* (Paris, 1958 [1947]), vol. 1, p. 22 and passim.

51. There were, for example, very elaborate shop libraries in at least several of the furniture manufacturers making high quality furniture from mid-century on. These libraries contained technical treatises on the property of wood and metal, geometry books, drawing manuals, decorative arts periodicals (sometimes in several languages), exhibition catalogues from fine arts as well as decorative arts shows, and histories of architecture and furniture. These libraries would loan books to the shops' workers so they could study them at home in their leisure. The deterioration of the trade-controlled culture of production was not, therefore, as complete or as linear as might be imagined.

Unfortunately one of these libraries, that of the Maison Schmidt, originally of the faubourg Saint Antoine, now of Saint Maur, was destroyed in 1986. Remnants of another, that of the Maison Rinck in the passage de la Bonne Graine in the faubourg, still exist and can be studied. Parts of the shop library of the Maison Fourdinois, including photographs and drawings, were also given to the Bibliothèque Forney and can be consulted there.

52. On the general history of the fairs, see John Allwood, *The Great Exhibitions* (London, 1977); Philippe Bouin and Christian-Philippe Chanut, *Histoire française des foires et des expositions universelles* (Paris, 1980); Maurice Isaac, *Les expositions internationales* (Paris, 1936); *Le livre des expositions universelles, 1851-1989* (Paris, 1983); Richard D. Mandell, *Paris 1900: The Great World's Fair* (Toronto, 1967); Werner Plum, *Les expositions universelles au 19e siècle: Spectacles du changement socio-culturel* (Bonn-Bad Godesberg, 1977); Paul Greenhalgh, *Ephemeral Vistas: The Expositions Universelles, Great Exhibitions, and World's Fairs, 1851-1939* (Manchester, 1988).

53. This "crisis" was widely discussed. See, for example, the many instances in the important magazine *Revue des arts décoratifs:* Georges Duplessis, "Le département des estampes à la Bibliothèque Nationale: Indications sommaires sur les documents utiles aux artistes industriels," *Revue des arts décoratifs* 6 (1885-86): 336; Victor Champier, "La maison modèle: Études et types d'ameublement," *Revue des arts décoratifs* 3 (1882-83): 20; "Le goût du vieux en art," *Revue des arts décoratifs* 5 (1884-85): 592-94; Henri Fourdinois, "Quelques réflexions sur le mobilier à propos de l'Union Centrale," *Revue des arts décoratifs* 3 (1882-83): 164-65.

54. See *Rapports des délégués des ouvriers parisiens à l'Exposition de Londres* (Paris, 1862); and *Exposition universelle de 1867. Commission ouvrière de 1867. Recueil des procès-verbaux des assemblées générales des délégués et des membres des bureaux électoraux . . . recueillis et mis en ordre par Eugène Tartaret,* 2 vols. (Paris, 1868-69).

55. See, for example, the debate between Kaplow and Rancière: Jeffry Kaplow, "Parisian Workers at the Universal Exhibitions of 1862 and 1867" (Paper presented at the conference on Work and Representations at Cornell University, 1984); Jacques Rancière and Patrice Vauday, "En allant à l'expo: L'ouvrier, sa femme et les machines," *Les révoltes logiques* 1 (1975): 5-22.

56. Madeleine Rebérioux, "Approches de l'histoire des expositions universelles

à Paris du Second Empire à 1900," *Bulletin du centre d'histoire économique et sociale de la région lyonnaise* 1 (1979): 198.

57. Ibid., p. 199.

58. The argument has been made that the artisans were completely uncensored in their reports. Mandell, *Paris 1900,* p. 13. The upholsters did, however, complain about the "narrowness" of the format. "Tapissiers," in *Exposition universelle de 1867,* ed. Devinck, vol. 3, p. 15. Most of my examples of artisanal opinion expressed at the fairs come from Devinck's three volumes. The texts are fuller than those in the Tartaret volume referred to in note 54 above.

59. "Tapissiers," p. 15.

60. For this kind of usage of *connaissances,* see Ludovic Simon's piece on the Bibliothèque Forney in which he praises it for providing the workers with *connaissances* and says nothing about *savoir.* "Une Grande Oeuvre" in *Ville de Paris,* July 4, 1884 (available in ADS VR 216). It is interesting that there is in French no commonly used word for skill—*habilité* or *qualification* is about as close as one comes.

61. They were not alone. Other artisans made similar objections. Poirier, Gobert, and Levallois, "Découpeurs, marqueteurs," in *Exposition universelle de 1867,* ed. Devinck, vol. 1, p. 19; C. Niviller, "Dessinateurs d'ameublements," in *Exposition universelle de 1867,* ed. Devinck, vol. 1, p. 22; Michel, Jules, Waaser, Lejeune, "Découpeurs à la mécanique," in *Exposition universelle de 1867,* ed. Devinck, vol. 1, p. 7; Destres and Spoetler, "Menuisiers en sièges," in *Exposition universelle de 1867,* ed. Devinck, vol. 2, p. 16.

62. Michel, Jules, Waaser, Lejeune, "Découpeurs à la mécanique," p. 8.

63. Ibid.

64. Descamps and Beaujean, "Tourneurs en chaises," in *Exposition universelle de 1867,* ed. Devinck, vol. 3, p. 8; Niviller, "Dessinateurs d'ameublements," p. 22.

65. Descamps and Beaujean, "Tourneurs en chaises," p. 8; Loremy and Crisey, "Doreurs sur bois," in *Exposition universelle de 1867,* ed. Devinck, vol. 1, p. 7.

66. Niviller, "Dessinateurs d'ameublements," p. 22.

67. Baude and Loizel, "Ébénistes," p. 13.

68. Niviller, "Dessinateurs d'ameublements," p. 22.

69. Ibid.

70. Baude and Loizel, "Ébénistes," p. 13.

71. Lesieur, Lagoutte, and J. Durand, "Menuisiers en meuble antique," in *Exposition universelle de 1867,* ed. Devinck, vol. 2, p. 1.

72. Ibid.

73. Ibid.

74. Baude and Loizel, "Ébénistes," pp. 22-23.

75. J. Fresson, *Conférences sur le meuble* (Paris, 1887), p. 66.

76. Descamps and Beaujean, "Tourneurs en chaises," p. 6; Stoerckel and Prevost, "Tourneurs sur bois," in *Exposition Universelle de 1867,* ed. Devinck, vol. 3, p. 17; Tabletterie et fantaisie de Paris," in *Exposition Universelle de 1867,*

ed. Devinck, vol. 3, p. 20; Loremy and Crisey, "Doreurs sur bois," p. 1; Lesieur, Lagoutte, and Durand, "Menuisiers en meuble antique," p. 1; Destres and Spoetler, "Menuisiers en sièges," p. 17.

77. Rebérioux, "Approches de l'histoire des expositions," p. 199.

78. Ibid., p. 201.

79. The discussion during the 1860s concerning the crisis of drawing made clear that only limited knowledge was appropriate. See, for example, Brongniart, "De l'enseignement du dessin en 1867," in *Exposition universelle de 1867,* ed. Michel Chevalier (Paris, 1868), pp. 402-10. On furniture makers revolutionary tendencies, see Auguste Van Doren, *L'ébénisterie à Bruxelles et à Paris* (Bruxelles, 1860), pp. 50, 52; and Thomas Funck-Bretano, "La Ville du Meuble," *La nouvelle revue* 76 (1892): 272.

MICHAEL HANAGAN

Commentary: For Reconstruction in Labor History

William Sewell may be right that there is no crisis in French labor history and that good work continues to be done, but there is more than the usual turmoil among labor historians. For decades, labor history has been a field strongly influenced by scholars, often Marxists, dissatisfied with the dominant political and economic order who sought to use labor history to explore alternative political possibilities and to persuade others of the plausibility of unpopular political movements. Frank Jellinek's concluding sentences in his study of the Paris Commune reveal this classic vision: "The Commune was only the first stage; the Russian October was the second. They are intimately linked, historically and traditionally, in the minds of those workers of France who, in numbers yearly increasing, demand each Whit Sunday at the Mur des Fédérés 'Les Soviets partout!' "[1] Workers, influenced by an analysis of historical events, surge forward to reproduce the event, only this time, learning from the past, they do so triumphantly.

Suppose the point of labor history is not to fight "in a battle fought over again / my king a lost king and lost soldiers my men" but to use the knowledge of the past to repeat successes and avoid defeats. Then, William Sewell's claim that "the organized working class seems less and less likely to perform the liberating role assigned to it in both revolutionary and reformist discourses about labor" raises fundamental questions. This is particularly the case since Sewell casts doubt on the *reformist* as well as the revolutionary enterprise of labor history. For those who share Sewell's concerns, proposals to rethink labor history need to address the issue of why study labor history at all. Does the study of labor history bear any but the most distant relationship to contemporary politics? Do other historical terrains provide more useful vantage points?

While the previous essays suggest many useful perspectives on labor history, I want to focus on the extent to which they present an approach to politics that includes strategies for organizing social groups in concerted opposition to state power or even for assuming state power. By *politics,* I mean practices relating to a polis, or in more modern terms, states. In my sense of the term, politics includes relations with local and national government as well as bureaucratic and judicial structures. I argue that labor history should focus on investigating the role of the working class in changing political institutions. This concern may seem unremarkable, but it is actually of decisive importance for it bears on our choice of investigative tools. Whatever else they have to offer, the efforts of post-modernists and adherents of critical theory to recast historical studies cannot adequately deal with popular struggles, political movements, and states. If these are our questions, then post-modernism and critical theory are not likely to be immediately involved in our answers. You cannot get here from there.

William Sewell's heroic efforts to rethink labor history reveal many of the difficulties endemic to post-modernist, "figurative and linguistic" frameworks. In place of materialist interpretations accepted by "most labor historians," Sewell seeks to combine a variety of perspectives: the later work of Michel Foucault, the cultural anthropology of Clifford Geertz, and the methodological individualism of the game theorists. Sewell attributes the current disarray in labor history to materialists who focus on "the economy" because they believe it is somehow particularly "material." Materialists come in great variety; they include Marvin Harris, David Harvey, Terry Eagleton, and Raymond Williams and such labor historians as E. P. Thompson and David Montgomery.[2] Yet none of these fits Sewell's description of materialists, and Sewell's own conception of materialism is curiously vague. At times he contrasts "material" with the mental, at other times with the cultural, and at other times with the immaterial. Sewell does not take into account that the foremost belief of modern materialists is the inextricable connection between matter and mind. Materialists are skeptical of the claims of "idealists" (most notably those in the Cartesian tradition) who see mind and matter as distinct entities which depend on nothing else for their existence.[3] Materialists may "privilege" the material insofar as they assert that mental processes grow out of material processes and that the physical world came before the human, but this is a far cry from asserting that cultural or intellectual processes are pale ghosts of flesh-and-blood impressions.

Instead of defining *materialism,* Sewell substitutes a long but highly interesting digression concerning proletarianization. Because materialist labor historians regard proletarianization as preeminently material, they have used it as an "omnibus, all-purpose causal force." Sewell's emphasis on the substantial degree of reskilling occurring over the course of industrialization is important for labor historians, but it is based on an interpretation of economic processes that is as material as anything to which he objects.[4]

Actually, the dichotomy between matter and mind Sewell attributes to materialists is characteristic of idealists who, since Plato, have argued for the existence of two separate and unequal worlds: the "pure" world of the idea and the contaminated world of the material. A striking example of an idealist view incorporated within Sewell's own rhetoric is his repeated reference to the "natural sciences" and the "human sciences." In this view, championed most prominently by Wilhelm Dilthey, the existence of human consciousness so distinguishes humans from everything else that knowledge must be divided into two separate fields. Of course, Dilthey insists that knowledge of the world of consciousness is more secure and well founded than that of the natural world.[5]

Never used by materialists, the rhetoric that Sewell employs to characterize materialist positions is the familiar rhetoric of idealism that seeks to portray materialism as its own perverse reflection. Sewell's version of materialism is not derived from materialists who "inverted" Augustinianism, as he claims, but is remarkably similar to Augustine's own portrait of Manichaeism, which identified the material with evil and the spiritual with the good. For Augustine, Manichaeism's great crime was to make the spiritual a passive force that was impinged on by the violent activity of the material world.[6] After adopting Christian orthodoxy, Augustine repudiated the radical Manichaean doctrine of his youth in which "my vision was limited with my eyes, to material bodies; with my mind, to phantasms. . . ."[7] What Augustine mistook for his own movement away from materialism was in fact only a movement within the idealist camp. Following Augustine's lead and continuing through to Sewell, idealist common sense sees materialism as an inversion of itself, with materialists giving the same sort of priority to matter that the idealist gives to ideas.

Sewell's references to "neural" functions and their "inextricable organic and phylogenetic connection" are not so much a synthesis of idealism and materialism as a reiteration of materialist positions; unfortunately, his commitment to materialistic explanation breaks down just at the point where it becomes most crucial. He undertakes the highly problematic task of reconciling methodological individualism, an extreme variety of individualism, with radically anti-individualist approaches to culture and power, approaches that have encountered resistance because of their inability to identify the human agents who constitute and maintain them. If dualism/idealism is to be avoided, mediating structures are necessary to bridge the connection between structures of power and autonomous individuals.

One can sympathize with Sewell's failure to specify mediating structures without conceding that his juxtaposition of subjectivist and antisubjectivist interpretations amounts to a "post-materialist" synthesis. Seeking to combine Foucault and Geertz with the methodological individualism of the game theorists is an extremely daring undertaking, and it is not easy to imagine the mediating structures that could unify them. Methodological individualism is the "doctrine that all social phenomena—their structure and their change—are in principle explicable in ways that only involve individuals—their properties, their goals, their beliefs and their actions."[8] It is difficult to see how an individualist perspective can be reconciled with Foucault's own enduring interest in showing the historical development of subjectivism. While Foucault's later work does show more concern with subjectivism, it makes no concessions to methodological individualism: "One has to dispense with the constituent subject, to get rid of the subject itself, that's to say to arrive at an analysis which can account for the constitution of the subject within a historical framework. And this is what I call genealogy."[9] Even after he discovered "bio- and micro-power," Foucault retained his longtime belief that "the individual is an effect of power."[10]

Beyond Sewell's assumptions concerning materialism, what is ultimately most arguable is the proposed intellectual division of labor within his system: Michel Foucault gets power; Clifford Geertz, meaning; and Gary Becker, scarcity. In the present context, I want to discuss Foucault's share of the spoils. What will it mean for labor history if we take Foucault's concept of power seriously and orient our research in a Foucauldian direction, abandoning the focus of labor history on collective social protest, organized political movements, and states?

Sewell finds an "expanded sense of the political" in Foucault's later works that certainly do extend our understanding of power in new and exciting directions, but he fails to note Foucault's severely contracted view of the role of political movements and state structures.[11] With considerable consistency over the course of his writings, Foucault argues, "We must escape from the limited field of judicial sovereignty and State institutions, and instead base our analysis of power on the study of the techniques and tactics of domination." Since the "seventeenth and eighteenth centuries," sovereignty has been displaced by a "disciplinary power" that lies outside state institutions but "fundamentally" determines and grounds them. Disciplinary power has made impossible all but the most primitive kinds of social solidarity and local rebellion. Foucault champions "local, discontinuous, disqualified, illegitimate knowledge against the claims of a unitary body of theory."[12]

Labor historians needs to consider Foucault's arguments in the light of their own studies of nineteenth- and twentieth-century labor history and social protest. Do we believe that state power is the phantom Foucault describes? Do we believe that state power only abets disciplinary power and that workers' movement were and are incapable of wresting serious concessions from the state? Do we believe that the history of the nineteenth and twentieth centuries can be meaningfully seen as the drying up of solidarity and the triumph of individuation? Labor historians who do not assent to these propositions cannot welcome Sewell's new synthesis wholeheartedly.

While Sewell's schema leaves little space for politics, Leora Auslander's contribution employs linguistic analysis to make a more political argument. Her efforts to use a linguistic analysis that is sensitive to gender issues in the study of labor history are both promising and exciting, although her advocacy of a politics of aestheticism for the French labor movement is more dubious. Auslander claims that aesthetic impulses were central to the concerns of cabinetmakers in mid-nineteenth century France and argues that the trade unionists who spoke for the labor movement in this period should have represented these concerns within the labor movement. According to Auslander, "taste" was considered feminine, and so the gendering of tastefulness may have led to silence on matters of beauty. In suppressing aesthetic expressions, trade unions "accepted and inverted the terms of conservative class definition" used by political economists. She uses the reports of artisans from the London expositions to uncover the aesthetic demands of artisans because artisans, especially in the 1860s, used the world's fairs to say things that were unsayable in the context of organized labor.

Auslander, however, neglects the political context of the expositions; reports from both London expositions figure importantly in French labor history. Artisans hoped to use the published reports from the congress to influence government policy and to promote artisanal organization. These reports were thoroughly political documents, and the language must be understood within a specific political context. Highly skilled artisans adopted an aesthetic language when addressing a dictator's government because it facilitated their nationalist appeals. An understanding of their choice of language reveals the manifold possibilities of aesthetic justifications as well as their potentially dangerous ramifications when used *in a political context* to defend *an existing division of labor.* Aesthetic arguments could be used for defending the integrity of artisanal culture but also for defending the exclusion of women from the trades.

"Taste" was not only associated with beauty/woman but also with the role of the artist/man. Associating artisans with artists permitted highly skilled work to be seen not only as masculine but also as quintessentially French. In the view of Henri Tolain, a bronze-carver, active secretary of the 1862 artisanal delegation, and a chief organizer of the artisanal participation in this exposition, industrialism spread so easily in England because of the "absence of an artistic sentiment among the working classes." Thankfully, however, France was different: "in our country artistic industry is in its natural climate. Intelligence and taste develop in this beautiful land."[13]

Nationalist arguments were used to persuade Napoleon III to legalize workers' organizations that would ensure the maintenance of quality production. But arguments that stressed the artistic distinctiveness of skilled workers also served to heighten their sense of separation from the great mass of French workers and even from other highly skilled workers. A combination of artisanal pride and elitism can be seen in the 1867 report of a stained-glass worker, who objected to the presence of a stained-glass exhibit next to the glass blowers' and crystal cutters' exhibits: "Today we are placed next to the machines. We demand that we not be separated any more at the expositions from the great family of artists, of which we are a branch." The stained-glass worker did not want to be associated with those portions of the glass industry that were partially mechanized and that "instead of practicing an art, engage in commercial speculation. . . . It is distressing to think that almost always rewards are given for quantity not quality. . . . Ignorance governs talent."[14] But what could glass blowers and crystal cutters think of an attitude that hardly promoted a sense of solidarity?

The identification of the artisan with the artist promoted elitist attitudes that led these workers to look down on less skilled workers as "men-machines" and to regard contemptuously the less skilled women workers, whose numbers were increasing in many trades. In 1867, a number of delegations of skilled workers demanded the legal prohibition of women from the skilled trades. In the tinsmiths' 1867 report, the relationship between professionalism and gender is elaborated: "To each his *metier:* to the man, wood and metal, to the woman, the family and textiles."[15]

Because they could foster individual competition among workers and rivalry among skilled occupations within the same trade unions, and because they stimulated workers' aspirations toward establishing their own shops, aesthetic politics were not encouraged by association-minded trade unionists, who generally employed a more universalist rhetoric that could appeal to all the workers in the shop. Auslander's criticism of trade union officials whose attention to wages, hours, and working conditions promoted "a falsely unified image of a working class" suggests that trade union officials should have tried to make the employers aware of the variety of heterogeneous positions among the workers they represented in labor negotiations. Auslander is right to point out that labor unity was the product of negotiation and strategic calculation, not an expression of an essentialist core of identity within the working class, but can the forging of labor unity within the work group be seen as "false," and can we blame labor organizations for ignoring such an aesthetic politics, no matter the reality of such sentiments on the personal level? A politics of aestheticism that is not expanded to encourage the widest possible democratic participation is a potentially dangerous political program. As Terry Eagleton notes, "The more fundamental political question is that of demanding an equal right with others to discover what one might become, not of assuming some already full-fashioned identity which is merely repressed."[16]

The value of combining linguistic analysis and attention to gender issues in labor history can be seen even more clearly in Laura Downs's interpretation of the neglected strike movement of May–June 1917. She shows how gender conceptions were used by French employers and conservative trade unionists, who attempted to delegitimate and ignore the strikes of women workers in the war industries. Women going on strike in the war industries could not be assigned the same meaning as men going out on strike in these same industries.

Employers and reformist trade unionists agreed that political significance could not be attributed to women's protests. The full range of nineteenth-century stereotypes of female behavior was used to explain women's militancy. Women were motivated only by "greed," they were manipulated by saboteurs, or they were constitutionally hysterical. Downs points out that the sexual lives of women militants were subjected to careful scrutiny by the police authorities, who were keen to find out whether female activists were promiscuous. In part, this interest stemmed from the theory that female activists were deviant characters. Although Downs does not explore this issue, it may also have been because the exposure of "promiscuous" behavior could be used to discredit activists in the working-class community.

The refusal of the authorities and male trade union leaders to accord the same significance to female strikers that they did to male strikers undoubtedly helped repress these strikes more effectively, since women were denied the advantages of labor solidarity and political support, but it also led to a major miscalculation about the larger trend of strike actions. The strikes of May–June 1917 can be seen as the first wave of a truly massive strike upheaval. The failure to recognize early symptoms in the May–June strikes left authorities and trade unionists unprepared for what was to come.

Where Auslander and Downs apply linguistic analysis to particular cases to demonstrate its value, Donald Reid puts the case at a more general level. He explains why he as a well-known labor historian adopted linguistic analysis. "When I first read Jacques Rancière's *La nuit des prolétaires* in Paris in 1981, I was disoriented" begins Reid's account of his conversion to linguistic analysis. Subscribing to a representational theory of truth and writing sociological history, Reid was torn by "inner doubts." Upon reading Rancière, he found himself "moved, like the workers Rancière describes, whose lives were changed in ways they never totally understood. . . . " Like Luther pondering Romans 1:17 with a "long and troubled conscience," Reid had his own cloacal experience.[17] His second book is on the sewermen of Paris, and he emerged from it with a new confidence in his own interpretation. Having assimilated the lessons of deconstructionism, he can now "understand how a society reveals itself in the process of endowing with value and values what it excludes and those charged with its exclusion."

Why then is Reid still so uneasy?: "Questioning the old life involves living the new, with its attendant accusations of immorality and infidelity. It is in the nature of things that each side will claim there is no looking back to the old life, but this very insistence should raise suspicions." Although a conversionary conviction animates his narrative, he asks, "Must our labor history become primarily an analysis of the linguistic construction of experience in the texts of outside observers . . . ?" If this were the case, "we would lose a lot" of the knowledge his old life as a "new labor historian" had uncovered, "the experience and thought of [the common] people." To unite these two perspectives, Reid stresses the need to "see language as consisting of signs that derive meaning from their relations to (and differences from) one another *as well as* from reference to contexts or social and material realities outside of language. . . . " So far so good, but how are languages linked to contexts, and what does Reid mean when he demands that labor historians recognize that their accounts "of social reality and the political and moral narrative it supports or reflects also *ultimately* [emphasis added] rely on linguistic constructs"?

After his linguistic turn, Reid still casts an uneasy glance behind. Perhaps his unease conceals an only half-formulated need for his brand of linguistic analysis to engage the major questions posed by a more politically oriented labor history. In his critique of Gareth Stedman Jones's study of Chartism, Marc Steinberg combines linguistically oriented interpretations with class-oriented analysis. In the Chartist movement, he suggests, "the use of radical discourses was fundamentally relational and grounded in class conflict. Its sources were multiple, and the meanings produced through them were attuned to both the structure of class relations and the context in which they were used."[18] Steinberg's analysis accepts the value of linguistic analysis but attempts to place such analysis within a framework that includes large-scale social protest and national politics. Might not an analysis that links linguistic contests to class contexts provide a starting point for identifying areas of agreement and disagreement in labor history?

Identifying myself more closely with the analysis of mass social protest than with the analysis of language communities, I think an engagement is necessary. Labor historians can benefit from linguistic analysis. The rhetoric of labor history is laden with an unproblematized reliance on dialectics, totalism, and teleology. The conceptual framework of labor history has been male oriented. Today, after the important work of feminist theory, much of it remains male, and many of its key debates are posed in terms of highly suspect dichotomies: reform/revolution, in-itself/for-itself, wageworker/housewife. A crying need of labor history is for greater awareness of "multiplicity" and attention to contests over meaning.[19]

Yet it is genuine dialogue and reconstruction that labor history offers linguistic analyses. Reid claims that "by rejecting a single counterparadigm, the linguistic turn can extend as well as challenge other explanatory systems." The radical implications of the principled rejection of all "single" counterparadigms are never elaborated in his essay, however. Doesn't the perpetual discovery of heterogeneity threaten in time to become a kind of monotonous homogeneity? By uncovering internal inadequacies, a linguistically informed analysis may reveal the subtle authoritarianism of ideological appeals and their oppressive character, but does such analysis provide any help in reconstructing the systems it has dissolved? Can Reid's linguistic analysis provide help in building a society based on multiplicity and heterogeneity, when such a political movement itself would require a degree of homogeneity and unified action over a wide-ranging political terrain?

The real difficulty in accepting Reid's call for a "linguistic turn" is not whether linguistic analysis is "apolitical" or useful. Linguistic analysis can be both political and useful. What is at stake are our priorities. Should labor history *concentrate* its attention on the analysis of significance within linguistic communities instead of on mass movements and political structures? The question is not whether there are benefits to a preoccupation with linguistic analysis but whether they justify the sacrifices. Numerous studies in European labor history, particularly works in French labor history, show how political movements that ignore states and the struggle for control of state institutions have been ultimately overwhelmed by and succumbed to state power.[20]

While Sewell, Auslander, and Reid adopt a post-modernist rhetoric, Christopher Johnson turns to one of the post-modernists' most celebrated opponents for help in reconstructing labor history.[21] The critical practice of Jürgen Habermas, the best-known contemporary exponent of the Frankfurt School of critical theory, reflects well the open-minded, thoughtful ethic embodied in his critical theory, and Johnson's extremely evenhanded summaries of opposing positions follow in this tradition. Johnson offers an introduction to Habermas's vision of the progressively more aggressive attack of the "system" on the "lifeworld," as the bureaucratizing tendencies of modern political and economic life impinge on the cultural presuppositions of daily life. Johnson also discusses Habermas's efforts to ground a universal moral code in the assumptions of everyday language practice.

In terms of the study of political change, the problematical part of Habermas's argument is his assumption of the need for a highly integrated social system. Habermas conceives that modern society requires *very tight integration;* it exists and has needs and even has self-acting powers of its own. Indeed, just as Talcott Parsons did, Habermas sees the fundamental problem of social theory as the rationalization of society, with "social differentiation" as a general process of development. Habermas, like Parsons before him, more or less assumes that modern societies are highly integrated and does not admit that this might be a contested proposition. His failure to consider alternatives and to confront the difficult problems of demonstrating system integration leads to the same kind of circular reasoning that eventually did in the Parsonian system. Following Karl Mannheim and George Herbert Mead, Parsons and Habermas accept the need for ever greater functional integration over the long haul. When confronted with evidence of heterogeneity and lack of integration, they perceive a crisis of the system; they never consider that such evidence could just as plausibly be used to challenge their assumption of growing integration.

Considered as a historical assumption, Habermas's unexamined postulate of a highly integrated system puts severe limits on the political role of labor history; for him, the political history of the labor movement reveals the failure of socialist revolution, but it has little other relevance. Moreover, those influenced by him, such as Claus Offe, invoke social control interpretations to explain the development of the modern welfare state, because they do not recognize that labor movements have played a continuing role in shaping welfare state policy and that some aspects of social policy may permanently embody democratic conquests. It does not seem to matter to them whether welfare programs are administered democratically or bureaucratically, whether they are funded by workers or employers, whether they provide universal entitlements or not. All these characteristics of different welfare states are seen as functional to capitalism in the long term or as temporary concessions to the needs of lifeworlds that must come into increasing contradiction with the needs of the capitalist order.[22] A failure to distinguish among welfare states and to realize the degree to which working-class and reform movements have shaped the growth of welfare states in some industrialized countries and not in others naturally makes Habermas oblivious to the importance of reformist and socialist movements in the history of advanced capitalism and to the role of the state as a terrain for struggle.[23]

Labor historians may not dismiss the systemic characteristics of capitalism discussed by Habermas, but they are usually much more likely to stress the structural and to emphasize the role of temporality and sequence in social development. While seldom making their assumptions explicit, labor historians generally seem to portray society as an ordered, independent but *loosely integrated,* constantly changing set of relations, rules, and roles that holds a collectivity of social groups together. As distinct from structuralist sociologists and Hegelian philosophers, labor historians usually portray a society that has an organization, properties, and powers of its own that emerge through collective actions over time. To survive, it must be collectively reproduced by groups and individuals, and it is extremely likely to be transformed into different structures by their actions.[24] From this common historical perspective, it makes sense to discriminate important differences among European and American welfare states and to distinguish long-term structural effects of historical victories and defeats of reform movements.

In different ways, it seems both natural and surprising that a hardened champion of 1848 like Christopher Johnson would be sympathetic to Habermas. After all, Habermas's argument that human liberation is implicit in every act in which we try to make ourselves understood against the forces of ignorance and prejudice does reprise a certain radicalism of the 1848 variety. Habermas's communicative ethic recalls the radicalism of Dussardier in Gustave Flaubert's *Sentimental Education.* To Dussardier the republic signified "universal emancipation and happiness," and his faith was that "if only people would try . . . with good faith, an understanding could be reached."[25] To associate Habermas (and

Johnson) with 1848 is not meant to be dismissive. More than any other moment, either before or since, the democratic faith of 1848 was able to rally masses of Western Europeans to insurrection, and perhaps it was the last great opportunity for socialist revolution in the industrializing West.

Nonetheless, a consideration of the experiences of 1848 raises some questions about the usefulness of Habermas's arguments. First of all, Johnson's own classic work on Cabet and the Icarians suggests that the so-called new social movements that emphasize life-style and identity are hardly the new factor in capitalist development that Habermas and his cothinkers suggest. More important, Johnson's study criticizes the utopian faith in autonomous social movements and the need for engaged involvement in mass politics on the national level. Johnson portrays Cabet as a man who "personally vacillated between direct political engagement and a policy of utopia as more important than limited progress."[26] In the book, Johnson's sympathies are with Cabet, the man promoting limited progress. But isn't Habermas closer to Cabet the utopian than to Cabet the political activist? What does Johnson make of Habermas's claim that "in the past decade or two, conflicts have developed in advanced Western societies that . . . no longer flare up in domains of material reproduction; they are no longer channeled through parties and associations: and they can no longer be allayed by compensations . . . they are carried out in subinstitutional—or at least extra-parliamentary—forms of protest"?[27] When Claus Offe discusses the new social movements he supports, doesn't he sound more like Cabet the utopian than Cabet the participant in larger political movements? "Social movements," Offe writes, "relate to other political actors and opponents not in terms of negotiations, compromise, reform, improvement or gradual progress to be brought about by organized pressures and tactics but, rather, in terms of sharp antinomies such as yes/no, them/us, the desirable and the intolerable, victory and defeat, now or never, etc. Such a logic of thresholds, obviously, hardly allows for practices of political exchange or gradualist tactics."[28]

Habermas's assumption of Parsons's sociological burden, the assumption that social systems require a consensus of values, also seriously misleads him about the present, for it encourages him to attach great significance to the existence of the variety of heterogeneous dissenting groups comprised under the heading of "new social movements." Deprived of the assumption of high integration, these groups look more like routine affairs under capitalism. If new social movements are not new but, as utopian socialists, prohibitionists, nonconfomist radicals, or Social Catholics, form one important strand present in most nineteenth- and twentieth-century reform movements, and if the presence of such movements is not the sign of inevitable breakdown, what hope remains? Isn't the real question whether these diverse groups can form long-standing political coalitions that fashion enduring political identities? In this light, it may be worthwhile to reflect on the achievements and failures of 1848. In February of 1848, the demand for a democratic republic was in many ways able to capture the allegiance of a variety of divided and different groups. The communicative ethic of Habermas attempts to establish a universal moral claim for the extension of democratic tolerance and discussion. While the force of such a claim may be real, will it ever be, by itself, sufficient to hold together a society of groups as they discover the extent of their divergence and difference? Regarding politics, it almost seems that Habermas relies on the independent workings of a capitalist order that will produce an ever-increasing proliferation of new social movements. Whether or not this occurs, won't it still be the task of men and women to unite these movements at both the local and national levels by means of rational discussion and democratically organized parties and movements?

Because post-modernism and critical theory fail to confront large-scale social movements and national politics, they abdicate the field of political analysis to those, such as Gertrude Himmelfarb, who would deny or discount the impact of popular struggles and social movements on national politics.[29] Ronald Aminzade's contribution to this collection attempts to emphasize and to refashion the connection between popular culture and social class and national politics. In his important essay, Aminzade argues that part of the reason for the disillusion with class analysis of political action is a faulty conception of class. Aminzade agrees with many of the critics that too often social class, seen as a question of internalized values, identity, or consciousness, has been arbitrarily designated the substance, while gender, race, religion, and ethnicity are only accidents. Aminzade draws on the conception of class developed by Adam Przeworski, a conception that has striking parallels with arguments made in gender studies by numerous feminist scholars. This conception of class has a number of attractive features. It avoids claims that religious issues in modern-day Northern Ireland or racism in the Reconstruction South or nationalism in the Austro-Hungarian Empire are or were "really" about class, without denying the possibility that elements of religious, race, or national issues can be transformed into class issues.

Aminzade attempts to redefine class as an essentially political kind of rhetoric. Class is not simply what people are but a structural possibility within working-class life. Important determinants of whether people choose to adopt class identities include political strategies, the structure of social movements, the character of ruling coalitions, and the available alternative identities. Implicit within this definition is a conception of political autonomy as a terrain of genuine freedom within a constrained environment, that is, an assertion of neither the outright independence of the political arena nor its subordination "in the last instance" to the economic base. Class rhetoric cannot be used plausibly by just anyone; its usage is shaped by the specific structure of class reproduction, and there is nothing inevitable about the choice of a class rhetoric. The possibilities of class action are constrained by the pace of industrialization and proletarianization, but social movement activists, rank-and-file workers, and ongoing political divisions all play a role in deciding the political rhetoric and identity assumed by popular movements. Struggles over republican ideology, party structure, and the gendering of popular republicanism all helped shape the character of social movements in nineteenth-century France.

Yet while Aminzade allows for a variety of alternatives to class formation, he gives us little basis for comprehending the range of choices available to workers or for understanding why workers would ever make nonclass choices. Why, for instance, might a nineteenth-century French worker join a Catholic labor organization that scorned class identification? Much recent work, such as that of William Gamson, James Scott, Sydney Tarrow, and Robert Wuthnow, provides important suggestions.[30] The work of Sydney Tarrow is particularly helpful. Tarrow combines long-term cultural traditions, oppositional political cultures, and social mobilization to analyze the emergence of collective beliefs and their relation to collective action. In the case of French Social Catholicism and its influence on working-class life, a consideration of these elements highlights the existence of nonclass forms of protest that were available in nineteenth-century France and, together with Aminzade's own analysis, helps us understand why some groups of workers chose these paths.

The neglect of Social Catholicism and its influence among workers in late nineteenth-century France reveals one of those blindspots in the labor history tradition that derive from a teleological view of working-class history. Because socialism represented the future, European labor historians paid almost exclusive attention to the socialist labor movement. As many historians have noted, Catholicism was a pervasive cultural and intellectual influence in nineteenth-century French life, and republicanism often defined itself in relationship to its Catholic opponent. Despite periods of rapprochment, French Catholics found themselves in increasing opposition to the holders of state power in France between 1830 and 1914. The years between 1902 and 1906 witnessed a high point of conflict in which Catholics often took to the streets to oppose church inventories by secular officials. Increasingly in the years after 1877, a

Social Catholic "oppositional political culture" came into existence. In contrast to a republicanism that defined itself in terms of individual rights, the general will, and a gendered conception of "fraternity," Social Catholicism emphasized corporatism and familism. Where republicanism attracted secular skilled workers, Social Catholicism won converts in areas of Catholic belief and among unskilled women workers. As Don Kalb has shown for Catholic shoemakers in Central Brabant, Social Catholicism was an ideal vehicle for mobilized skilled workers and homeworkers who worked for small independent proprietors who employed family and friends.[31] All the more interesting, although many early working-class Social Catholics vehemently denied "class feelings," in time the Catholic trade union movement evolved into a genuine path to class formation, paralleling secular republicanism. The manner in which the Catholic labor movement became a variant type of class formation rather than an alternative to it deserves the close attention of labor historians.

Aminzade's concluding comment about the need to see historical change as "path-dependent, in which past choices at key forks in the road helped determine the subsequent trajectory" is an exciting new kind of historicism. The idea of historical development as a branching process is an important and intriguing idea that both provides support and raises problems for traditional class analysis. Implicit within this model of branching development when considered on an international scale is the possibility of an enduring reconfiguration of national politics in ways that retain class interest as a political force but relegate class movements themselves to a secondary or peripheral role.

Together, Przeworski's concept of class, a "path-dependent" concept of development, and the ongoing explorations of proletarianization can provide the basis for a revitalized labor history that would include not simply the study of the development of class consciousness but also the study of historical alternatives to class consciousness and the exploration of the ways in which class impulses are at once reshaped and retained within nonclass popular social movements. In contrast to the retreat from national politics and organized political movements implicit in so much of the work of Foucault and Habermas, this labor history would encompass an even wider variety of popular movements and political struggles within its purview. To assess the political possibilities open to labor movements within modern-day countries, we will need to understand the historical ways in which class has been reconfigured within the political systems of individual nations. Key moments in the branching process will need to be identified, and the specific ways in which class has been reconfigured must be delineated.

The results of such an analysis will not justify an appeal to class consciousness as a universal political solution in the traditional Marxist manner. As Adam Przeworski has noted, he is not a Leninist but a follower of that "other great Russian socialist thinker, Georgij Konstantinowich Pessim."[32] Nonetheless, the conclusions to be drawn from Aminzade's and Przeworski's arguments are not necessarily so pessimistic. Such a branching analysis, combined with a new conception of class as a structural choice, will highlight the important ways in which class developments shaped and continue to shape political process in advanced industrial countries. Instead of oscillating between a revolutionary utopianism and a despairing pessimism, labor historians can provide a more balanced perspective, based not only on a greater awareness of the relationship between labor's past and present but also on a new, if tempered and chastened, understanding of the unexploited possibilities for class actions contained within the present situation as well as a new awareness of the alternatives to class action.

In conclusion, the invigorating and stimulating currents of the new linguistic turn of labor history cannot be denied, but the wisdom of recentering labor history around linguistic analysis cannot be affirmed. In expressing my doubts, I am conscious of evaluating and interrogating these new approaches in terms that are not theirs and that many will find entirely beside the point. To accuse Michel Foucault of failing to discuss the role of national political movements is to summon him to a tribunal whose legitimacy he would not recognize; in his view, the whole project of seeking to discuss the strategy and tactics of large-scale movements is pretentious and absurd—and, ultimately, repressive. Even those who do not share Foucault's dismissal of theoretical discussion in politics as useless may find my concerns irrelevant. It may be that nationwide political popular movements, mass struggles, and democratic social reforms belong so thoroughly to the past that only antiquarians should be concerned with them. Yet it may be wise to contemplate whether the failure to consider a role for such movements is not symptomatic of pessimism and despair, derived not so much from an analysis of the past as from the serious defeats of progressive causes at the present time. If the virtue of history is to provide an enlarged perspective on human affairs, then it may be well to consider with what certainty we want to eliminate systematic discussion and analysis of large-scale political movements from our deliberations.

Notes

1. Frank Jellinek, *The Paris Commune of 1871* (New York, 1965), p. 429.

2. Marvin Harris, *Cultural Materialism: The Struggle for a Science of Culture* (New York, 1979); David Harvey, *The Condition of Postmodernity: An Enquiry into the Origins of Cultural Change* (Oxford, 1989); Terry Eagleton, *Criticism and Ideology: A Study in Marxist Literary Theory* (London, 1976); Raymond Williams, *Problems in Materialism and Culture* (London, 1980); E. P. Thompson, *The Making of the English Working Class* (London, 1963); David Montgomery, *Worker's Control in America: Studies in the History of Work, Technology, and Labor Struggles* (Cambridge, 1979).

3. To get an idea of contemporary debates between materialists and idealists, see C. V. Borst, ed. *The Mind/Brain Identity Theory* (New York, 1970).

4. For an interesting discussion of craft skills and the issue of reskilling, see Charles More, *Skill and the English Working Class, 1870-1914* (New York, 1980).

5. See Peter T. Manicas, *A History and Philosophy of the Social Sciences* (Oxford, 1987), chap. 7.

6. Peter Brown, *Augustine of Hippo* (Berkeley, Calif., 1969). Brown notes that the Manichees were the " 'Bolsheviks' of the fourth century" (p. 46).

7. Augustine, *Confessions* (Washington D.C., 1953).

8. Jon Elster, *Making Sense of Marx* (Cambridge, 1985), p. 5. On Elster, see Elliott Sober, Andrew Levine, and Erik Olin Wright, "Marxism and Methodological Individualism," *New Left Review*, no. 162 (1987): 67-83.

9. Michel Foucault, "Truth and Power," in *Power/Knowledge: Selected Interviews and Other Writings*, ed. Colin Gordon (New York, 1980), p. 117. See also Hubert L. Dreyfus and Paul Rabinow, *Michel Foucault: Beyond Structuralism and Hermeneutics* (Chicago, 1982), chaps. 8, 9.

10. Michael Foucault, "Two Lectures," in *Power/Knowledge*, ed. Gordon, p. 98.

11. On this point, see Sheldon S. Wolin, "On the Theory and Practice of Political Power," in *After Foucault: Humanistic Knowledge, Postmodern Challenges*, ed. Jonathan Arac (New Brunswick, N.J., 1988), pp. 179-202; and Michael Gane, ed., *Towards a Critique of Foucault* (London, 1986).

12. Foucault, "Two Lectures," p. 83.

13. Quoted in Daniel Willbach, "Work and Its Satisfactions: Origins of the French Labor Movement" (Ph.D. diss., University of Michigan, 1977), pp. 226-27.

14. Quoted in Ibid., p. 219.

15. Quoted in Ibid., p. 407.

16. Terry Eagleton, *The Ideology of the Aesthetics* (Oxford, 1990), p. 414.

17. On Luther's struggle, see Martin Brecht, *Martin Luther: His Road to Reformation, 1483-1521* (Philadelphia, 1985). Brecht is skeptical of Luther's "cloacal" experience (pp. 225-27).

18. Marc W. Steinberg, "Talkin' Class: Discourse, Ideology, and Their Roles in Class Conflict," in *Bringing Class Back In*, ed. Scott McNall (Boulder, Colo.,

1991), pp. 265-66. On deconstructionism, see Louis Menand, "Signs of the Times," *New York Review of Books,* Nov. 21, 1991.

19. See, for example, Julia Wrigley, *Class Politics and Public Schools: Chicago 1900-1950* (New Brunswick, N.J., 1982).

20. On the danger of the disappearance of politics in cultural analysis, see the contributions of Ellen Dubois, Mary Jo Buhle, and Temma Kaplan, "Politics and Culture in Women's History," *Feminist Studies* 6 (1980): 29-48.

21. For Habermas's critique of post-modernism, see *The Philosophical Discourse of Modernity,* trans. Frederick Lawrence (Cambridge, Mass., 1987). An important treatment of this same topic is Christopher Norris, *What's Wrong with Postmodernism: Critical Theory and the Ends of Philosophy* (Baltimore, 1990).

22. See David Held, *Introduction to Critical Theory: Horkheimer to Habermas* (Berkeley, Calif., 1980), pp. 366-67; and Russell Keat, *The Politics of Social Theory: Habermas, Freud, and the Critique of Positivism* (Chicago, 1981).

23. See Frances Mascia-Lees, Patricia Sharpe, and Coleen Ballerino Cohen, "The Postmodern Turn in Anthropology: Caution from a Feminist Perspective," *Signs* 15 (1989): 7-33; and Joan Wallach Scott, *Gender and the Politics of History* (New York, 1988).

24. See Christopher Lloyd, *Explanation in Social History* (Oxford, 1986), chap. 8.

25. Gustave Flaubert, *Sentimental Education* (London, 1961), pp. 217, 370.

26. Christopher H. Johnson, *Utopian Communism in France* (Ithaca, N.Y., 1974), p. 297.

27. Jürgen Habermas, *The Theory of Communicative Action,* trans. Thomas McCarthy (Boston, 1987), vol. 2, p. 392. See also Jean L. Cohen, "Strategy or Identity: New Theoretical Paradigms and Contemporary Social Movements," *Social Research* 52 (1985): 663-716.

28. Claus Offe, "New Social Movements: Challenging the Boundaries of Institutional Politics," *Social Research* 52 (1985): 830.

29. See "In Jefferson Lecture, Historian Assails New Approaches to Studying the Past," *Chronicle of Higher Education,* May 1, 1991.

30. William A. Gamson, "Political Discourse and Collective Action," in *International Social Movement Research,* ed. Bert Klandermans, Hanspeter Kriesi, and Sidney Tarrow (Greenwich, Conn., 1988), pp. 219-24; James C. Scott, *Domination and the Arts of Resistance: Hidden Transcripts* (New Haven, Conn., 1990); Sidney Tarrow, "Mentalities, Political Cultures, and Collective Action Frames: Constructing Meanings through Action," in *Frontiers of Social Movement Research,* ed. Aldon Morris and Carole Mueller (New Haven, Conn., forthcoming); Robert Wuthnow, *Communities of Discourse: Ideology and Social Structure in the Reformation, the Enlightenment, and European Socialism* (Cambridge, Mass., 1989).

31. Don Kalb, "Moral Production, Class Capacities, and Communal Commotion: An Illustration from Central Brabant Shoemaking (c. 1900-20)," *Social History* 16 (1991): 279-98.

32. Adam Przeworski, *Capitalism and Social Democracy* (Cambridge, 1985), p. 239.

GAY L. GULLICKSON

Commentary: New Labor History from the Perspective of a Women's Historian

William Sewell and Donald Reid use the term *crisis* in speaking of the current state of labor history, although they are not in agreement with each other. Reid declares the field to be "ripe for a mid-life crisis," while Sewell declares it is not in crisis but is lacking intellectual vitality. In a similar vein, Ronald Aminzade declares that class analysis is "neither dead nor buried" but is suffering, perhaps, because "class-reductionist explanations of politics have been thoroughly discredited." Despite their differing formulations of the current health of the field, the fact that the Sewell, Reid, and Aminzade contemplate the possibility of a crisis or death in the field is telling. As they and Christopher Johnson acknowledge in one way or another, it has become virtually impossible, given the current state of the labor movement in the West and the implications of feminist scholarship, linguistic analysis, and political theory, for labor historians to continue to ask the same questions, use the same paradigms, and write the same narratives that they have in the past.

Regardless of whether we regard labor history as being in a state of crisis or malaise, the questions posed by the historians in this volume and under discussion within the field in general are portentous. They not only reflect disarray but also pose enormous opportunities for the field. Labor historians appear to be poised on the threshold of an exciting new era, similar to the one they stood on in the 1960s and 1970s when the work of E. P. Thompson and others shifted the focus of labor history from leaders, organizations, and ideas to the workplace, community organization, and working-class culture.

The questions currently being asked by labor historians cover considerable terrain. Have we identified the right factors in our studies of class formation? Have we created the right (or the most useful) paradigms? What role did gender conceptualizations play in the formation of the working class and vice versa? What is the proper subject of labor history? What are the proper boundaries of the field? If we combine the study of class with the study of gender, what happens to the major questions, issues, topics, and tropes of these fields? What story or narrative are we to tell? How significant was the world outside the workplace to the formation of working-class culture? Should we focus more on the encounters between workers and bourgeois? Between men and women, husbands and wives, mothers and sons? Should we write a dual-focus narrative, a two-gender labor history, and if so, how are we to do it? Is linguistic analysis a useful tool for labor historians, or will it lead us away from real people, meaningful insights, and causal analyses into the esoteric realms of intellectual history? How did the labor movement become bureaucratized? How are we to relate theory to narrative? What is the relationship between economic change, class formation, and politics? And so the questions go.

Out of these and the host of other questions that might be addressed in relation to these essays, I would like to single out three overlapping issues that appear and reappear when one asks questions about integrating the study of gender and class, women and men: narratives, boundaries, and identity.

Narratives

Since the 1960s, the main objective of both the new (male) labor history and women's labor history has been to analyze the effects of industrialization on workers. Both fields have focused on the experiences of workers during and after the transition from an artisan-and-merchant-based economic system to factory-based capitalism, although as we move toward the end of the twentieth century, historians like Laura Lee Downs have begun to turn their attention to the period of "mature" industrialization. There are, however, important differences in the stories or major narratives told in each field. For male labor history, proletarianization has been the primary paradigm.[1] It has formed the structure for the narratives and has been the way in which historians have understood

or have made sense out of the history of male workers. Proletarianization
is a complex and important concept. As Sewell observes, it combines
"under a single aegis a number of empirically distinct processes." Most
important to the field, however, is the way in which it has placed the
working man in the center of history. When it is the operative paradigm
in labor history, technological developments and changes in the workplace
(especially the creation of the factory) are explored through their effects
on the worker. Questions of deskilling and reskilling, the formation of
class consciousness, and the origins of militancy are all pursued in terms
of the creation of either the proletarian or the proletariat.

Proletarianization has not played the same role in women's labor
history as it has in men's. This is not to say that women's historians have
not been concerned with the effects of industrialization on working
women. Indeed, this has been a major theme of research in women's
history beginning with Alice Clark's *Working Life of Women in the
Seventeenth Century* (1919) and Ivy Pinchbeck's *Women Workers and
the Industrial Revolution, 1750–1850* (1930), picking up again almost
half a century later with Louise Tilly and Joan Scott's *Women, Work, and
Family* (1978), and continuing down to the present day in Mary Blewett's
Men, Women, and Work (1988) and Laura Downs's essay in this volume.
This research on women workers has added immensely to our understanding of the process of industrialization and its effects on workers, and
in many ways parallels the research in the new labor history that focuses
on male workers.[2]

Nor is it accurate to say that women's historians have been oblivious to
the power of the concept of proletarianization. Indeed, its paradigmatic
power is so great that when I wrote *The Spinners and Weavers of Auffay,*
a study of the effects of proto-industrialization on the women and men of
the pays de Caux, I claimed significance for my findings under this
rubric. I explored whether the demographic behavior of proto-industrial
workers fit the pattern of their urban proletarian counterparts and argued
that proto-industrialization "allowed most families to resist the lure of
urban factory jobs and to maintain the traditional family economy until
well into the second half of the nineteenth century."[3] In short, I argued,
while proto-industrialization created a kind of halfway house between
cottage industries and factories, it delayed "real" proletarianization in the
Caux. Both for my own work and for that of other historians writing
about women workers, however, proletarianization appears more as a
touchstone than as an organizing paradigm for the narrative.

What makes women's labor history significantly different from men's is
the historian's need to account for two phenomena rather than one: the
impact of industrialization on women who stayed in the paid labor force

(or who were subsequently drawn into it); and the removal and withdrawal of women from paid employment as work moved into factories. No single paradigm has informed our understanding of these dual processes, partly because proletarianization as it has been defined and conceived by historians is a process that fits men's but not women's economic and cultural experiences, and partly because it is inherently difficult to develop one narrative structure or one organizing principle to account for the varied effects of industrialization on working-class women. As a result, women's labor narratives revolve around the related but separate themes of the sexual division of labor and the separation of spheres. These twin themes have allowed female labor historians to account for the impact of industrialization on women who stayed in the paid labor force and for the removal and withdrawal of women from it.

The separation of spheres has functioned in much of the women's history written in the last two decades in the same way that proletarianization has functioned in the new (male) labor history. It has been the trope that has, as Linda Kerber observed, "helped historians select what to study and how to report what they found."[4] Historians have used this trope so effectively and so consistently that it has "predisposed" readers to find arguments making use of it persuasive.[5] Marxist feminists have been drawn to the trope of separate spheres not just because it has played a dominant role in histories of bourgeois women but also because one of its earliest formulations is found in Friedrich Engels's conceptualization of the public and the private.[6] Even for historians focusing on women workers, the separation of spheres has formed a central, if unspoken, theme and organizing principle as they have sorted out the experiences of single, married, and widowed workers; addressed the problems of working wives and mothers; and explored how working women have coped with their own and society's feelings about their participation in the public sphere of work.[7]

The sexual division of labor is a closely related, but nevertheless distinct, concept. The conceptualization of some tasks as "women's work" and others as "men's work" has had a profound effect on women's employment opportunities, wages, and status within the workplace, the home, and the political arena. Demonstrating that the sexual division of labor was a product of a patriarchal value system and not a logical outcome of capitalism has been an important part of women's labor history.[8] Indeed, questions about the relationship between gender and skill have played much the same role in women's labor history that the question of the relationship between skill and militancy has played in male labor history.

As William Sewell points out, these sexual divisions of the labor force, based largely on a conceptualization of women as "incapable of or unsuited for" most tasks that were defined as skilled, was part of a web of mutually reinforcing assumptions and practices that severely limited women's job opportunities and wages. As Anne Phillips and Barbara Taylor put it, "Skill definitions are saturated with sexual bias."[9] Far from being based on some objective criteria, they have been "imposed on certain types of work by virtue of the sex and power of the workers who perform it."[10] Work performed by women that demands dexterity thus has generally been regarded as less skilled than work performed by men that demands strength, and when women and men have performed similar tasks, women's work has generally been classified as less skilled than men's. The paper box and carton industries are a classic case in point. As Phillips and Taylor explain the situation, "Paper boxes are produced by women working on hand-fed machines; the work is considered —and paid—as unskilled labour. Cartons are produced [by men] under a more automated process, and the work hence requires less individual concentration but it is treated as semi-skilled. [Moreover] . . . because of the similarities between the work of men and women in the carton industry . . . women in carton production are considered more skilled than [women] box workers."[11]

The significance of the sexual division of labor and the separation of spheres as motivating questions and concepts in women's labor history is also demonstrated in Jean Quataert's study of the transition to capitalism in the German states. Quataert demonstrates how economic interests could lead to the denigration of women's work when those interests interacted with sexual divisions of labor and public-private distinctions. The dilemma for women began in the seventeenth century, when "guildsmen established elaborate rules and regulations . . . that distinguished between professional, organized work, on the one hand, and nonprofessional, unregulated household labor, on the other."[12] As the distinction between professional public work and nonprofessional household work gained definitional power, men and especially women who worked at home in the textile and garment industries found their skills devalued, their professionalism undermined, and their wages debased. Since women rather than men were also culturally assigned responsibility for housework, the public-private distinctions had more serious consequences for women than for men, as all of their work, paid and nonpaid alike, came to be identified as housework. The enduring consequences of this identification of women with domesticity can be seen at the end of the nineteenth century, when elderly women who "spun, washed, ironed, or embroidered" for others in their own homes were denied pensions, while shoemakers and tailor apprentices, who also worked in their homes for customers, were granted them.[13] In large part, Quataert's research is directed toward determining the origins of the identification of women with domesticity, that is, the separation of spheres. That she sees it as an intellectual construct created by artisans by the time of the Thirty Years' War is interesting, not only because her research contributes to our understanding of women's labor history but also because it demonstrates the centrality of the separate spheres trope to our understanding of women's past.

Writing from a more avowedly feminist perspective than Quataert's, Phillips and Taylor called for Marxists to "rethink economic categories in the light of feminism" and to recognize that "gender hierarchy enters directly into the development of capitalist relations." This and their subsequent demand that "the socialist movement [be] freed from its ideology of masculine skills" so it could "confront the nature of capitalist work" are explicitly political in nature.[14] The article also makes, however, an implicit plea for labor historians to rethink the categories of skilled, semiskilled, and unskilled labor and to analyze the formative role gender conceptualizations have played in the development of Western capitalism.

Joan Scott made what had been an implicit challenge to labor historians explicit when she asked historians to analyze the role gender conceptualizations have played not only in the development of Western capitalism but also in their own conceptualization of that process. Scott argues that the narratives of class formation created by E. P. Thompson, Gareth Stedman Jones, and others have replicated rather than analyzed the gender values of the working men about whom they write.[15] Drawing on the insights provided by literary criticism to analyze "the contents and the textual strategies"[16] of *The Making of the English Working Class,* Scott argues that this formative work in the new labor history coded all that Thompson regarded as positive in the development of a working-class consciousness and movement as masculine and all that was negative as feminine.[17] As a result, proletarianization became a male, not a female, experience in the hands of Thompson and the labor historians who followed him.

What is most important about Scott's analysis is her point that while "women are fleeting actors in the pages of the book, the feminine is a central figure in the representation of working-class politics."[18] It is this representation that Scott now asks us to recognize and analyze. In the past two decades, women's historians have gone a long way toward restoring our sense of women as actors in the economic and political arenas and our understanding of the process of industrialization, but their work has remained largely on a track parallel to men's labor history, because of the sexual division of labor and the different metaphors used by historians to order and make sense out of their subject matter. Scott argues that we need to go beyond the writing of parallel histories for men and women, hoping that somewhere they will join to form one narrative, to a recognition of the role gender has played in the consciousness and politics of our subjects and in our reconstructions of the past.

Following in Scott's footsteps, I want to suggest that we also need to reformulate the tropes and paradigms that have informed and structured our understandings of men's and women's labor history. We need to amend proletarianization so that it becomes a concept encompassing the experiences of men *and* women, and we need to abandon the dualism of the separate spheres trope. Each has served us well in the past two decades. Each has allowed us to think in causal terms and has encouraged us to search for the values and structures that have informed, constrained, and encouraged individual and collective action. But each has also begun to predetermine and limit our view of the past. The conceptualization of class as a male experience and domesticity as a female experience misconstrues and oversimplifies the complexity of the processes and experiences we are trying to understand and explain. In short, we need to find a structure for our narratives and ways of understanding the past that will allow us to write a two-gender history that does not define one sex or the other (either implicitly or explicitly) as the enemy (or even as the "other") and that does not perpetuate the gender biases of our sources or our subjects.

Boundaries

I assume that such a new narrative will alter the boundaries of labor history. Since the 1960s, labor history has centered on workplaces, community organizing, and working-class culture. Defined out of most studies have been the home (the domestic sphere); political movements led by, motivated by, or concerned with noneconomic, nonmaterial, and nonsocialist interests; and the nonmaterial interests of workers. As the essays in this collection demonstrate, there are many aspects of workers' lives that it is time to include in our histories, many new questions to ask, and many new analytical techniques to use.

Christopher Johnson calls for expanding the boundaries of labor history in his discussion of Habermas's conception of the lifeworld and the "everyday life" historians in Germany. As he cogently notes, the labor movement became bureaucratized or "systematized" and divorced from a wide variety of lifeworld problems, even though movements developed around them "in the heyday of union and mass party formation." Labor historians have seldom explored the meaning and importance of these (nonmaterial) issues to workers or how and why labor organizations failed to champion them. To explore the lifeworld of workers and labor unions' and parties' disengagement from their members is to expand the boundaries of labor history in a variety of directions.

Leora Auslander pushes at the boundaries of labor history by challenging the notion of a unified working-class consciousness. She urges historians to look beyond the discourses of organized labor to find the variety of issues and interests that concerned working men and women. She examines, as a case in point, the significance of knowledge, skill, craft sense, and the creation of beauty for workers in the furniture trades. Far from claiming that such things were of equal concern in other trades, she argues for an exploration of the differences among working-class experiences and values. Responding to some labor historians' suspicions about the "instability and alien nature of linguistically informed history," Donald Reid calls for historians to take up "the linguistic challenge" and to explore the "ways in which language constructs rather than reflects identity, interests, intentions, and actions." Ronald Aminzade expands the boundaries of traditional labor histories in a variety of ways. He urges historians exploring the translation of class interests into political objectives to bear in mind that "institutions, such as political parties, and ideologies, like republicanism, play a key role in this process"; he calls on historians to situate local studies in the context of the international economy; and he demonstrates that the ideology and practice of republicanism, which shaped collective perceptions of class interests, political alliances, and the character of local politics, were "based on populist and fraternal (i.e., gendered) understandings of politics."

William Sewell calls for a comprehensive and radical overhaul of labor history, including the elimination of the paradigms and dichotomies that have informed work in the past, and a variety of theoretical strategies, most notably linguistic analysis. In particular, Sewell challenges the logic by which historians have distinguished the material from the nonmaterial/ideal/cultural, thereby defining the boundaries of their field, and asks us to "imagine a world in which every social relationship is simultaneously constituted by meaning, by scarcity, and by power."

Finally, Laura Downs's case study of the 1917 Parisian munitions strikes challenges historians' "classic distinction between 'narrow' struggles over shop-floor conditions and the more 'political' strike, motivated by broader concerns," and their "dismissive view of women's protest as preeminently unpolitical." Downs's work implicitly pushes at the boundaries of the subject matter of labor history by challenging historians to examine what they have and have not allowed themselves to see and analyze in their histories.

Taking up the challenges laid down by the historians in this volume will lead us to new questions, new ways of reading texts, and new ways of writing history, all of which will ultimately lead to a more complex model of reality, more inclusive narratives, and, I would say, better history.

Identity

In addition to pushing at the boundaries of labor history, the questions currently being asked about the significance and role of gender conceptions in the past have profound implications for the major subject of labor history—the male worker. He is *the proletarian,* especially when he works in heavy industry. Proletarianization happened to him. The questions that now arise are what about women workers and what about the women in the families of male workers? Were they being similarly proletarianized or did they somehow stand outside the process? Have we defined the process or concept correctly if only the experiences of men fit the definition?

My first introduction to the issue of class identity came in the spring of 1961 when Mr. Davis, my American Problems teacher at David Douglas High School in semirural, semisuburban Portland, Oregon, looked at me and said, "What class do you belong to?" This was a question no one had asked me before, and I did not know the answer. I rapidly considered the only three alternatives I knew—upper class, middle class, and working class—and responded, "the middle class." Mr. Davis then proceeded to ask a variety of other students the same question, and everyone of them gave the same response. We all declared ourselves members of the middle class. I am sure that Mr. Davis knew then what I figured out much later—none of us had given the correct answer. None of us (with one or two possible exceptions) was a child of the middle class. Our mothers were housewives or worked as clerks in stores, and our fathers held working-class or lower-middle-class jobs.

Reading these essays has reminded me of this experience, not simply because my friends and I made the classic American assumption that if we were Americans we must be middle class but also because I truly did not know the answer to the question. At age seventeen, I had no class identity. Later, I learned to identify myself as a child of the lower middle class, based on my father's occupation, but I learned this from reading books, not from my family. Now I ask myself why I privileged my father's occupation in determining my class origins. What about my mother's occupation? My grandparents' occupations? My family's values, educational levels, aspirations, income, friends, leisure activities, political views, attitudes toward unions, religious beliefs, racial attitudes, gender conceptions, cultural interests, class consciousness (or lack of class consciousness), and so forth? Why were all of these aspects of my family's life irrelevant in determining the class to which we belonged, and should they have been irrelevant?

The answer to this last question lies in the history of the conceptualization of proletarianization, in the fact that in its essence the concept is male. This is the point that Joan Scott makes in her analysis of *The Making of the English Working Class,* and it is a point the new labor historians in this collection either implicitly or explicitly accept. If we fully explore the intertwining of our senses of gender and class and move away from defining proletarianization as a process defined in terms of male experiences (and, as Auslander points out, as a unified, naturalized, and normative male experience), the subjects and narrative structures of our labor histories will become more complex, more varied, and more encompassing. Surely, however, male (and sometimes female) workers were not the only members of society who experienced proletarianization. The process also affected the experiences, values, and consciousness of other family members. Not all members of a family may have related to the process in the same way, but to leave everyone other than the male worker out of our analyses is surely to misunderstand the process. Just as Jacques Rancière has focused our attention on the significance of contacts between workers and bourgeois in forming the consciousness of workers,[19] so we should also focus on the significance of contacts between employed men and unemployed women, between men in one occupation and their wives in another, between sons and mothers, and between fathers and daughters in the process of class formation.

In a paper on Cockney mothers and sons delivered at the 1990 Berkshire Conference in Women's History, Ellen Ross explored the differences between the culturally sanctioned and dichotomous male and female roles, the collusion of some wives and husbands in playing out their roles, and the alliances between mothers and sons that existed in virtually all families. One son, distressed by his father's meanness to his mother, declared to his "mum" that when he grew up he was not going to be like "Dad." He was going to be nice.[20] How he behaved as an adult is undocumented, but while he and some other sons may have rejected the standard male role, others gradually adopted their father's behavior and ceased to ally with their mothers. Either way, the relationships between boys and their mothers played a role in forming their consciousness, and either way, sons grew up to be members of the working class. In addition, of course, the daughters in these families also grew up not just to marry into the working class but to be members of it, although most of them would not work consistently in the public sphere and have traditionally been ignored by labor historians.

Women's historians and new labor historians like those in this volume have sensitized us to the importance of exploring women's roles and activities as well as the variety of male-female, male-male, and female-female relationships in the formation of class consciousness. What linguistic analysis alerts us to is the importance of analyzing the language used by men and women in their encounters and in their statements on virtually all subjects, not as a reflection of reality but as the shaper and creator of it. In short, historians are moving toward a far broader conceptualization of the subject of labor history, a conceptualization that will not only analyze gender relationships and gender concepts but also encompass women as subjects.

Writing A New Labor History

One of the most interesting aspects of the essays in this collection is the degree to which they respond not just to the challenge to write linguistically informed history but also to Joan Scott's challenge to historians to displace the universal male subject of history and to analyze the role of gender in the past and in our own narratives. The challenge these historians see and to which they respond goes far beyond integrating information about women and men or including the private sphere in analyses of class formation. They call for historians to analyze the ways gender structured the experiences and perceptions of people in the past, the way it has structured the narratives or stories we tell (e.g., through the creation of dichotomous male-female, good-bad contrasts), and the way it has informed the analytical judgments we as historians make.

Reid supports Scott's call for labor historians to abandon the unitary narrative that focuses on the creation of *the worker,* who is always gendered and always male. Sewell celebrates the theoretical struggles taking place within women's history and calls for similar theoretical debates and explorations within labor history. Indeed, the kind of rethinking and reevaluating he hopes for in labor history is modeled after the "fundamental and ever-vigilant challenging, rethinking, or unthinking of conventional categories" that feminists have called for and have begun to undertake in a variety of intellectual fields.

In his agenda for French labor history, Aminzade declares that "class formation is a gendered process" and asks historians to "explore the gendered character of ideas and institutions even when women are absent from the scene." Johnson urges us to situate labor history within the lifeworld of workers, thereby implicitly opening the possibility of a labor history that includes women and women's concerns (including "the multiple unaddressed claims of women for equality") in history. Even more significant, Johnson's praise of Joan Landes's exposure of the "masculinity that inhered in the thought and practice of the classical bourgeois public sphere and Habermas's failure to consider this in emphasizing its 'utopian' potential" signals his readiness to consider the ways in which masculinity inhered in the thought and practice of male artisans and workers.[21]

Auslander studies primarily male workers, but in her expressed desire for historians to consider the diversity of workers' interests and consciousness, she takes an important step toward fulfilling Scott's demand that we displace and problematize the universal male subject of history. Similarly, when she analyzes the multiple, context-dependent discourses of workers, she builds on Scott's argument that language shapes rather than reflects experience. Downs not only looks at women workers but also introduces gender as a category of analysis by examining the ways in which women workers have been perceived and described by their contemporaries and historians. In both senses, her work is informed by the theoretical and empirical studies of Scott.

The self-reflection, evaluation, and innovation apparent in these essays leads me to declare that the new French labor history is neither dead nor in crisis but is alive and well and is moving into an exciting new era of broadly inclusive narratives built around a new understanding of the process of proletarianization and a new awareness of the role gender conceptions and language have played in the past and in our histories.

Notes

1. As the essays in this volume demonstrate, proletarianization appears under a variety of guises or titles in labor histories. It sometimes appears as class formation or the development of class consciousness. I do not mean to imply that proletarianization is the only paradigm of the new labor history. Other major paradigms include the creation of bourgeois hegemony (Aminzade) or materialism (Sewell).

2. Alice Clark, *The Working Life of Women in the Seventeenth Century* (London, 1919; 1968); Ivy Pinchbeck, *Women Workers and the Industrial Revolution, 1750-1850* (New York, 1930); Louise A. Tilly and Joan W. Scott, *Women, Work, and Family* (New York, 1978); Mary H. Blewett, *Men, Women, and Work: Class, Gender, and Protest in the New England Shoe Industry, 1780-1910* (Urbana, Ill., 1988). Also important among the histories written early in the twentieth century is Frances Collier, *The Family Economy of the Working Classes in the Cotton Industry, 1784-1833* (Manchester, 1964). Written as a master's thesis, this work was available only in manuscript form until 1964.

3. Gay L. Gullickson, *The Spinners and Weavers of Auffay* (Cambridge, 1986), p. 201.

4. Linda K. Kerber, "Separate Spheres, Female Worlds, Woman's Place: The Rhetoric of Women's History," *Journal of American History* 75 (1988): 11.

5. Ibid., p. 10.

6. Friedrich Engels, *The Origin of the Family, Private Property, and the State* (New York, 1972). See for instance, Juliet Mitchell, *Women, the Longest Revolution* (London, 1984).

7. See, for instance, Tilly and Scott, *Women, Work, and Family;* Joan W. Scott, "'L'ouvrière! Mot impie, sordide . . .': Women Workers in the Discourse of French Political Economy, 1840-1860," in her *Gender and the Politics of History* (New York, 1988), pp. 139-63; Olwen Hufton, "Women and the Family Economy in Eighteenth-Century France," *French Historical Studies* 9 (1975): 1-22; Mary Lynn Stewart, *Women, Work, and the French State* (Montreal, 1989); Michelle Perrot, "L'éloge de la ménagère dans le discours des ouvriers français au XIXe siècle," *Romantisme,* no. 13 (1976): 105-21; Marilyn Boxer, "Women in Industrial Homework: The Flowermakers of Paris in the Belle Epoque," *French Historical Studies* 12 (1982): 401-23.

8. Alice Kessler-Harris, *Out to Work: A History of Wage-Earning Women in the United States* (New York, 1982). In the most recent women's labor history, *sexual division of labor* has been replaced by *gender division of labor.* The change signals an increasing emphasis on the cultural rather than physiological nature of these labor divisions. The terms are synonomous in meaning, however, and those historians who have written and spoken of the sexual division of labor have always treated these divisions as culturally imposed.

9. Anne Phillips and Barbara Taylor, "Sex and Skill: Notes towards a Feminist Economics," *Feminist Review,* no. 6 (1980): 79.

10. Ibid.

11. Ibid., p. 84.

12. Jean Quataert, "The Shaping of Women's Work in Manufacturing: Guilds, Households, and the State in Central Europe, 1648-1870," *American Historical Review* 90 (1985): 1147.

13. Ibid., p. 1146.

14. Phillips and Taylor, "Sex and Skill," p. 87.

15. Joan W. Scott, "On Language, Gender, and Working-Class History" and "Women in *The Making of the English Working Class,*" in her *Gender and the Politics of History.*

16. Scott, "Women in *The Making,*" p. 71.

17. Ibid., pp. 78-79. The dichotomies in Thompson's text work roughly as follows. Men who worked acquired class consciousness and engaged in rational political struggles; women were tied to the domestic sphere and religious reform movements that together functioned to "compromise or subvert" class consciousness.

18. Ibid., p. 76.

19. Jacques Rancière, *The Nights of Labor: The Worker's Dream in Nineteenth-Century France,* trans. John Drury (Philadelphia, 1989).

20. Ellen Ross, unpublished paper, June 1990.

21. Aminzade actually makes this case in his analysis of the significance of the masculine vision of "fraternity" that inhered in artisan and working-class culture.

Selected Bibliography

Theoretical and Interdisciplinary Works

Abelson, Elaine, David Abraham, and Marjorie Murphy. "Interview with Joan Scott." *Radical History Review*, no. 45 (1989): 41-59.

Adorno, Theodor. *Negative Dialectics*. London, 1973.

Althusser, Louis. *Lenin and Philosophy and Other Essays*. New York, 1971.

Anderson, Perry. *Considerations on Western Marxism*. London, 1976.

Arato, Andrew, and Eike Gebhardt, eds.. *The Essential Frankfurt School Reader*. New York, 1978.

Axelrod, Robert. *The Evolution of Cooperation*. New York, 1984.

Baudrillard, Jean. *Le miroir de la production*. Paris, 1985.

———. *Le système des objets*. Paris, 1968.

Becker, Gary S. *A Treatise on the Family*. Cambridge, Mass., 1981.

Bennett, Judith. "Feminism and History." *Gender and History* 1 (1989): 250-64.

Bernstein, Richard, ed. *Habermas and Modernity*. Cambridge, Mass., 1985.

Bettelheim, Charles. *Les luttes de classes en URSS*. Paris, 1974.

Bourdieu, Pierre. "What Makes a Social Class? On the Theoretical and Practical Existence of Groups." *Berkeley Journal of Sociology* 32 (1987): 1-17.

Bowles, Samuel, and Herbert Gintis. *Democracy and Capitalism: Property, Community, and the Contradictions of Modern Social Thought*. New York, 1986.

Burawoy, Michael. *Manufacturing Consent: Changes in the Labor Process under Monopoly Capitalism*. Chicago, 1979.

———. *The Politics of Production: Factory Regimes under Capitalism and Socialism*. London, 1985.

Certeau, Michel de. *The Practices of Everyday Life*. Trans. Steven F. Randall. Berkeley, Calif., 1984.

Cockburn, Cynthia. *Brothers: Male Dominance and Technological Change.* London, 1983.

Cohen, Jean L. "Strategy or Identity: New Theoretical Paradigms and Contemporary Social Movements." *Social Research* 52 (1985): 663-716.

Coleman, D. C. "Proto-industrialization: A Concept Too Many." *Economic History Review,* 2d series, 36 (1983): 435-48.

Coleman, James S. *Foundations of Social Theory.* Cambridge, Mass., 1989.

Derrida, Jacques. *Of Grammatology.* Trans. Gayatri Chakravorty Spivak. Baltimore, 1974.

Dickson, Tony, and David Judge, eds.. *The Politics of Industrial Closure.* London, 1987.

Donald, James, and Stuart Hall, eds. *Politics and Ideology.* New York, 1986.

Dreyfus, Hubert, and Paul Rabinow. *Michel Foucault: Beyond Structuralism and Hermeneutics.* Chicago, 1982.

Dubois, Ellen, Mary Jo Buhle, and Temma Kaplan. "Politics and Culture in Women's History." *Feminist Studies* 6 (1980): 29-48.

Eagleton, Terry. *Criticism and Ideology: A Study in Marxist Literary Theory.* London, 1976.

———. *The Ideology of the Aesthetics.* Oxford, 1990.

Edwards, Richard, David Gordon, and Michael Reich. *Segmented Work, Divided Workers: The Historical Transformation of Labor in the United States.* Cambridge, 1982.

Elster, Jon. *Cement of Society.* Cambridge, 1989.

———. *Making Sense of Marx.* Cambridge, 1985.

———. *Nuts and Bolts for the Social Sciences.* Cambridge, 1989.

———. *Rational Choice.* Oxford, 1986.

———. *Solomonic Judgements.* Cambridge, 1989.

Fagin, Leonard, and Martin Little. *Foresaken Families.* Harmondsworth, England, 1984.

Flax, Jane. "Postmodernism and Gender Relations in Feminist Theory." *Signs* 12 (1987): 621-43.

Foucault, Michel. *Discipline and Punish: The Birth of the Prison.* Trans. Alan Sheridan. New York, 1977.

———. *The Foucault Reader.* Ed. Paul Rabinow. New York, 1984.

———. *The History of Sexuality.* Trans. Alan Sheridan. 3 vols. New York, 1978-86.

———. *Language, Counter-Memory and Practice.* Ithaca, N.Y., 1973.

———. *The Order of Things: An Archeology of the Human Sciences.* New York, 1973.

———. *Power/Knowledge: Selected Interviews and Other Writings.* Ed. Colin Gordon. New York, 1980.

Gamson, William. "Political Discourse and Collective Action." In *International Social Movement Research,* ed. Bert Klandermans, Hanspeter Kriesi, and Sidney Tarrow. Greenwich, Conn., 1988.

Gane, Michael, ed. *Towards a Critique of Foucault.* London, 1986.

Geertz, Clifford. "Blurred Genres: The Reconfiguration of Social Thought." In

Local Knowledge: Further Essays in Interpretive Anthropology. New York, 1983.
——. *The Interpretation of Cultures.* New York, 1973.
——. *Negara: The Theater State in Nineteenth-Century Bali.* Princeton, N.J., 1980.
Gerson, Barbara. *All the Livelong Day: The Meaning and Demeaning of Routine Work.* New York, 1975.
Goffman, Erving. *Forms of Talk.* Philadelphia, 1981.
Gorz, André. *Critique of Economic Reason.* London, 1989.
——. *Farewell to the Working Class.* London, 1982.
Gramsci, Antonio. *Selections from the Prison Notebooks.* Trans. Quintin Hoare and Geoffrey Nowell Smith. London, 1971.
Gumperz, John. *Discourse Strategies.* Cambridge, 1982.
Habermas, Jürgen. *Autonomy and Solidarity—Interviews with Jürgen Habermas.* Ed. Peter Dews. London, 1986.
——. *Legitimization Crisis.* Trans. Thomas McCarthy. Boston, 1975.
——. *The Philosophical Discourse of Modernity.* Trans. Frederick Lawrence. Cambridge, Mass., 1987.
——. *The Structural Transformation of the Public Sphere: An Inquiry into a Category of Bourgeois Society.* Trans. Thomas Burger. Cambridge, Mass., 1989.
——. *The Theory of Communicative Action.* Trans. Thomas McCarthy. 2 vols. Boston, 1987.
Hall, Stuart. "The Problem of Ideology—Marxism without Guarantees." In *Marx 100 Years On,* ed. Betty Matthews. London, 1983.
——, ed. *Culture, Media, Language: Working Papers in Cultural Studies, 1972-79.* London, 1980.
Hardin, Russell. *Collective Action.* Baltimore, 1982.
Harding, Neil. *Lenin's Political Thought.* 2 vols. New York, 1977-81.
Harding, Sandra. "The Instability of the Analytic Categories of Feminist Theory." *Signs* 11 (1986): 645-64.
Harris, Marvin. *Cultural Materialism: The Struggle for a Science of Culture.* New York, 1979.
Harvey, David. *The Condition of Postmodernity: An Enquiry into the Origins of Cultural Change.* Oxford, 1989.
Hechter, Michael. *Principles of Group Solidarity.* Berkeley, Calif., 1987.
Held, David. *Introduction to Critical Theory: Horkheimer to Habermas.* Berkeley, Calif., 1980.
Hollinger, David. "The Return of the Prodigal: The Persistence of Historical Knowing." *American Historical Review* 94 (1989): 610-21.
Hutton, Patrick. "The Foucault Phenomenon and Contemporary French Historiography." *Historical Reflections* 17 (1991): 77-102.
Jay, Martin. *Fin-de-siècle Socialism.* New York, 1988.
——. *Marxism and Totality.* Berkeley, Calif., 1984.
——. "Should Intellectual History Take a Linguistic Turn? Reflections on the

Habermas-Godamer Debate." In *Modern European Intellectual History: Reappraisals and New Perspectives,* ed. Dominick LaCapra and Steven Kaplan. Ithaca, N.Y., 1982.

Keat, Russell. *The Politics of Social Theory: Habermas, Freud, and the Critique of Positivism.* Chicago, 1981.

LaCapra, Dominick. *Rethinking Intellectual History: Texts, Contexts, Language.* Ithaca, N.Y., 1983.

Lakatos, Imre. *The Methodology of Scientific Research Programmes.* Cambridge, 1978.

Lamont, Michèle. "How to Become a Famous French Philosopher: The Case of Jacques Derrida." *American Journal of Sociology* 93 (1987): 584-622.

Laquer, Walter, and George Mosse, eds. *The New History: Trends in Historical Research and Writing since World War II.* New York, 1966.

Lehman, David. *Signs of the Times: Deconstruction and the Fall of Paul de Man.* New York, 1990.

Lloyd, Christopher. *Explanation in Social History.* Oxford, 1986.

Lukács, Georg. *History and Class Consciousness.* London, 1968.

McCarthy, Thomas. *The Critical Theory of Jürgen Habermas.* Cambridge, Mass., 1978.

McCloskey, Donald. *The Rhetoric of Economics.* Madison, Wis., 1985.

Mansbridge, Jane. *Beyond Adversary Democracy.* New York, 1980.

Mascia-Lees, Frances, Patricia Sharp, and Coleen Ballerino Cohen. "The Postmodern Turn in Anthropology: Caution from a Feminist Perspective." *Signs* 15 (1989): 7-33.

Mehlman, Jeffrey. *Revolution and Repetition: Marx/Hugo/Balzac.* Berkeley, Calif., 1977.

Modell, John. "A Note on Scholarly Caution in a Period of Revisionism and Interdisciplinarity." In *Social History and Issues in Human Consciousness,* ed. Andrew Barnes and Peter Stearns. New York, 1989.

Mouffe, Chantel, and Ernesto Laclau. *Hegemony and Socialist Strategy: Toward a Radical Democratic Politics.* London, 1975.

Mouzelis, Nicos. *Politics in the Semi-Periphery.* New York, 1986.

——. "Reductionism in Marxist Theory." *Telos* 45 (1980): 173-85.

Nelson, John S., Allan Megill, and Donald N. McCloskey, eds. *The Rhetoric of the Human Sciences: Language and Argument in Scholarship and Public Affairs.* Madison, Wis., 1987.

Newman, Louise. "Critical Theory and the History of Women: What Is at Stake in Deconstructing Women's History." *Journal of Women's History* 2 (1991): 58-68.

Norris, Christopher. *What's Wrong with Postmodernism: Critical Theory and the Ends of Philosophy.* Baltimore, 1990.

Novick, Peter. *That Noble Dream: The "Objectivity Question" and the American Historical Profession.* Cambridge, 1988.

Offe, Claus. "New Social Movements: Challenging the Boundaries of Institutional Politics." *Social Research* 52 (1985): 817-68.

——, ed. *Disorganized Capitalism.* Cambridge, 1985.

Olson, Mancur. *The Logic of Collective Action.* Cambridge, Mass., 1963.

Palmer, Bryan D. *Descent into Discourse: The Reification of Language and the Writing of Social History.* Philadelphia, 1990.

Phillips, Anne, and Barbara Taylor. "Sex and Skill: Notes towards a Feminist Economics." *Feminist Review,* no. 6 (1980): 79-88.

Przeworski, Adam. *Capitalism and Social Democracy.* Cambridge, 1985.

Rancière, Jacques. "The Myth of the Artisan: Critique of a Category of Social History." *International Labor and Working-Class History,* no. 24 (1983): 1-16.

——. *The Nights of Labor: The Worker's Dream in Nineteenth-Century France.* Trans. John Drury. Philadelphia, 1989.

——. *Le philosophe et ses pauvres.* Paris: Fayard, 1977.

Rancière, Jacques, and Patrice Vauday. "En allant à l'expo: L'ouvrier, sa femme et les machines." *Les révoltes logiques* 1 (1975): 5-22.

Reddy, William M. *Money and Liberty in Europe: A Critique of Historical Understanding.* Cambridge, 1987.

Reid, Donald. "The Night of the Proletarians: Deconstruction and Social History." *Radical History Review,* nos. 28-30 (1984): 444-63.

Reynolds, Sian, ed. *Women, State, and Revolution: Essays on Power and Gender in Europe since 1789.* Amherst, Mass., 1987.

Riley, Denise. *Am I That Name? Feminism and the Category of "Woman" in History.* Minneapolis, 1987.

Sabel, Charles, and Michael Piore. *The Second Industrial Divide: Possibilities for Prosperity.* New York, 1984.

Schervisch, Paul. *The Structural Determinants of Unemployment: Vulnerability and Power in Market Relations.* New York, 1983.

Schöttler, Peter. "Historians and Discourse Analysis." *History Workshop,* no. 27 (1989): 37-65.

Schwartz, Olivier. *Le monde privé des ouvriers: Hommes et femmes du Nord.* Paris, 1990.

Scott, Joan Wallach. *Gender and the Politics of History.* New York, 1988.

Sewell, William H., Jr. "Review of *Gender and the Politics of History,* by Joan Wallach Scott." *History and Theory* 29 (1990): 71-81.

Sirianni, Carmen. *Workers' Control and Socialist Democracy: The Soviet Experience in Comparative Perspective.* London, 1982.

Skocpol, Theda, ed. *Vision and Method in Historical Sociology.* Cambridge, 1984.

Skocpol, Theda, and Michael Burawoy, eds.. *Marxist Inquiries: Studies of Labor, Class, and States.* Chicago, 1982.

Sober, Elliott, Andrew Levine, and Erik Olin Wright. "Marxism and Methodological Individualism." *New Left Review,* no. 162 (1987): 67-83.

Spiegel, Gabrielle. "History, Historicism, and the Social Logic of the Text in the Middle Ages." *Speculum* 65 (1990): 59-86.

Stallybrass, Peter. "Marx and Heterogeneity: Thinking and the Lumpenproletariat." *Representations* 31 (1990): 69-95.

Stansell, Christine. "A Response to Joan Scott." *International Labor and Working-Class History,* no. 31 (1987): 24–29.
Staudohar, Paul, and Holly Brown, eds. *Deindustrialization and Plant Closure.* Lexington, Mass., 1987.
Stearns, Peter. "Encountering Postmodernism." *Journal of Social History* 24 (1990): 449–52.
Steinberg, Marc. "Talkin' Class: Discourse, Ideology, and Their Roles in Class Conflict." In *Bringing Class Back In,* ed. Scott McNall. Boulder, Colo., 1991.
Therborn, Göran. *The Ideology of Power and the Power of Ideology.* London, 1980.
Tilly, Louise. "Gender, Women's History and Social History." *Social Science History* 13 (1989): 438–62.
Toews, John E., "Intellectual History after the Linguistic Turn: The Autonomy of Meaning and the Irreducibility of Experience." *American Historical Review* 92 (1987): 879–907.
White, Steven K. *The Recent Work of Jürgen Habermas: Reason, Justice, and Modernity.* Cambridge, 1988.
Williams, Raymond. *Problems in Materialism and Culture.* London, 1980.
Wolin, Sheldon. "On the Theory and Practice of Political Power." In *After Foucault: Humanistic Knowledge, Postmodern Challenges,* ed. Jonathan Arac. New Brunswick, N.J., 1988.
Wood, Ellen Meiksins. *The Retreat from Class.* London, 1986.
Wright, Erik Olin. *Class, Crisis, and the State.* London, 1978.
———. *Classes.* London, 1985.
Zeitlin, Maurice, ed. *Classes, Class Conflict, and the State: Empirical Studies in Class Analysis.* Cambridge, Mass., 1980.

Historical Works

Accampo, Elinor. *Industrialization, Family Life, and Class Relations in Saint-Chamond, 1815–1914.* Berkeley, Calif., 1989.
Aminzade, Ronald. *Class, Politics, and Early Industrial Capitalism: A Study of Mid-Nineteenth-Century Toulouse, France.* Albany, N.Y., 1981.
———. "Reinterpreting Capitalist Industrialization: A Study of Nineteenth-Century France." In *Work in France: Representations, Meaning, Organization, and Practice,* ed. Steven Kaplan and Cynthia Koepp. Ithaca, N.Y., 1986.
Amann, Peter. *Revolution and Mass Democracy: The Paris Club Movement in 1848.* Princeton, N.J., 1975.
Baron, Ava, ed. *Work Engendered: Toward a New History of American Labor.* Ithaca, N.Y., 1991.
Berlanstein, Lenard R. *Big Business and Industrial Conflict in Nineteenth-Century France: A Social History of the Parisian Gas Company.* Berkeley, Calif., 1991.
———. *The Working People of Paris, 1871–1914.* Baltimore, 1984.

Bezucha, Robert. *The Lyon Uprising of 1834: Social and Political Conflict in the Early July Monarchy.* Cambridge, Mass., 1974.

Blewett, Mary H. *Men, Women, and Work: Class, Gender, and Protest in the New England Shoe Industry, 1780-1910.* Urbana, Ill., 1988.

Bloch, Marc. *French Rural History: An Essay on Its Basic Characteristics.* Trans. Janet Sondheimer. Berkeley, Calif., 1970.

Braun, Rudolf. *Industrialisierung und Volksleben.* 2 vols. Zurich, 1960.

Bythell, Duncan. *The Handloom Weavers.* Cambridge, 1969.

———. *The Sweated Trades: Outwork in Nineteenth-Century Britain.* Cambridge, 1985.

Censer, Jack R., ed. *The French Revolution and Intellectual History.* Chicago, 1989.

Chanut, Philippe. *Histoire française des foires et des expositions universelles.* Paris, 1980.

Chatelain, Abel. *Les migrants temporaires en France de 1800 à 1914.* 2 vols. Lille, 1977.

Clark, Christopher. *The Roots of Rural Capitalism: Western Massachusetts, 1780-1860.* Ithaca, N.Y., 1990.

Clawson, Mary Ann. *Constructing Brotherhood: Class, Gender, and Fraternalism.* Princeton, N.J., 1989.

———. "Early Modern Fraternalism and the Patriarchal Family." *Feminist Studies* 6 (1980): 368-91.

Corbin, Alain. *Archaïsme et modernité en Limousin au XIXe siècle.* 2 vols. Paris, 1975.

Cottereau, Alain, "The Distinctiveness of Working-Class Cultures in France, 1848-1900." In *Working-Class Formation: Nineteenth-Century Patterns in Western Europe and the United States,* ed. Ira Katznelson and Aristide Zolberg. Princeton, N.J., 1986.

———. "Usure au travail, destins masculins et destins feminins dans les cultures ouvrières en France au XIXè siècle." *Le mouvement social,* no. 124 (1983): 71-112.

Cross, Gary. *Immigrant Workers in Industrial France: The Making of a New Laboring Class.* Philadelphia, 1983.

———, ed. *Worktime and Industrialization.* Philadelphia, 1988.

Darnton, Robert. *The Great Cat Massacre and Other Episodes in French Cultural History.* New York, 1984.

Davis, Natalie Zemon. *Society and Culture in Early Modern France.* Stanford, Calif., 1975.

Eley, Geoffrey. "Labor History, Social History, *Alltagsgeschichte:* Experience, Culture, and the Politics of the Everyday—a New Direction for German Social History?" *Journal of Modern History* 61 (1989): 297-343.

Elwitt, Sanford. "Politics and Ideology in the French Labor Movement." *Journal of Modern History* 49 (1977): 468-80.

Fitzpatrick, Sheila, ed. *Cultural Revolution in Russia, 1928-1931.* Bloomington, Ill., 1978.

Fontaine, Laurence. *Le voyage et la mémoire: Colporteurs de l'Oisans au XIXe siècle.* Lyon, 1984.

Furet, François. *Penser la Révolution française.* Paris, 1978.

Gallie, Duncan. *Social Inequality and Class Radicalism in France and Britain.* Cambridge, 1983.

Garden, Maurice. *Lyon et les lyonnais au XVIIIe siècle.* Paris, 1970.

Gaxie, Daniel, ed. *Explication du vote: Un bilan des études électorales en France.* Paris, 1985.

Goldstein, Jan. *Console and Classify: The French Psychiatric Profession in the Nineteenth Century.* Cambridge, 1987.

Goldstein, Leslie. "Early Feminist Themes in French Utopian Socialism." *Journal of the History of Ideas* 43 (1982): 91-108.

Gullickson, Gay. *Spinners and Weavers of Auffay.* Cambridge, 1986.

Hanagan, Michael. *Nascent Proletarians: Class Formation in Post-Revolutionary France.* Oxford, 1989.

Hochschild, Arlie. *The Managed Heart: Commercialization of Human Feeling.* Berkeley, Calif., 1983.

Hufton, Olwen. "Women and the Family Economy in Eighteenth-Century France." *French Historical Studies* 9 (1975): 1-22.

Hunt, Lynn, ed. *The New Cultural History.* Berkeley, Calif., 1989.

Johnson, Christopher. "Economic Change and Artisan Discontent: The Tailors' History, 1800-1848." In *Revolution and Reaction,* ed. Roger Price. London, 1975.

——. "Patterns of Proletarianization: Parisian Tailors and Lodève Woolen Workers." In *Consciousness and Class Experience in Nineteenth-Century Europe,* ed. John Merriman. New York, 1979.

Jones, Gareth Stedman. *Languages of Class: Studies in English Working Class History, 1832-1982.* Cambridge, 1983.

Jones, P. M. *The Peasantry in the French Revolution.* Cambridge, 1988.

Judt, Tony. "A Clown in Regal Purple: Social History and the Historians." *History Workshop,* no. 7 (1979): 67-93.

Julliard, Jacques. *Fernand Pelloutier et les origines du syndicalisme d'action directe.* Paris, 1971.

Kerber, Linda. "Separate Spheres, Female Worlds, Woman's Place: The Rhetoric of Women's History." *Journal of American History* 75 (1988): 9-39.

Lachmann, Richard. "Elite Conflict and State Formation in Sixteenth- and Seventeenth-Century England and France." *American Sociological Review* 54 (1989): 141-62.

Landes, Joan. *Women and the Public Sphere in the Age of the French Revolution.* Ithaca, N.Y., 1988.

Lequin, Yves. *Les ouvriers de la région lyonnaise (1848-1914).* 2 vols. Lyon, 1977.

Levine, David. *Family Formation in the Age of Nascent Capitalism.* New York, 1977.

——. "Punctuated Equilibrium: The Modernization of the Proletarian Family in the Age of Ascendant Capitalism." *International Labor and Working-Class History,* no. 39 (1991): 3-20.

Maza, Sara. "Politics, Culture, and the Origins of the French Revolution." *Journal of Modern History* 61 (1989): 703-23.

Mendels, Franklin. "Protoindustrialization: The First Phase of the Industrializing Process." *Journal of Economic History* 32 (1972): 241-61.

Merriman, John, ed. *Consciousness and Class Experience in Nineteenth-Century Europe.* New York, 1979.

Montgomery, David. *Workers' Control in America: Studies in the History of Work, Technology, and Labor Struggles.* Cambridge, 1979.

More, Charles. *Skill and the English Working Class, 1870-1914.* New York, 1980.

Moss, Bernard. *The Origins of the French Labor Movement, 1830-1914: The Socialism of Skilled Workers.* Berkeley, Calif., 1976.

Murard, Lion, and Patrick Zylberman. *L'Haleine des Faubourgs: Ville, habitat, et santé au XIXe siècle.* Fontenay-sous-bois, 1978.

——. *Le petit travailleur infatigable: Ville-usines, habitat et intimités au XIXe siècle.* Paris, 1976.

Nathans, Benjamin. "Habermas's 'Public Sphere' in the Era of the French Revolution." *French Historical Studies* 16 (1990): 620-44.

Nicolet, Claude. *L'idée républicaine en France, 1789-1924.* Paris, 1982.

Perrot, Michelle. "L'éloge de la ménagère dans le discours des ouvriers français au XIXe siècle." *Romantisme,* no. 13 (1976): 105-21.

——. "A Nineteenth-Century Work Experience as Related in a Worker's Autobiography: Norbert Truquin." In *Work in France: Representations, Meaning, Organization, and Practice,* ed. Steven Kaplan and Cynthia Koepp. Ithaca, N.Y., 1986.

——. "On the Formation of the French Working Class." In *Working-Class Formation: Nineteenth-Century Patterns in Western Europe and the United States,* ed. Ira Katznelson and Aristide Zolberg. Princeton, N.J., 1986.

——. *Les ouvriers en grève: France, 1871-1890.* 2 vols. Paris, 1974.

Quataert, Jean. "The Shaping of Women's Work in Manufacturing: Guilds, Households, and the State in Central Europe, 1648-1870." *American Historical Review* 90 (1985): 1122-48.

Rabinbach, Anson. *The Human Motor: Energy, Fatigue, and the Origins of Modernity.* New York, 1990.

Reddy, William. *The Rise of Market Culture: The Textile Trade and French Society, 1750-1900.* Cambridge, 1984.

Reid, Donald. *The Miners of Decazeville: A Geneology of Deindustrialization.* Cambridge, Mass., 1985.

——. *Paris Sewers and Sewermen: Realities and Representations.* Cambridge, Mass., 1991.

——. "The Role of Mine Safety in the Development of Working-Class Consciousness and Organization." *French Historical Studies* 12 (1981): 98-119.

Rosenhaft, Eve. *Beating the Fascists? The German Communists and Political Violence, 1929-1933.* Cambridge, 1983.

Rule, John. "The Property of Skill in the Period of Manufacture." In *The Historical Meanings of Work,* ed. Patrick Joyce. Cambridge, 1987.

Sabel, Charles, and Jonathan Zeitlin, "Historical Alternatives to Mass Production: Politics, Markets, and Technology in Nineteenth-Century Industrialization." *Past and Present,* no. 108 (1985): 133-74.

Samuel, Raphael. "Workshop of the World: Steam Power and Hand Technology in Mid-Victorian Britain." *History Workshop,* no. 3 (1977): 6-72.

Scott, Joan Wallach. *The Glassworkers of Carmaux: French Craftsmen and Political Action in a Nineteenth-Century City.* Cambridge, Mass., 1974.

Sewell, William H., Jr. *Structure and Mobility: The Men and Women of Marseille, 1820-1870.* Cambridge, 1985.

———. "Uneven Development, the Autonomy of Politics, and the Dockworkers of Nineteenth-Century Marseille." *American Historical Review* 93 (1988): 604-37.

———. *Work and Revolution in France: The Language of Labor from the Old Regime to 1848.* Cambridge, 1980.

Sonenscher, Michael. *The Hatters of Eighteenth-Century France.* Berkeley, Calif., 1987.

———. "Mythical Work: Workshop and Production and the Compagnonnages of Eighteenth-Century France. In *The Historical Meanings of Work,* ed. Patrick Joyce. Cambridge, 1987.

———. *Work and Wages: Natural Law, Politics, and the Eighteenth-Century French Trades.* Cambridge, 1989.

Stein, Margot. "The Meaning of Skill: The Case of the French Engine-Drivers, 1837-1917." *Politics and Society* 8 (1979): 399-427.

Stewart, Mary Lynn. *Women, Work, and the French State.* Montreal, 1989.

Thompson, E. P. *The Making of the English Working Class.* London, 1963; New York, 1966.

Thomson, James K. J. *Clermont-de-Lodève, 1633-1789.* Cambridge, 1983.

Tilly, Charles. *The Contentious French.* Cambridge, 1986.

———. "Demographic Origins of the European Proletariat: A Proletarian World." In *Proletarianization and Family History,* ed. David Levine. Orlando, Fla., 1984.

———. "Retrieving European Lives." In *Reliving the Past: The Worlds of Social History,* ed. Olivier Zunz. Chapel Hill, N.C., 1985.

Tilly, Louise A., and Joan W. Scott. *Women, Work, and Family.* New York, 1978.

Tomlins, Christopher L. *The State and the Unions: Labor Relations, Law, and the Organized Labor Movement in America, 1880-1960.* Cambridge, 1985.

Traugott, Mark. *Armies of the Poor: Determinants of Working-Class Participation in the Paris Insurrection of June 1848.* Princeton, N.J., 1985.

Trempé, Rolande. *Les mineurs de Carmaux, 1848-1914.* 2 vols. Paris, 1971.

Truant, Cynthia. "Solidarity and Symbolism among Journeymen Artisans: The

Case of Compagnonnage." *Comparative Studies in Society and History* 21 (1979): 214–26.

Weissbach, Lee Shai. "Artisanal Responses to Artistic Decline: The Cabinet-makers of Paris in the Era of Industrialization." *Journal of Social History* 16 (1982): 67–81.

Wuthnow, Robert. *Communities of Discourse: Ideology and Social Structure in the Reformation, the Enlightenment, and European Socialism.* Cambridge, Mass., 1989.

Zylberberg-Hocquard, Marie-Hélène. *Femmes et féminisme dans le mouvement ouvrier français.* Paris, 1981.

Notes on Contributors

RONALD AMINZADE is an associate professor of sociology at the University of Minnesota. He is the author of *Class, Politics, and Early Industrial Capitalism* (1981) and is preparing for publication "Visions of the Republic: A Comparative Study of Local Politics in Mid-Nineteenth-Century France."

LEORA AUSLANDER is an assistant professor of history at the University of Chicago. She is preparing for publication "Taste and Power: The Life-Cycle of Parisian Furniture, 1750–1940."

LENARD R. BERLANSTEIN is a professor of history at the University of Virginia. He is the author of *The Barristers of Toulouse in the Eighteenth Century* (1975), *The Working People of Paris, 1871–1914* (1984), and *Big Business and Industrial Conflict in Nineteenth-Century France* (1991).

LAURA LEE DOWNS is an assistant professor of history at the University of Michigan. She is preparing for publication "Manufacturing Inequality: The Construction of a Gender-Stratified Labor Force in the Metalworking Factories of France and Britain, 1914–1939."

GAY L. GULLICKSON is an associate professor of history at the University of Maryland. She is the author of *Spinners and Weavers of Auffy: Rural Industry and the Sexual Division of Labor in a French Village, 1750–1850* (1986). Her current project is a study of women in the Paris Commune of 1871.

MICHAEL HANAGAN is teaching at the Center for Historical Studies at the New School for Social Research. He is the author of *The Logic of*

Solidarity: Artisans and Industrial Workers in Three French Towns, 1871-1914 (1980) and *Nascent Proletarians: Class Formation in Post-Revolutionary France* (1989) and has edited several collections of essays on the formation of a working class.

CHRISTOPHER H. JOHNSON is a professor of history at Wayne State University. He is the author of *Utopian Communism in France: Cabet and the Icarians, 1839-1851* (1974) and *Maurice Sugar: Law, Labor, and the Left in Detroit, 1912-1950.* He is preparing for publication "The Life and Death of Industrial Languedoc, 1700-1920."

DONALD REID is an associate professor of history at the University of North Carolina, Chapel Hill. He has published *The Miners of Decazeville: A Genealogy of Deindustrialization* (1985) and *Paris Sewers and Sewermen: Realities and Representations* (1991).

WILLIAM H. SEWELL, JR., is a professor of history and political science at the University of Chicago. He has published *Work and Revolution in France: The Language of Labor from the Old Regime to 1848* (1980) and *Structure and Mobility: The Men and Women of Marseille, 1820-1870* (1985).

Index

Académie des Sciences Morales et Politiques, 159
Adorno, Theodor: as theorist of domination, 70, 77, 79
Advertising: and the economy, 19, 168
Agulhon, Maurice, 39
Alienation, 75-76, 80. *See also* Marxism
Althusser, Louis: and contributions to Marxism, 23, 70
Anarchism, 68
Anderson, Perry, 69
Annales school: influence on labor history, 3, 28
Anthropology: influence on labor history, 3, 28, 30, 40, 55, 79. *See also* Geertz, Clifford
Anti-Semitism, 68
Apprenticeship: deterioration of, 59, 155-59, 170; organization of, 20, 93, 153-54
Arato, Andrew, 69
Aristocracy: in political life, 6, 21
Artisans: competence of, 150, 152-53, 165-71; deteriorating conditions for, 59-62; in labor movements, 2, 7, 16, 93, 96-97, 101, 104, 160, 186, 196; and women, 204-5, 207, 211
Audiganne, Armand, 48, 159, 164
Austro-Hungarian Empire: and class protest, 194

Automobile industry: in 1950s, 57

Babeuf, Gracchus, 162
Bataille, Georges, 66
Becker, Gary, 29, 185
Belle Epoque, 41
Berlin, 71
Biology: and conceptualization in social thought, 24-25
Bolsheviks. *See* Communism
Bordeaux (France), 155
Blake, William, 39
Bloch, Marc, 37*n*12
Bowles, Samuel, 23
Boston, 149
Boulogne-Billancourt (France), 123, 125, 130, 132
Bourgeoisie: as dominant class, 6, 67, 77-78, 96; formation of, 74, 98, 203, 209; and workers, 40, 50, 101, 158, 164, 170
Brabant: workers in, 196
Burawoy, Michael, 26-27
Bureaucracy: and labor movements, 76, 80, 84, 191-92, 206

Cabet, Étienne, 59, 95, 104, 193
Cabinetmakers. *See* Furniture makers
Capitalism: and handicrafts, 156, 162; mechanics of, 19, 69-70, 75-77, 192,

Capitalism (*Cont'd*)
    203, 205; shaping working class, 3, 8,
    17, 60, 95, 97. *See also* Class analysis
Carbonari societies, 104
Carmaux (France), 44
Cartesian thought. *See* Descartes, René
Carton making, 204
Center for Social Theory and Comparative
    History (UCLA), 28
Chartism, 4, 90
Chatelain, Abel, 56
Child labor. *See* Apprenticeship
Chile: Communism in, 69
China: revolution in, 69
Christian thought: as foundation of histori-
    cal concepts, 21-22, 24, 37n11, 184
Citizenship: and workers' protest, 103-4
Citroën, André, 136
Class analysis: critique of, 5-6, 31-32,
    47-48, 56, 64; defense of, 10, 90-97;
    refinement of, 108-9, 161, 194-97. *See
    also* Marxism
Class conflict, 2, 6, 7-8, 48, 109n5. *See also*
    Proletarianization
Class consciousness: critique of, 39, 44, 48,
    68, 105, 149, 188; and politics, 196-97;
    research on, 111n16, 151, 163, 202;
    sources of, 2, 4-5, 10-11, 31-32, 48, 57,
    93-94, 208-9, 211n1; and women,
    206-7, 210, 212n17
Clerical workers, 17. *See also* Bourgeoisie
Cochin, Augustin, 87n20
Collective bargaining, 76
Collective protest. *See* Class consciousness;
    Labor Politics
Committee for Historical Studies (New
    School for Social Research), 28
Communicative interaction, 57, 63, 77-78,
    81. *See also* Habermas, Jürgen
Communism: and labor history, 5, 43, 57,
    67, 69, 74-75
Compagnonnages. *See* Journeymen's
    associations
Condorcet, Marquis de, 103
Confédération Générale du Travail, 117,
    135
Consumerism: and working class, 76,
    157-58, 164, 169
Cottereau, Alain, 62, 102
Craft knowledge: definition of, 151-52;

transmission of, 156, 165-66, 170;
    workers' discourses about, 160, 162-63,
    167-68, 171
Crafts. *See* Artisans
Craft sense: definition of, 151-52; transmis-
    sion of, 156, 160, 164, 170, 171
Critical theory. *See* Frankfurt school;
    Habermas, Jürgen
Culture: as autonomous force, 3-4, 6, 9, 11,
    17-19, 26, 212n8; defining social rela-
    tions, 30, 32, 61, 63, 107
Culture of production: 156-60, 163-64, 167,
    169-70

Davis, Natalie, 3
Deconstruction: applied, 21-26, 50, 189-90;
    of class, 6, 8-9, 15-16, 55; critique of,
    87n16, 105; methods of, 47. *See also*
    Derrida, Jacques; Feminist theory
Deindustrialization, 17, 40, 70-71
De Man, Paul, 42, 64, 86n16
Democracy: and labor policies, 101-2, 106,
    113n31
Demography: and labor history, 38n29, 48,
    59
Depression of 1930s, 71
Derrida, Jacques, 6, 34, 51, 64, 66, 77,
    87n16
Descartes, René, 63, 72, 77, 183
Deskilling, 18, 151, 202
Dilthey, Wilhelm, 184
Disciplinary techniques: and social power,
    31, 186. *See also* Foucault, Michel
Discourses: critique of, 41, 55-56, 63, 190;
    and identity, 6-12, 65, 91-92, 101,
    207; of labor, 107, 160-61, 163, 169;
    in theory, 30, 33
Domesticity: assumptions about, 103, 132,
    204-6. *See also* Gender; Separation of
    spheres
Donzelot, Jacques, 56
Draft dodgers: in labor rhetoric and protest,
    125-26
Dressmakers, 128-29
Durkheim, Émile, 78-79

Eagleton, Terry, 183, 188
Eastern Europe: revolution in, 67
Economic determinism: and class, 59, 73,
    108, 194-95; critique of, 19, 23, 32;

Economic determinism (*Cont'd*) reductionism of, 62, 64, 90–92. *See also* Materialism

Economics, contribution to labor history of, 28–29, 32

Eighteenth century. *See* Pre-industrial work

Elster, Jon, 73–74

Elwitt, Sanford, 69

Employers: as allies of workers, 93, 95; combating workers, 115–18, 125, 129, 131, 134, 136, 188; deploying labor, 155, 166–68

Engels, Friedrich, 203

England: production in, 187

Enlightenment: and social thought, 21–22, 31, 63, 70, 77, 79, 81, 157

Estates General, 113n31

Ethnicity: and workers' identity, 5

European Economic Community (ECC), 71

"Everyday life" history, 84, 206

Factory production, 2, 17, 27, 59–60, 97, 202. *See also* Munitions workers

Family ideology, 155–56

Fascism: and social thought, 70

Fédération des Métaux, 119–20, 135

Femininity: and meanings, 159, 162, 164, 169. *See also* Masculinity

Feminism: impact on labor history, 5, 15–16. *See also* Feminist theory

Feminist theory: conceptualization of, 200, 203, 205; contributions to labor history, 5, 8–9, 15–16, 104–5, 161, 178n50, 190; and politics, 30–32, 81

Ferry, Jules, 111n21

Fordism, 71, 77

Foremen: and labor protest, 120–21, 126, 129

Foucault, Michel: concept of power of, 31–32, 34, 56, 64, 66, 186, 196–97; philosophy of, 3, 6, 51, 70, 80–81, 183, 185. *See also* Post-structuralism

Fourierists, 40, 104

France: labor history of, 1, 4, 45; politics in, 6, 21, 95–96, 103, 165; workers in, 7, 48, 56, 59–61, 90, 159, 170. *See also* Artisans; Republicanism

Frankfurt school, 70, 191

Fraternalism: and politics, 99, 103, 104, 112n26, 213n21

French Revolution of 1789: historiography of, 5–6, 64, 66, 91, 100, 109n5; and institutional change, 8, 61–62, 77, 157; politics of, 103, 105, 113n31

Freudianism: and feminist thought, 15–16

Functionalism: and evolution of historiography, 63–64

Furet, François, 64, 87n20, 91, 100

Furniture makers: collective identity of, 10, 159–64, 186–88; organization of, 149–50, 164–71; training of, 151–59

Gallo, Max, 115

Gambetta, Léon, 106

Game theory: and history, 29, 183, 185

Garden, Maurice, 58

Garment workers. *See* Tailors: Seamstresses

Gay rights: and labor protest, 81

Geertz, Clifford: influence of, 3, 27, 55, 63, 183; notion of culture of, 24–25, 30, 61, 185

Gender: and class, 7–11, 31, 55, 65, 201–7, 209–10; defining attributes, 16, 34, 51, 158, 169, 186–88; and politics, 44, 80, 103, 105, 107, 127, 163. *See also* Feminist theory

General Agreement on Tariffs and Trade (GATT), 71

Genovese, Eugene, 69

Germany: labor in, 204, 206; during World War I, 115, 130, 132, 136

Gintis, Herbert, 23

Girondins, 103

Glassworkers, 2, 44–45

Goldberg, Harvey, 44

Gorz, Andre, 71

Göttingen (Germany), 58

Gramsci, Antonio, 23, 31–32, 36n8, 67–70

Grévy, Jules, 111n21

Guilds, 20, 204. *See also* Journeymen's associations

Guizot, François, 79

Habermas, Jürgen: conception of social change of, 76–84, 191–94, 206; influence of, 10, 55, 57, 62, 72, 196. *See also* Communicative interaction; Lifeworld

Handicrafts. *See* Artisans

Harris, Marvin, 183

Harvey, David, 183

Havel, Vaclav, 66
Hegel, Georg Friedrich, 22, 67, 72, 192
Heidigger, Martin, 64, 66, 77
Hegemony, 67, 96. *See also* Gramsci, Antonio
Himmelfarb, Gertrude, 194
History and Society Program (University of Minnesota), 28
Hobsbawm, Eric, 3
Hochschild, Arlie, 26
Horkheimer, Max, 70, 79
Husserl, Edmund, 61, 78

Icarians. *See* Cabet, Étienne
Idealism: in historical conceptualization, 22–24, 37n11, 183–84, 207. *See also* Materialism
Identity: of workers. *See* Class consciousness
Imperialism: and labor movements, 76
Industrial Revolution: and labor history, 2
Intellectual history: trends in, 1, 3, 16, 36n8, 201
Interdisciplinary studies: significance to labor history, 27–29, 33–35
International Monetary Fund: and managed capitalism, 71
Interpretive systems: in labor history, 27–32, 35, 47, 49

Jacobinism: and leftist politics, 50, 74, 103, 111n21, 127
Jansenism: and social thought, 50
Jaurès, Jean, 44
Jay, Martin, 69
Jellinek, Frank, 182
Johnson, Barbara, 63
Jones, Gareth Stedman, 4, 16, 41, 56, 190, 205
Jouhaux, Léon, 117, 122, 135
Journeymen, 59–60, 93, 153–56. *See also* Artisans
Journeymen's associations: and transmission of skill, 104, 156–57, 159–62, 174n23
July Monarchy: politics in, 95

Kant, Immanuel, 63, 72
Kerber, Linda, 203
Keynes, John Maynard, 76

Labor history. *See* New labor history
Labor politics: consequences of, 17, 80–81,

191; determinants of, 91–94, 98–99, 112n26, 196–97; in labor history, 202, 206. *See also* Class conflict; Socialism
Labor process. *See* Proletarianization
Labrousse, Ernest, 64
Laclau, Ernesto, 23, 30
Landes, Joan, 82, 211
Language: as system of meanings. *See* Post-structuralism; Linguistic turn
Languedoc: industry in, 71
Ledru-Rollin, Alexandre, 106, 112n21
Lefebvre, Georges, 5
Legitimism: in local politics, 96
Leninism: and social practice, 40, 66, 68, 75, 87n20, 197
Le Play, Frédéric, 165
Liberalism, 23, 48, 68, 75, 96, 100–102, 105, 111n21
Lichtheim, George, 75
Lifeworld: changes in, 61–62, 65, 81, 84; as conception of society, 57–59, 78–79, 191–92, 206, 210
Linguistics, 41
Linguistic turn: agenda of, 6, 46–51, 189–90, 201, 207; critique of, 41–43, 105, 186; uses of, 9–10, 197. *See also* Post-structuralism
Literary criticism: and historical methodology, 3, 28–30, 41, 64, 205
Locke, John, 22
London: labor movements in, 165, 186, 209
Louis-Napoléon. *See* Napoléon III
Lukács, Georg, 67, 70
Lumpenproletariat, 48, 91

Macé, Jean, 106
Making of the English Working Class, The. *See* Thompson, E. P.
Mannheim, Karl, 191
Marcuse, Herbert, 70
Markets: influence of, 26, 48, 58, 62, 64, 76, 78, 98
Marx, Karl, 19, 22, 47–49, 59, 67, 71–76. *See also* Marxism
Marxism: critique of, 22–23, 56–57, 62, 65–69, 91, 205; in labor history, 3, 16, 44, 55, 97, 182, 203; philosophical basis of, 70–74, 81; revision in, 4, 9–10, 31–32, 36n8
Masculinity: and aesthetic appreciation, 156, 159, 161–62, 169–70; and labor

Masculinity (*Cont'd*)
  movements, 127, 133, 156, 177n45; and
  republican rhetoric, 103–4, 112n26
Masonic lodges: as sources of republican
  political culture, 104
Materialism: conceptual weaknesses of,
  17–26, 65–67, 183–84; defense of,
  42–43, 55–56, 94, 108; as orientation in
  labor history, 7, 9, 34, 50, 221n1; philo-
  sophical basis of, 21–24, 37n11. *See also*
  Marxism
Mead, George Herbert, 78–79, 191
Mehring, Franz, 75
Merchant capitalism: transforming produc-
  tion methods, 59–60
Merrheim, Alphonse, 117, 120, 135
Merriman, John, 64
Metalworkers, 114, 117, 125, 127. *See also*
  Munitions workers
Middle Ages, 159
Mill, John Stuart, 78
Miners, coal, 48
Ministry of Armaments (France), 120–22,
  131, 135
Mobile Guard, 91. *See also* Revolutions of
  1848
Money: as symbol, 19, 59, 79. *See also*
  Wages
Montesquieu, Baron de (Charles de
  Sécondat), 22
Montgomery, David, 5, 20, 69, 183
Moral proletarians: as concept in labor his-
  tory, 49–50
Mouffe, Chantel, 23, 30
Munitions workers: organized protest of, 10,
  119–30, 207–8; repression of, 131–36;
  work conditions of, 114–19, 141n31. *See
  also* Women workers
Mutual aid societies, 159–61

Napoléon III, 165, 187
Narratives: conventions of in labor history,
  48, 51, 127, 201–3, 209; innovations
  in, 40, 42–44, 189, 204–6, 210; uses of,
  108
Nationalism: and workers identities, 68, 104,
  187
Neumann, Franz, 70
New labor history: conventions of, 1–5,
  12n2, 18, 43–44, 149–50, 163, 182–83,
  192; critiques of, 8, 15–16, 48, 200–201,

211n1; future of, 11, 46, 84, 108, 190,
  206; and theory, 114–16, 160–61
Newton, Isaac, 21
Nietzsche, Friedrich, 64, 66, 77
Normalization: techniques of, 3, 56. *See also*
  Foucault, Michel

Offe, Clause, 191, 193
Old Regime. *See* Pre-industrial work
Olsen, Mancur, 29
Oxymorons, 26–27, 34

Palmer, Bryan, 6–7, 41–42, 45, 55–56, 63.
  See also Post-structuralism
Parent-Duchâtelet, A.-J.-B., 41, 49–50
Paris: workers in, 41, 49, 91, 114, 123, 128,
  160, 165. *See also* Munitions workers;
  Sewermen
Paris Commune: in revolutionary tradition,
  182
Parsons, Talcott, 191, 193
Path-dependent analysis, 96, 108, 196–97
Patriarchy, 8, 31, 203. *See also* Feminist
  theory
Perrot, Michelle, 172n4
Pessim Georgij Konstantinowich, 197
Philadelphia: labor congress at, 169
Physiocrats: social thought of, 22
Piece rates. *See* Wages
Plato: impact on conceptualization in labor
  history, 40, 184
Police: used against labor protest, 124–26,
  130–32, 134, 136
Political culture: and workers' movements,
  61, 64
Political economy: and rhetoric of labor
  movements, 157–59, 161–62, 169–70
Political parties. *See* Labor politics; Socialism
Political science: impact on labor history,
  28–29, 32, 90, 200
Politics: as autonomous force, 30–34, 91,
  98–100
Poni, Carlo, 58
Popular culture: and working-class culture,
  194, 196, 201
Populism: and workers' protest, 23, 93, 102
Positivism: critique of, 6
Post-Marxism, 23, 64, 70. *See also* Marxism
Post-materialism. *See* Materialism
Post-modernism, 81, 191, 194. *See also*
  Linguistic turn; Post-structuralism

Post-structuralism: agenda of, 6–11, 63–65, 91, 183; critique of, 14*n*26, 41–42; implications of, 4, 46–49, 105. *See also* Palmer, Bryan

Power: conceptualizations for labor history, 31–32, 34, 43, 51, 56, 59, 64, 76, 185–86. *See also* Foucault, Michel

Pre-industrial work: modes of, 2, 7, 153, 154, 155, 157, 168, 170. *See also* Artisans

Prezeworski, Adam, 110*n*9, 194, 196–97

Producers' cooperatives: as effort to control production, 160

Program on the Comparative Study of Social Transformation, 28

Program on Rhetoric of Inquiry (University of Iowa), 28

Proletarianization: and class formation, 2–3, 11, 57–58, 91, 172*n*5; problematical nature of, 7–8, 18, 60–61; process of, 160, 167; research on, 10, 97–99, 184, 196

Proto-industry: and new methods of labor deployment, 58, 202. *See also* Proletarianization

Public sphere: and political change, 8, 77–78, 82, 84, 203

Quataert, Jean, 204

Rabinbach, Arson, 48

Radicalism: English, 4; French, 102, 111*n*21

Railroads: as political issue, 98, 101

Rancière, Jacques: and analysis of artisans, 10, 16, 61–62, 209; and critique of labor history, 3, 7, 39–41, 51, 56–57, 189

Rational choice theory, 29, 34

Rationalization: as historical process, 70, 75, 78–80

Ready-made manufacturing, 59, 158. *See also* Proletarianization

Reddy, William: and critique of class analysis, 4–7, 19, 26–27, 42, 47, 91

Reformism: and workers' politics, 15, 197

Renault Automobile Company: and workers' protest, 124–25, 129, 131–32

Representations: of social experience, 48–49, 63

Republicanism: ideology of, 99–104, 195, 207; notion of representation in, 105–8; social basis of, 93, 95–96

Reskilling: and class formation, 18, 184, 202

Revisionism: in labor history. *See* New labor history; Post-structuralism

Revolutions of 1848: and workers' movements, 61, 74, 78, 80, 90–91, 106, 192–94

Ricoeur, Paul, 78

Rites of passage, 3

Ritual: as used by historians, 3, 103, 156

Romania, 69

Ross, Ellen, 209

Rouen (France): nineteenth-century politics in, 94–96

Rousseau, Jean-Jacques: republican ideology of, 103, 111*n*21, 112*n*31

Rudé, George, 5

Russian Revolution: and workers' politics, 68, 87*n*20, 182

Saint Augustine: social thought of, 37*n*11, 184

Saint-Étienne (France): nineteenth-century politics in, 94–96

Saint-Simonians, 40, 104

Sansculottes: contributions to workers' politics, 103, 105, 107

Schama, Simon, 64

Schutz, Alfred, 78

Scott, Joan: gender analysis of, 8, 16, 51, 65–66, 105, 205, 209–11; revisionism of, 30, 41–44, 56, 63; scholarship in labor history of, 2, 4, 7, 11, 46, 202

Seamstresses, 7, 59

Second Empire (France): politics in, 111*n*21

Semiotics, 30

Semiskilled workers, 154

Separation of spheres: as theme in labor history, 203–4

Service workers, 17

Sewell, William H.: and critique of materialism, 3, 39, 44, 47; evaluation of, 182–86, 210; and linguistic analysis, 41–42, 91

Sewermen (Parisian): politics of, 41, 49–50, 189–90

Sexual division of labor, 11, 202–6, 212*n*17

Shoemakers, 196

Shop chiefs: role in repression of workers, 120–21

Shopkeepers, 94, 101

Skill: creation of, 20, 33, 60, 154, 156, 160, 162, 164, 167, 170, 207; and protest,

Skill (*Cont'd*)
  2, 6, 40, 187, 205; and work, 57, 76,
    202
Skocpol, Theda, 90
Social Catholicism: and labor movements,
    193, 195-96
Social history, 28, 41-42, 46, 48, 56, 63. *See
    also* New labor history
Socialism: ideology of, 17, 43-44, 67, 74,
    100-102, 104, 193; origins of, 1, 4, 62,
    97; politics, of, 135, 161, 191
Sociology: contributions to labor history, 30,
    140, 192
Soldiers: and workers' protest, 117, 127
Sonenscher, Michael, 7, 57, 60-62, 64-65
Soviet Union: labor in, 67-68
Speech communities, 10, 161, 178n50, 190
Stained-glass workers, 187
Stalinism: and labor ideology, 32, 57, 67,
    69-70
State-centered social theory, 90-92, 109n1
States: economic role of, 70, 73, 78-80, 161,
    165, 169; formation of, 3, 66; power of,
    90, 185-86, 191. *See also* Welfare state
Steinberg, Marc, 190
Stone, Lawrence, 14n26
Strike of 1917: origins of, 114-19; participa-
    tion in, 119-30; repression of, 130-36
Strikes: causes of, 8, 177n44; consequences
    of, 76, 159-61; meaning of, 27, 165. *See
    also* Proletarianization; Strike of 1917
Structuralism, 64, 192
Subjectivism: and conceptualization in labor
    history, 72, 185
Syndicalism, 68
Systems analysis, 66-67

Tailors, 7, 59-60
Tariffs, 98, 101
Taste: in handicraft production, 150,
    158-59, 161-69, 171, 175n30, 186, 207.
    See also Furniture makers
Textile workers, 4, 58, 187
Third Republic (France): 50, 195-96
Thirty Years' War: and changes in work
    regimes, 205
Thomas, Albert, 122, 131
Thompson, E. P.: critique of, 42, 44, 183,

    205, 209; innovations of, 1, 3, 5, 23, 35,
      39-40, 200
Tilly, Charles, 3-4, 58
Tocqueville, Alexis de, 87n20
Tolain, Henri, 187
Totalism, 69, 190
Toulouse (France): nineteenth-century poli-
    tics in, 94-97, 106
Tour de France, 156. *See also* Journeymen's
    associations
Trade unions: formation of, 1, 96, 150; logic
    of, 76, 159-65, 169-70, 177n44; sex-
    ual politics of, 117-18, 126, 131, 136,
    186-88
Traugott, Mark, 90
Tristan, Flora, 104, 112n28

Universal expositions. *See* World's fairs
Universities: intellectual life at, 27-28
University of Wisconsin, 44, 59
Utopianism, 193, 197

Vienna: labor congresses at, 169
Villermé, Louis, 161

Wages: determinants of, 33-34, 59; levels
    of, 110n8, 118, 135, 141n31; protest
    over, 91, 93, 121-22, 133, 150, 160,
    162-63, 165, 167, 188
Weber, Max, 70, 79
Welfare state, 50, 70, 81, 192
White-collar workers, 101
Williams, Raymond, 183
Women's history: conceptualization in,
    202-6, 209-10, 212n8; innovations in,
    1-2, 15, 46. *See also* Gender
Women workers: attributions of, 187-89;
    conditions of, 8, 11, 17, 33, 56, 158; pro-
    test of, 112n29, 116, 118, 127. *See also*
    Munitions workers
Workplace. *See* Proletarianization
World Bank, 71
World's fairs: as forum for labor protest, 150,
    159, 164-171, 186
World War I: impact on workers, 10, 115.
    See also Munitions workers; Strike of
    1917